KV-637-693

Contents

Preface

This book is intended to provide an introduction to economics for students who have no prior knowledge of the subject. This means that we have tried to explain all the terms and concepts used, and may mean that those readers who have some prior acquaintance with economics will find that parts of the book cover ground with which they are already familiar. It is still worth while to go over those sections again so that the explanations given here can be fitted in with the explanations of new areas, thereby providing a comprehensive account.

In very broad terms, there are two major types of economic models or two main areas of economic theory. These are referred to as micro and macro.

Micro-economics deals with the economic behaviour of individuals. This includes individual persons as consumers and workers, and individual producers or entrepreneurs.

Macro-economics deals with activity at the level of the economy as a whole. It, too, is based on the decisions and actions of individual economic agents but combines these to examine developments at the level of the whole economy rather than at the level of individual firms or industries.

Chapters 2 to 9 can be regarded as dealing with the micro side and Chapters 10 to 21 with the macro.

It is perfectly possible to look at macro issues before the micro ones. This book, however, starts with the micro, and it is suggested that this order be followed, since various economic terms and concepts are explained in that order. To start with the macro chapters could mean that some terms are used without further explanation because these have been given earlier in the micro chapters.

While this volume is particularly suited to those students preparing for the examination in Economics for the new syllabus of the Institute of Chartered Secretaries and Administrators, it will also be appropriate for those taking other examinations for professional qualifications and for those preparing for academic examinations. In addition, it is intended to provide an introduction to economics for those who are not preparing for any examination but just want to know more about an important subject.

I want to thank Bill Conboy, an old friend and colleague, who read the first draft and made many helpful comments which had the clarity of exposition obtained from many years of teaching economics, and the clarity of presentation one expects from a qualified draughtsman. I am indebted to my son, Toby, for producing all the diagrams on our computer. Caroline Wise, Nicola Ralph and Sybil Owen typed the draft with speed, friendliness, and tolerance of my bad handwriting and poor typing.

May 1986   Derek Robinson

Part one

Introduction

CHAPTER 1

The subject and methodology of economics

Economics is about the production and distribution of income and wealth. Another way of looking at economics is to say that it is about the production and distribution of goods and services. These are the things we can buy with our income and wealth. The subjects we shall be examining include some of the most important issues in our societies, such as the causes of employment and unemployment, inflation, why countries trade with each other, and the importance of the balance of payments. Of course we cannot deal with these important topics immediately. We must first set out the basic concepts and methods of analysis used by economists. To begin with, therefore, we shall use quite simple concepts; once these have been understood we can move on and apply them to the real world.

Remember, the whole purpose of economics is to help us to understand the real world, the world in which we live and the economy in which we operate. We live in different economies – some of us in what are called developed economies and others in what are referred to as developing economies. There are considerable differences between these two broad groups and among the members of each group. It is extremely unlikely, therefore, that the problems in each individual country will be exactly the same. Indeed, it is equally unlikely that the problems in any one country will remain the same for long periods of time. While the main emphasis in this book will be on the United Kingdom, we shall refer to other types of economy and, where appropriate, bring out major differences between them. The basic methods of analysis should be the same, but different assumptions about people's behaviour might be necessary.

Economic theory is an attempt to explain people's behaviour in certain specified situations. For example, what will happen if the price of one good rises and everything else remains the same? In the real world it is almost impossible that the price of only one good could rise and *everything* else remain the same. The increase in the price of that good would affect someone's income. However, because initially we want to consider only the effects of the rise in price of that single good or commodity, we *assume* or specify that everything else remains the same, even though we know that this will not be the case. Economists use the Latin term *ceteris paribus* to indicate that everything else remains the same.

As we go through the book there will be various other special or technical terms introduced. It is important to note whenever we use a term in a special or technical sense. There are a number of words which we use in economics which are also used in an everyday sense with a different meaning. We give some words a special meaning in economics and care must be taken not to confuse the two usages. For example, the word 'investment' in normal or everyday usage can mean the buying of stocks and shares or the depositing of money in a bank or building society. In economics it does not mean either of these things; it means the purchase of capital equipment to be used in production, or the production of goods for inventories or, sometimes, government expenditure. We shall go into this in detail in Chapter 12.

The general approach we take in economics is to start our analysis from an assumed position or some assumed state of the economy. We then postulate that something changes and work through the effects of that change. This sort of theoretical analysis is therefore the application of logic or reason to a specified set of circumstances or conditions using various assumptions which we make about people's behaviour. These assumptions are absolutely crucial.

For example, we often assume that entrepreneurs are profit-maximisers. An entrepreneur is the individual responsible for organising and financing production. The word entrepreneur suggests a single individual but could equally well refer to a joint-stock company, so that to refer to an entrepreneur could mean a small businessman employing two or three workers or a massive multinational corporation. Profit-maximising means acting in such a way as to get the maximum amount of profit that it is believed can be obtained. We have good reason to believe that many entrepreneurs in the real world are not always profit-*maximisers*. They do not necessarily seek to extract every single last penny or cent of profit. Nevertheless, we may often assume that they do, and we make this assumption not because we wish to stereotype entrepreneurs or producers as exploiting profiteers, but because we must make some assumption about people's motivation before we can undertake economic analysis.

If we wish to find out how a producer decides how many people to employ and how many goods to produce we must assume something about his motivation. If we assume that he is profit-maximising we can then work out how he will make his initial decisions and how he will respond to certain changes in relevant variables. If he is *maximising* profits then we can be fairly certain what he will or should do in specified situations. If we assume that he merely seeks to obtain some 'reasonable' or 'customary' level of profit it is much more difficult for us to explain and forecast his behaviour.

This might correspond very well with the real world, where many important economic changes are indeterminate within broad ranges of forecast behaviour. For theoretical analysis, and to establish the concepts we need to have at our disposal in order to undertake economic analysis of the real world, we must first make the assumptions necessary for us to establish precise relationships. We obtain determinacy in economic theory because of the assumptions we make about the way people behave and will behave. It is necessary for us to do this, but we should never forget that the determinacy of our economic model is derived from the assumptions we have made. If those assumptions do not reflect the way people behave in the real world, the results obtained from our economic analysis or model will not explain or forecast what will happen in the real world.

The assumptions we make and the way in which we conclude that people behave and respond to changes are, collectively, what we mean by an economic model. Economists have to build models of an economy in order to analyse and forecast what will happen in different situations. A model can be simple or extremely complicated. We shall start with quite simple models and add complications as we go along in order to try to make the simple or basic models correspond more closely to the real world.

An economic model can be regarded as similar to a toy or model train or motor car with a clockwork engine. We can wind it up by feeding into the model appropriate assumptions, but the engine of the model, that which makes it run and decides in which direction and how fast and how far it will run once we have started it, consists of the motives we assume are held by the various economic agents.

Economic agents merely means all those who play any part in decisions and actions which affect the economy. You and I are economic agents. Within our total economy we are very unimportant as economic agents because there are millions of other economic agents whose actions might be different from ours and so swamp any effects our particular actions might have. But if all the others, or a large majority of them, act in the same way as we do as consumers or as workers, it is possible to group us all together and refer to the body of consumers or workers as a single category of economic agent. Similarly, trade unions are economic agents, and they may behave differently from the way in which individual workers behave. Entrepreneurs are economic agents and there may be sufficient similarities and differences among the great variety of entrepreneurs for us to regard them as different groups. Small agricultural producers may behave very similarly, as may small manufacturing producers. Large corporations may behave in broadly the same way as each other but differently from small producers, and multinational corporations may behave yet differently again.

State or government organisations might behave in a distinctly different way from all of these other producers. They may not be profit-maximising or even profit-making. They may be intended or instructed to operate at a loss.

There is sometimes an argument about whether economics is, or is not, a science. The answer may well depend on what you mean by a science, and quite frankly the question is not really important, or even perhaps relevant to our study. If a science is able to predict accurately what will happen as a result of specified changes to particular variables, and this prediction can provide the basis for accurate forecasts of real world developments, then economics is not yet a science. We just do not know enough about how economic agents will react to changes in prices, in their income, or in their behaviour, to be able to make totally reliable forecasts. The main reason for this is that economic agents can, and do, change their motivation and behaviour. They do not all, or always, respond in the same way to the same changes, or even continue to act consistently in circumstances where there are no changes in external economic variables. Because economic agents, people like you and me, are human beings, they can and do change their behaviour and motivations.

If the debate is about whether or not economic theory can provide specific determinate solutions to changes in specified economic variables, so that economic models can provide unambiguous answers when something changes, the answer is probably yes. But this is only because the assumptions fed into the model must, if the model is logically consistent, provide that solution. It does not mean that the real world will behave in the way the model predicts. This will depend on the validity or the relevance of the assumptions to the real world. Any model or economic theory is, for practical purposes, only as good as the assumptions on which it is based. This does not mean that we should not bother with economic theory or with economic models. If we did that we would have nothing to guide us in our analysis of the real world economic issues. Rather, it means that we should always try to make our assumptions as realistic as we can. There is nothing necessarily inconsistent in making different assumptions about the motivation and behaviour of economic agents in different economies, or in the same economy at different times.

Some of the assumptions made in the early chapters may seem unreasonably simple and inappropriate. They are merely to provide a starting point. Later we will amend and build on them.

While many of the examples presented here are taken from the United Kingdom, other countries are used to illustrate different conditions or circumstances where appropriate. The basic methods of analysis are relevant to all market economies, i.e. economies where the forces of demand and supply play the major role in determining prices, wages and other economic variables. There are some economies where decisions are based on administrative plans. These planned economies operate by different criteria and are not discussed in this book.

There is one final point we should make. Economists do not always agree. They differ in the assumptions they make about how economic agents act in specific economic conditions, and therefore may arrive at different conclusions about the effects of any given particular changes in the same economic forces in the same circumstances.

We shall concentrate on two main schools of economic thought. A school of economic thought consists of economists who have common views about how economic agents behave and how the economy will react to specified changes. The general approach adopted in this book is a Keynesian one. This reflects the analysis and interpretation of economic behaviour expounded by John Maynard Keynes, a British economist who wrote various influential works in the 1930s and 1940s. The other main approach discussed is known as monetarism. This interpretation goes back much earlier to eighteenth- and nineteenth-century writers and has been revived and reinterpreted by modern economists. The most well-known current monetarist writer is Milton Friedman of the United States.

The main cause of the differences between these two schools, and for that matter among other views, is the different interpretation placed on the behaviour of economic agents. Some of the difference arises from the ways in which evidence is interpreted, and some from disagreement about the choice of evidence needed to explain economic behaviour. In analysing economic problems in the real world we can never collect all the relevant information, and we can never repeat our analyses, since we can never find two exactly identical situations from which to compare results.

We cannot assert that one school of thought or method of analysis is correct and demonstrate this by rigorous proof. All we can do is conclude that one interpretation seems to explain the evidence more satisfactorily than do other explanations. This is a question of judgement. The important thing is that whatever theoretical approach or school of analysis we adopt, we should be able to justify its relevance and appropriateness to the questions we are examining. We have to be able to say why we choose one set of assumptions about how economic agents behave rather than some set of alternative assumptions. Having done this, we must then ensure that our reasoning is consistent – both in terms of its own logic, and with the evidence. This may mean that two different economists, or economics students, can arrive at different answers to the same question. Each answer will then be tested by the two criteria of consistency.

Part two

Micro-economics

CHAPTER 2

Production

Production of goods takes place by combining different factor inputs. We shall consider three factors: land, capital and labour. Land can be used for agricultural purposes or it can provide the site for factories. Capital, when referred to as a factor of production, means capital equipment such as machinery – ranging from a simple spade to the most complex automated production process such as a steel-rolling mill. It should be noted that when we use the term *capital* to refer to a factor of production we always mean *physical* capital equipment and not money or financial capital. This is one of those occasions when we give a special or technical meaning in economics to a word that is used differently in an everyday sense.

Labour is the application of human effort to production. Just as there are many different types of machines or capital equipment, so there are many different types of labour. We distinguish between the different sorts of labour by having different occupations which denote different kinds of skills or abilities. These can be seen as different qualities of labour. We can also distinguish different types of labour which have the same skills, according to the quantity of labour-effort which individuals supply in a given time period. For example, two typists may have the same quality of typing skill – they each make the same number of mistakes per thousand words – but one can type 40 words a minute and the other can type 60. Two tea pluckers may be equally skilful but one may be able to pluck half as much again as the other.

The factors of production need raw materials or product inputs to work on. Production is the process of transforming a set of raw materials into different goods or commodities. Sometimes the raw material inputs may be manufactured or semi-manufactured products rather than basic raw materials. A flour mill has wheat as its raw material input which it transforms or processes into flour. A bakery may then buy that flour as its raw material input and transform or process it into bread.

The law of varying proportions

This odd-sounding term is one of the most important concepts in economics. It says that the application of increasing amounts of one factor to fixed amounts of other factors will lead first to increasing and then to decreasing returns. Before we can see the implications of this 'law', which is really a general rule rather than a piece of legislation or law of nature, it is necessary to examine the various parts of the statement.

We will assume that the factors land and capital are fixed and given. 'Fixed' means that the quantity cannot be altered. 'Given' means that we assume a particular combination for purposes of illustration. To take a simple example we will assume that the land and capital consist of a small workshop with an electric saw and various carpenter's tools, such as a hammer, plane and chisel.

Because land and capital are assumed given and constant they are the *fixed* factors of production. The amount of labour can be changed so that labour is the *variable* factor. We could make labour the fixed factor and capital the variable one if we wished.

If only one man were employed in the workshop he would be able to produce, say, one chair each working day. He would have to do all the tasks himself, so that he would have to plane the wood, cut it to the required sizes and shapes, and then nail together the parts to make a chair. The various items of capital equipment would be idle for long periods since the worker would be able to use each of them for only part of his working day. If a second man were employed we would expect the total output to rise more than proportionately to the increase in labour. We might, therefore, find that the total output from two workers was three chairs a day. If a third man were employed output might rise to six chairs a day. This is what is meant by increasing returns. As more variable factors are used the return from each additional worker rises.

The change in output resulting from the employment of additional workers, with constant amounts of other factors of production, is shown in Table 2.1. The first column shows the number of workers. The second shows total output, in this example the number of chairs. Column three shows *average product*, which is the total output divided by the number of units of labour input. This is actually a measure of labour productivity. If we had divided by the number of units of capital we would have obtained capital productivity. Usually we measure labour productivity, and when we read that productivity is rising by 2 per cent a year, what this generally means is that total output divided by some measure of labour input is 2 per cent higher than it was in the previous year. However, such statements do not, strictly speaking, mean that the actual productivity of labour has risen, because it is never the case in the real world that the amount of other factors of production has remained constant over the two years.

Table 2.1. Average and marginal physical productivity

Number of workers	Total chairs produced	Average physical product (APP)	Marginal physical product (MPP)
1	1	1	1
2	3	1.5	2
3	6	2	3
4	10	2.5	4
5	15	3	5
6	21	3.5	6
7	26	3.7	5
8	30	3.75	4
9	33	3.67	3
10	35	3.5	2

Column four shows *marginal* product. Marginal means the change in the total resulting from the employment or use of the last unit of the variable factor. It is obtained by subtracting the total output from the employment of, say, three men from that resulting from the employment of four men – which gives the marginal product of the fourth worker.

You can see from the table that marginal product rises up to the sixth worker and then begins to decline, although total product or output continues to rise. After the sixth worker each additional worker adds something to total output – the total number of chairs produced goes up – but he adds less to the total than did the previous worker. The average and marginal products of labour from Table 2.1 are shown in Fig. 2.1.

The term 'decreasing returns' means that the marginal product is falling so that the increase in total output resulting from the employment of an additional unit of the variable factor (in this example, labour) is less than the increase resulting from the employment of the previous unit of the variable factor. In Table 2.1 there are increasing returns up to the sixth worker, and diminishing returns from the seventh worker onwards.

There are two main reasons why average and marginal product should

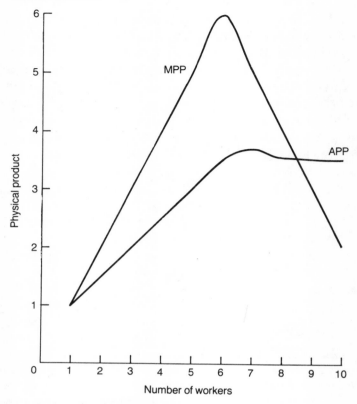

Fig. 2.1 Average and marginal physical productivity

change in this way. The first is the specialisation or division of labour. If only one worker was employed he would have to perform all the tasks we described earlier. As more workers are employed each one can specialise because the various tasks are divided among them; thus each worker can become more efficient at this particular task. There will also be less time wasted in moving from one task to another, so that each worker will spend more of his working day actually producing chairs. Secondly, however, there will come a point when, with the given fixed factors of production, each additional worker will add less to total output because there will be insufficient room or tools for him to work effectively. The particular combination of the electric saw and other tools that are assumed at the beginning of the analysis are appropriate to a given number of workers; if more workers are employed there will not be enough capital equipment for them to be fully or properly employed. The marginal product obtained by employing them will therefore be less than the marginal product from the number of workers for which the workshop was designed, or for which the capital equipment was appropriate.

We have to emphasise one reason which does *not* explain the rise and fall in marginal product. It is not because some workers are better than others. Indeed, we actually specify in this analysis that workers are homogeneous; this means that they are identical in all respects. They are equally efficient, equally skilled and work equally hard. We know in the real world that workers are *heterogeneous*. They differ in their skills, abilities, application, motivation and in the pace at which they work, as we suggested with the typists and tea pluckers earlier. What we are saying here is that even if we ignore all these differences among individuals and assume that workers are homogeneous, there will still be rising, then falling, marginal productivity of labour. If one individual worker were better (or worse) than the others, then it is possible that his individual marginal product would be higher (or lower) than that shown in Table 2.1, but this possibility is ignored in this example.

However, we have to complicate the assumption about homogeneity. We have seen that the specialisation or division of labour is an important cause of rising marginal productivity. This means that while the different workers were equal in skill and ability at the time they were employed, they became unequal in *specific* skills once they had been employed and had some experience of performing certain tasks. The man who spends all his working time making chair legs will do this better and make more chair legs a day than those who do other tasks. The worker who runs the electric saw will become better at doing that than the others because he becomes more experienced and specialised. We still assume homogeneity within a specialised task, so that every leg-maker is equally good and indistinguishable from every other leg-maker, but the leg-makers are better at making legs than are the other non-specialist leg-maker workers. This is true of each of the other specialised tasks.

This has an important implication for production methods. The amount and type of capital equipment used may call for considerable specialisation or division of labour. The obvious example is an assembly-production method in an automobile factory, but the same division of labour can be found in a mass-production clothing factory where machinists may do very specialised tasks, such as making buttonholes in shirts or sewing pockets in trousers. To obtain the highest average and marginal product of labour with given capital may require particular forms of work organisation which may lead to a very narrow specialisation and considerable division of labour. The assumption that labour is homogeneous relates only to the specific occupation or type of work that is being referred to.

There is one other point that we should note about this simple explanation. In Table 2.1 we assumed that one man would produce one chair in a day and that two men would produce three chairs and so on. These figures depend on an assumption about the type of labour effort-input forthcoming. It may be that if we were to measure actual outputs from this carpenter's shop we would find that the marginal products were only half as much as we state in Table 2.1, or they could be twice as high. Until we know the amount and type of labour effort-input represented by eight hours' work from the assumed homogeneous labour, we cannot actually calculate the outputs. In one economy outputs may be higher with identical capital equipment than in another, owing to differences in the quality of labour or because of variations in what is regarded as a normal or usual day's effort. Similarly, the labour effort-input from a given workforce with the same capital equipment can change through time. If this occurs there will be a change in the average and marginal products.

In the same way, if the amount or quality – i.e. the type – of capital equipment should change, we would expect the average and marginal products of labour to alter.

It is possible that very narrow specialisation of tasks affects the morale and attitudes, and so the level or effectiveness, of labour effort-input. This would not prevent the emergence of increasing and decreasing returns but would mean that the level of output per worker would be lower. This is illustrated in Fig. 2.2, where curve MP_1 shows the marginal product of labour before the loss of morale and curve MP_2 shows the marginal product of labour following the reduced labour morale effort-input. Conversely, if labour can be induced to work harder, or if the workforce receives additional appropriate training, marginal productivity of labour may increase from MP_2 to MP_1. The amount of labour effort-input obtained or expected per unit of time worked is influenced by social factors and is neither constant nor necessarily known.

The short and the long run

In economic analysis we do not allow the amount or type of the fixed factors to alter in the short run. Put differently, we say that in the short run the fixed factors are fixed. That is how we define the short run – it is that period in which some factors are fixed, and so cannot be altered in either amount or type. The variable factor can be altered in the short run, as we

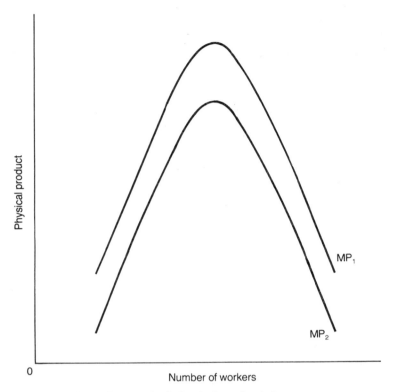

Fig. 2.2 Shifting the marginal physical productivity curve

employed more labour while the quantity of capital could not be altered.

In the long run all factors can be altered so that we could, in our example of the chair-making factory, have bought more tools or another electric saw in the long run. If we had done this we would expect all the marginal and average products of labour to alter.

Employment and marginal productivity

We can use the concept of marginal product to shed some light on the question of how the level of employment is determined. The marginal product shown in Table 2.1 is the marginal *physical* product, or MPP. It is physical product because we measured output in units of chairs produced, i.e. the physical product. If we assume that each worker is paid the equivalent of three chairs for a day's work, then from Table 2.1 we can see that the employer of this factory would employ nine workers. If the *tenth* worker were employed he would add only *two* chairs to total output, but the employer would have to pay him the equivalent of three chairs. If the employer had stopped hiring workers at the *third* man, who also has an MPP of three chairs, he would be making a loss since the first *two* workers added less than three chairs to output yet were paid the equivalent of three chairs, and each worker between the *third* and the *ninth* added more than three chairs to total output.

This relationship becomes easier to understand if we convert the marginal physical productivities of each worker into marginal revenue productivities (MRP). This is done by multiplying the units of physical output by the price each unit of output will obtain. Thus, if each chair is

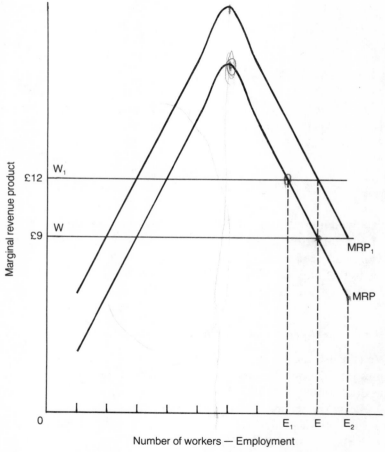

Fig. 2.3 Marginal revenue product, wages and the level of employment

sold for £3, the MRP of each worker is obtained by multiplying his MPP by £3. This gives us a simple formula: MRP=MPP (P) where P is the price of each unit of output.

Figure 2.3 shows the MRP curve and the assumed wage level of £9 a day. The level of employment is E on the horizontal axis. If only E_1 workers were employed the entrepreneur could gain by increasing employment and output since the MRP is higher than the wage. If more than E workers are employed, say E_2, the entrepreneur is paying out more in wages than he receives from selling the product of the extra workers (E-E_2) and so is incurring a loss on those workers. Once the level of wages and the MRP are known, the level of employment of profit-maximising employees is also known.

If the MRP is given and there is an increase in wages from W to W_1, the level of employment will fall from E to E_1, as shown in Fig. 2.3.

However, if it is possible to increase the MRP to MRP_1, the level of employment may remain at E. If the price of chairs is outside the control of the entrepreneur so that he cannot alter the price he charges for each of his chairs that he sells, the only way that MRP can rise to MRP_1 is if there is an increase in MPP. If MPP increases, perhaps because workers increase their effort-input, then there can be an increase in wages to W_1 without employment falling. We can now see one aspect of the importance of the assumption that labour is homogeneous and that the effort-input remains constant. If this occurs, an increase in wages with constant MRP will lead to less employment.

CHAPTER 3

Costs and supply

We have seen that when engaged in the production of goods, an entrepreneur uses both fixed and variable factors of production. The amount of variable factors used can be changed immediately, or at very short notice. Fixed factors are different in that once they have been engaged or bought, the entrepreneur has to pay for them even if he does not use them. Also, he cannot increase the fixed factors in the short run – which is why they are called fixed factors. The short run is also the length of time it takes for the entrepreneur to obtain more fixed factors if he is expanding or seeking to obtain more of them, or it is the time taken to dispose of the fixed factors he already has if he is reducing production. The short run is not, therefore, a constant period of time. It will vary from industry to industry depending on the type of capital equipment used and the time taken for a firm to obtain more of them. For example, we might expect a tailor's shop or garment-making factory to be able to increase its capital equipment (a fixed factor) more quickly than an oil refinery. It might be possible to obtain an additional sewing machine in a few days but it may be two or three years before additional refining plant can be designed, made and installed. Even with the sewing machine the short run could be quite lengthy if the additional machine had to be imported, with the consequential delays this might involve.

As we have two types of factors – fixed and variable – so we can regard the firm or entrepreneur as having two types of costs – fixed costs and variable costs.

Fixed costs

Fixed costs are the costs of employing the fixed factors of production. For simplicity of explanation we will assume that the fixed factors of production are land and capital equipment. In order to produce the firm has to have a plant, factory or workshop (we can use these terms interchangeably). These factors might have been bought or rented for a given period. In either case the firm has to meet those costs for some time period. If they are bought a certain sum will have been spent on them. If they are rented a certain sum will have to be paid for the length of the rental agreement. They can therefore be seen as fixed lump-sum costs, which have to be met whether or not any production takes place. Because they are a fixed sum, for as long as that quantity of fixed factors remains given or constant, it is clear that the amount of fixed costs per unit of output will decrease as output increases. Moreover, the average fixed costs per unit of output (AFC) will decrease in a special way. This is illustrated in Fig. 3.1, which

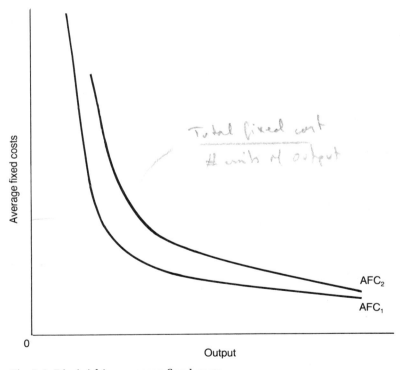

Fig. 3.1 Diminishing average fixed costs

shows two separate average fixed cost curves. AFC_1 represents a particular size of plant and AFC_2 is the curve for a plant which is twice as large, so that the total fixed costs are twice as large as in AFC_1 and the AFC per unit of output are also twice as large for each level of output.

The AFC is obtained by dividing the total fixed cost (TFC) by the number of units of output. The slope of an AFC curve is always the same as the curve is a rectangular hyperbola. All that this means is that for every level of output on that curve the AFC multiplied by the number of units of output comes to the same total – the TFC. This has to be so because the AFC is simply the TFC divided by the particular number of units of output shown on the horizontal scale of Fig. 3.1.

A universal rule therefore is that as output increases average fixed costs decline, but at a diminishing rate.

Remember also that some fixed costs have to be met whether production takes place or not. They cannot be avoided unless the firm goes out of business. Even then it may have to pay some fixed costs if it is committed to a rental agreement for some time ahead. There are other fixed costs which might have to be met if the firm operates at all but which might be avoidable if the firm closes down. If the firm produces only one unit of output it might have to pay a standing electricity or water charge, rates or a local tax, and insurance. If it closes down it might escape these costs.

The key feature of fixed costs is that once incurred, i.e. for a given amount of fixed factors, they do not vary with the level of output.

Variable costs

The costs of the variable factors do vary with the level of output. Remember, variable factors can be changed in the short run. We are assuming that labour is a variable factor, so that the entrepreneur can hire more or less labour as he wishes, and we are assuming that he can vary the amount of labour he uses immediately. In the real world this may not be the case. It may take time before additional workers can be recruited and trained, and there may be laws or collective agreements which prevent an employer from dismissing workers at immediate notice. For analytical purposes, in order to understand how the employer's costs are determined, we will ignore these complications, although in reality they may be very important.

We are now assuming that the employer can recruit as much homogeneous labour as he wishes at the prevailing wage level. This means that if he wants more labour he can immediately obtain as many additional workers as he wishes at the same wage as he is already paying his existing workforce. The new recruits are assumed to be homogeneous with the existing workforce so that they are equally efficient as the existing workers. We are also assuming that the cost of the raw materials for each unit of output remains constant irrespective of the level of output. If the factory is producing chairs, the cost of timber for each chair made is assumed to be the same whether the firm produces one, ten or 100 chairs a day. We are also assuming that any other variable costs of production are constant for each unit of output so that the cost of electricity to run the electric saw is assumed to be the same for each chair no matter how many chairs are produced. The total electric bill will vary directly and exactly according to the output of chairs. If 20 chairs are produced, the total electric bill is assumed to be twice the amount of producing ten chairs, so that the raw material and other variable input costs are assumed to be constant per unit of output.

The average labour costs per unit of output will, however, not remain the same per unit of output, even though the wage paid to each additional worker is the same. As output increases the labour cost or wages-per-unit of output will vary, even though each worker costs the employer the same amount since wages are assumed to be fixed and constant. This apparent contradiction is explained by and derived from the law of varying proportions, which we discussed in Chapter 2.

There we explained that the MPP and APP per worker, with a given amount of fixed factors of production, first rose and then fell. If each worker is paid the same wage this means that the average labour cost per unit of output will first fall and then rise. The labour cost per unit of output is determined by dividing the amount of output by the labour cost which we are assuming is the same as wages. Average labour costs are therefore obtained from total wages/total output, which is the same as $E \cdot W / E \cdot APP$ where E is the number of workers employed; W is the wage per worker; and APP is the average physical productivity. The wage cost per unit of output resulting from employing an additional worker is the wage of that worker divided by his marginal physical productivity, or W/MPP.

We have seen in Chapter 2 that with a given amount of fixed factors MPP first rises and then falls as more workers are employed. As we can see from Table 3.1 this means that average and marginal labour costs per unit of output will first fall and then rise as more workers are employed and output increases.

We therefore have two sorts of variable costs. There are those which we will assume are constant per unit of output irrespective of the level of

Table 3.1. Average and marginal labour costs per unit of output

Number of workers (1)	Wage per worker (2)	Total wages (3)	Total chairs produced (4)	Average labour cost (5)	Marginal labour cost (6)
1	10	10	1	10	10
2	10	20	3	6.67	5
3	10	30	6	5	3.3
4	10	40	10	4	2.5
5	10	50	15	3.33	2
6	10	60	21	2.86	1.67
7	10	70	26	2.69	2
8	10	80	30	2.67	2.5
9	10	90	33	2.73	3.33
10	10	100	35	2.86	5

Notes: 1. Column (5) is column (3) divided by column (4).
2. Column (6) is the change in column (3) for each number of workers employed, divided by the change in column (4). Strictly speaking, this shows how unit labour costs vary as additional workers are employed. It is assumed that each worker must be employed for a full day at a wage of £10 rather than only for the time taken to produce one extra chair.

output, such as the raw materials used in production, and there are labour costs which will vary with the level of output as a result of the law of varying proportions. We can add these together to obtain an average variable cost curve, as shown in Fig. 3.2. The figure also shows the AFC curve. If we add these together we obtain the ATC or average total cost curve. This shows the average costs per unit produced with the given amount of fixed factors.

In addition the figure shows the marginal cost curve (MC). This is the change in total cost which is incurred as a result of producing one additional unit of output. It is therefore made up of the marginal labour cost per unit of output plus the raw material costs and any additional costs such as extra electricity used to produce one more unit of output.

There is one important feature of the ATC and MC curves which should be noted. The MC curve *always* cuts the ATC curve at the lowest point on the ATC curve. This is because the change in ATC as output is increased depends on what is happening to MC. The change in ATC as a result of producing one more unit of output depends on how the MC of that additional unit compare with the ATC for the current level of output, since the new ATC, including the extra unit of output, is the previous ATC plus the MC of the extra unit divided by the previous level of output plus 1. It is the same arithmetical principle as we find with average cricket scores. If a batsman has an average of 50 runs an innings (and we assume he has no Not Out innings so every innings is counted in the denominator), whether

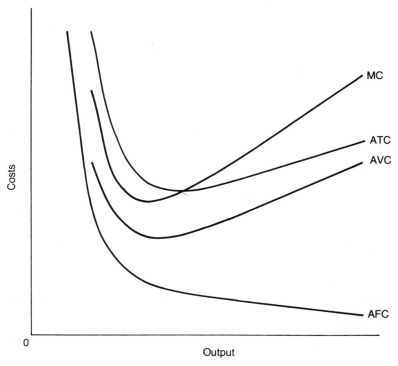

Fig. 3.2 Average fixed, variable, total and marginal costs

his average score goes up, falls or remains constant depends on how many runs he scores in his next or marginal innings. If he scores more than 50 his average will rise. If he scores less than 50 it will fall, and if he scores exactly 50 it will remain constant.

Thus, when MC are falling ATC are also falling. When MC begin to rise ATC will continue to fall as long as the MC are less than the ATC. When MC are larger than ATC the ATC will increase just as scores of more than 50 will pull up the batting average. Where the ATC is at its lowest point it will equal the MC, for if at that point the MC were higher than the ATC, the ATC would in fact have to be rising, and conversely if the MC were lower than the ATC.

As we shall see later, the fact that the MC always cuts the ATC at the lowest point on the ATC curve has important consequences for production and resource allocation decisions. The level of output where MC=AC is the most efficient level of output for that plant, given the amount and type of capital equipment and given the level of effort-input of its workforce, for that is the level of output where average costs are lowest. From now on we shall refer to ATC simply as AC, so that when we refer to average costs we mean average total costs which include both fixed and variable costs.

We have been able to derive short-run cost curves for a firm which will apply for as long as the fixed factors remain the same, on the assumption that the firm can obtain as many units of homogeneous variable factors that it wishes at the prevailing wages or costs. It has not been necessary for us to know or make any assumptions about the level of demand. On the assumptions made, the short-run costs are totally independent of the level of demand. The cost curves are short-run costs because they apply only as long as the fixed factors remain constant, and this is what we mean by the short run.

Long-run cost curves

The amount of fixed factors can be changed in the long run. When this happens a new set of cost curves will have to be drawn up. The fixed costs will change as the amount of fixed factors is altered, and the variable costs are also likely to change. We illustrated in Fig. 3.1 how the fixed costs may change: as the amount of fixed factors is increased the AFC curve moves from AFC_1 to AFC_2. There is a whole series of possible amounts of fixed factors which the entrepreneur could choose to install.

For each amount of fixed factors there will be a corresponding AVC curve. The amount of variable factors necessary to produce a given level of output will change according to the *type* of fixed factors which are used. Capital equipment or machinery can be designed so that it uses more or less labour to produce a given level of output. In the example of the chair factory the entrepreneur could have used handsaws instead of an electric saw. This would have reduced his fixed costs but might have increased his total costs because more labour would have been needed to produce the same amount of sawn wood using handsaws. In agricultural production a tractor can be bought so that crops are transported by mechanical means instead of being carried by agricultural labourers. Fewer units of the variable factor labour will then be needed to produce the same amount of output which, in this example, is the volume of crops transported from one place to another.

If more fixed factors are used we would expect the optimum level of output for that plant or factory to increase. With only a small level of output the AFC would tend to be high, and the more fixed factors that are used the more efficient it is to operate the plant at a scale which fully utilises them. We expect therefore to find that there are *economies of scale*; as production is expanded by the addition of more units of fixed factors of production the AC falls. There are a number of reasons for this.

We can distinguish economies which are internal to the plant and those which are external.

Internal economies

Technical economies As plants and the capital equipment they use get bigger, production costs increase at a slower rate. The larger the capital equipment the less, proportionately, is the amount of labour needed. Generally speaking, a machine that is twice as large as the one it replaces does not need twice as many workers to operate or maintain it. A lorry with a load capacity of 20 tons needs only one driver, but two ten-ton lorries would each need a driver. The initial costs in setting up a production process may be high, as with the development and tooling-up required to manufacture a new model of a car. The greater the output over which these costs can be spread, the lower the cost per unit produced. Large-scale assembly-line or flow production methods will result in less idle machine time, since work can be passed on from one process to the next without the machine standing unused. As more output will be produced from the capital equipment, the capital costs per unit of output will be lower. There will also be economies of scale resulting from the specialisation or division of labour.

Managerial economies This can be seen as part of the specialisation of labour. Expert accountants, engineers and a specialist company secretary can be employed by a large plant, each specialist making a particular contribution depending on his or her expertise. A small plant might not be able to afford to hire the different specialists, and if it did, they would be underemployed or idle for part of their working day. Some costs do not rise proportionately to the size of the transactions. Even if a larger company employs more specialist accountants and finance staff so that it pays higher wages to its finance staff than does a small company, it may still be the case that the cost of preparing invoices and paying bills falls per item of transaction. It is unlikely that it will cost 100 times as much to process a cheque for £100,000 as it does to process one for £1,000.

Financial economies Larger companies can obtain finance more easily and cheaply than can smaller companies, and need to maintain proportionately lower reserves. The cost of raising new finance by issuing new shares does not rise proportionately with the size of the new issue. Larger firms can borrow at lower rates of interest.

Marketing economies These may be available for both buying and selling. A large firm buying large quantities of raw materials in bulk will probably be able to buy at a lower price than a firm taking smaller quantities. On the selling side, a large firm may benefit from joint distribution of various products. It may be able to ensure that all its delivery vans and lorries carry full loads as it is supplying a number of different products to a number of purchasers in one locality. Or it may obtain bulk load discounts from other providers of transport facilities. If there is advertising, the cost per unit sold will not rise proportionately.

Research and development economies A large firm can finance research and development more easily than can a small firm, and by spreading the cost over a larger amount of output this will result in a relatively lower increase in R & D costs per unit of output.

Risk-bearing economies A large firm can spread the risks of loss over a number of different products. It therefore needs to keep fewer reserves in relation to total turnover. It may be better able to try out new products if the effects of a product failure will not threaten the future existence of the whole firm. A small firm may be unable to take the same risks and may be reluctant to do so if failure of the new product meant that the firm might go bankrupt. However, as we shall discuss in Chapter 8, it does not follow that large firms will take more risks or that small firms will not engage in R & D or make significant technological breakthroughs. What the existence of these economies of scale means is that it is relatively cheaper and easier for a large firm to undertake these activities as it is able to benefit from the spreading of expenditure over a larger amount of output.

External economies

There may be external economies of scale which accrue to all firms in an industry or locality. These are not the result of the relative size of individual firms but arise from factors external to each firm or plant.

Labour supply If there is a tradition of certain sorts of work in a locality, such as mining in South Yorkshire or sugar growing in the West Indies or Mauritius, the labour supply in those areas may have some knowledge of the industry and be more willing to work in it than if the firm were setting up in an area with no tradition of that sort of employment. There may be a supply of unemployed workers with the necessary skills. Local education and training facilities may provide the specialist skills and occupations needed.

Trade associations Firms in the same industry may form an association to provide research facilities which help all firms. They may also advertise and encourage consumption of the product in general rather than the product of a single producer, thus increasing demand for the output of each firm – which can allow each firm to operate on a lower cost curve and obtain returns to scale.

Transport and ancillary services If a number of firms in the same industry are located near each other there may be improvements in the common services used by them. A sugar mill may be provided close by if there are four or five sugar estates, but this might not be an economic proposition for any one estate. Specialist repair services and other firms providing semi-manufactured inputs may be attracted by the presence of a number of firms as potential customers, and this can lower input costs.

Economies of the plant and the firm

Most of the internal economies of scale we have listed apply to a particular plant or factory. Many firms are multi-plant firms or companies in that they own a number of plants. There may be additional economies of scale to a multi-plant firm even when it has exhausted the plant-level economies of scale. The financial and managerial economies may still apply. A large company may be able to obtain economies from a central finance or marketing organisation by utilising the expertise in all its plants. It may obtain larger discounts from bulk purchasing if it co-ordinates the buying of all raw materials and inputs. It may recruit better personnel if it can offer promotion by transferring people among the various plants.

The search for further economies of scale at the level of the company may lead it to *horizontal* integration. This involves replicating the activity of one plant in a number of others so that the various plants are basically doing the same thing, producing the same products. An example of this is a company which has a number of bakeries in different parts of the country, each one making the same product. Horizontal integration can provide economies of scale when there are limits to the technical or other economies of scale at the level of the plant, but when there are still other economies, such as bulk purchasing, advertising of a brand or company name, utilisation of central financial reserves and specialist expertise, which can be applied to other aspects of production and sales. In the case of bakeries the cost of transport of the finished product, and the possible loss of quality resulting from the time taken to deliver it from a single large plant to different parts of the country, might explain the replication of a number of bakeries owned by the same company.

Services provide many examples of horizontal integration. Chains of shops, such as that of Bata selling Bata shoes, are intended to provide a source of outlet for the product in a number of localities. Customers might not be prepared to travel large distances to buy this particular brand of shoes, so retail outlets are small and conveniently placed. The production of shoes might have considerable economies of scale in the one plant, so it would make sense to have one large factory making the shoes and a number of shops selling them.

Vertical integration takes place when there are economies of scale available to the company as a result of undertaking activity at different stages of the production process. Thus, a bakery might buy or establish a flour-milling plant or its own retail shops. This can allow central expertise and finance to be used over a larger range of activity, thereby reducing the unit costs, and may permit specialised knowledge of the productive or marketing process to be used more effectively. It can also allow the company to benefit by bulk purchases and to cut out the profits of intermediary producers.

Diversified or conglomerate integration

Some companies have expanded, generally by taking over or merging with other firms, into quite different types of activity, so that there has been neither horizontal nor vertical integration. These are generally referred to as conglomerates. Economies of scale might be achieved by the use of the central managerial expertise, financial resources, marketing skills or superior general managerial abilities. In other cases the diversification might be deliberately designed to spread the risks of the company so that it will be less seriously affected by future changes in consumers' tastes and demand. For example, some chocolate and sweets manufacturers have diversified into food production. This will not only give them new markets should the public taste for sweets decline, but will also allow them to take advantage of some of their existing specialisations and economies of scale. They can use their expertise in producing under hygienic conditions and sell the new products under their established brand name. They may have well-developed connections with many retail outlets so that their marketing staff can easily adapt to the new products.

Diseconomies of scale

However, at some point diseconomies of scale occur. As plants get beyond a certain size they become less efficient, and MC and AC begin to rise. There may be various reasons for this.

The plant may simply become too big to organise and manage very efficiently. As organisations grow beyond a certain point it becomes much more difficult to organise and integrate their activities. It is not possible for a single manager to control all the activities, and even though the use of specialists can bring economies of scale, at some point it becomes so difficult to integrate the various specialist activities that diseconomies set in. Co-ordinating the work of the various sections begins to pose problems, and communication among the various departments becomes more and more difficult. Inter-departmental rivalries may develop which impede co-ordination and create inefficiencies.

The need to have specialist departments with arrangements for co-ordination and managerial hierarchies may add considerably to the costs as more and more specialists are employed. In short, the organisation can become 'top-heavy'.

Large plants and firms may also become 'institutionalised' and impersonal. Individual workers may not have a feeling of identity with the firm. With small firms the employer may know all his employees individually and they may feel part of the organisation, committed to its aims and well-being, and so have more motivation. In large establishments the workers may feel 'alienated', and their morale and productivity may suffer. In addition, the large-scale operation may require very narrow specialisation of labour, so that there is little or no job satisfaction because workers are employed on repetitive routine work processes. This is obviously noticeable in the case of assembly-line production. In the terms we introduced in Chapter 2, this means that the effort-input suffers because of the size of the plant, or as a result of the work organisation and job content. We cannot always separate these two elements. The main cause of the diseconomies may be simply the sheer size of the plant, which causes poor morale, reduced effort-input and lack of commitment, or it may be the work organisation and job content which is associated with, or the result of, large plants.

There is a tendency in large plants for more industrial disputes to arise, for absenteeism to be higher and for there to be more labour turnover. Each of these can increase costs per unit of output and so lead to diseconomies of scale. The features which contribute to economies of scale at the level of the plant can be seen as *technologically possible economies of scale*. Technology and work organisation with the division or specialisation of labour may permit these economies to be achieved. However, *sociological diseconomies of scale* may prevent the technologically possible economies from being achieved. The sort of labour effort-input resulting from large-scale production with narrow divisions of labour, and the organisational and institutional features which are often associated with large plants, may create social pressures which lead to lower effort-input, more industrial unrest, less commitment to the firm, and so on, the total effect of which causes average costs to increase.

It should be noted that these sociological diseconomies can be seen as contradicting the assumption about labour homogeneity. If workers are homogeneous so that they provide the same effort-input irrespective of the size of plant, the diseconomies may not arise. We can still try to keep the homogeneity assumption by saying that the jobs are different in the large firms because they involve much narrower tasks and are much more restricted and repetitively routine, so the question of homogeneity between the two types of workers does not arise. They are different occupations and all that the homogeneity assumption requires is that workers in each of the two separate occupations be identical. However, even though this may often be the case, there can be some occupations which are almost identical whether they are in large or small firms, e.g. a driver, and there can still be differences in attitudes, morale and effort-input.

The series of possible short-run cost curves facing a firm will probably look something like those shown in Fig. 3.3. There is a very large range of possible amounts of fixed factors which the firm could use. Each of these provides a short-run cost curve because once the firm has selected that combination of fixed factors it is burdened with those fixed costs for the short-run period. It can, after that short-run period, choose to move to any other of the short-run cost curves, each of which represents a different amount of fixed factors. As a result of economies and diseconomies of scale

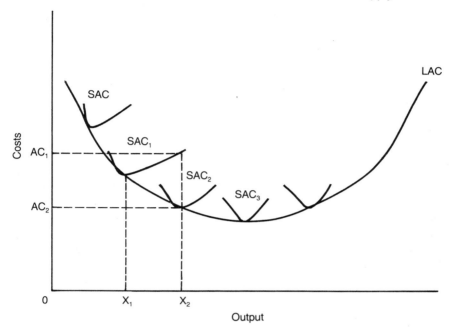

Fig. 3.3 Short-run and long-run cost curves

we would expect the short-run cost curves first to fall and then rise as the optimum level of output for which each short-run cost curve is designed to produce increases.

The lowest point on each short-run cost curve, where the MC=AC for that short-run curve, is the most efficient, i.e. the optimum size of plant for producing that level of output. Thus in Fig. 3.3 the level of output OX_1 can be produced most efficiently by using the amount of fixed factors represented by short-run cost curve SAC_1. If the level of output OX_2 is required this can be produced from SAC_1 at an average cost of OAC_1. However, if the firm expands to SAC_2 it can produce output OX_2 at an average cost of OAC_2. This is obviously more efficient. What the firm seeks to do therefore is to have the amount of fixed factors represented by the short-run cost curve which can produce its planned level of output most efficiently. It can always produce any given level of output from more than one SAC, as we have just seen. But there is only one SAC which produces that level of output most efficiently.

We can join together or combine the various SACs to obtain a long-run cost curve (LAC). We do this by joining the various SACs as represented by the LAC in Fig. 3.3. You will see from the way the LAC is drawn that it does not actually touch the lowest point on each SAC except for SAC_3, which is the lowest of all the possible SACs.

Each SAC, and thus the LAC, represents the costs of producing different amounts of output by using different amounts of fixed factors. Different amounts of variable factors will also be used. The SAC represent the costs of producing the appropriate levels of output from given technology. Thus SAC_1 in Fig. 3.3 may represent the production costs if the fixed factors of production consist of two handsaws and a given combination of hammers, planes, chisels, etc. SAC_2 represents the costs if three handsaws and the same combination of other tools are used, and SAC_3 shows the costs if an electric saw is used.

However, if a new type of electric saw was developed which, for the same cost, was more efficient, it would be necessary to draw a completely new set of SACs and so a new LAC. In the same way, if the effort-input from each worker increased, all the SACs and the LAC would be reduced; they would rise if the effort-input per worker was reduced.

Choice of plant size and combination of factors

A company has to choose on which SAC it wishes to operate. In some cases the decision about which short-run cost curve to establish is a long-term decision. A car assembly plant, a concrete-making factory, an oil refinery or a brewery each represents one SAC in that in time they can each be altered by the addition or removal of some of the fixed factors. However, once the decision to build these plants has been made, a large amount of capital has been invested and it may be a number of years before the size of the plant can be extended.

The firm must also decide on the particular combinations of fixed and variable factors it wishes to employ. As we have seen, it can use different combinations of capital and labour to produce the same total output. We can distinguish between *capital-intensive* and *labour-intensive* methods of production according to whether a firm uses more capital or more labour. It can decide to move to a new SAC. We shall discuss this choice in more detail in Chapter 10.

We have seen that an SAC curve first falls and then rises. The rate at which it changes indicates the effects on a firm's costs of producing levels of output which are not the optimum level for that SAC. If a firm is certain that it will wish to produce exactly the optimum of its SAC it may not matter whether the SAC changes sharply or slowly. Figure 3.4 shows two

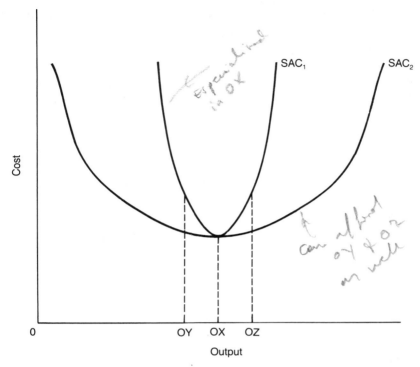

Fig. 3.4 Cost curves of different types of organisation

possible SACs for the same optimum level of output OX. SAC_1 is designed to produce exactly OX and if output departs from this by only small amounts, say OY or OZ, average and marginal costs increase sharply.

SAC_2 is designed to produce OX equally efficiently, but uses a different combination of fixed factors. It may use different sorts of machines, different technology or different mixes of fixed and variable factors. This particular plant can produce amounts OY or OZ at costs which are very little higher than the optimum costs of producing OX. This is a much better SAC for a firm. It provides a range of output levels over which costs are almost constant, thereby reducing the risks or uncertainties to the firm – which may be unsure of the actual level of output it wishes to produce in the future. The best thing for the firm is if it can organise its production so that it has constant costs, or constant returns to scale, over a wide range of output. In this case, fluctuations in output will not cause sharply rising costs. It may seek to do this by designing its production methods so that for a single SAC it has a range of output with constant costs, i.e. its SAC is flatbottomed. Or it may have a number of SACs which are very similar in their level of optimum production costs so that while each SAC is not flatbottomed, the LAC is fairly flat.

The shape of the SAC depends on the law of varying proportions and on how the various factors of production and the technology used combine to determine the MPP. The LAC depends on economies and diseconomies of scale.

CHAPTER 4

Consumer demand

Consumers have limited means. No matter how rich we may be there is some limit to our wealth and income. We have to make two types of decision. The first, which we shall discuss in Chapter 11, is how to decide between spending and saving. The second, which we are considering here, is how to allocate our spending among the various goods and services available to us. At this stage we shall assume that each individual has a certain amount of money to spend on goods and services and that he spends all of it. This is the same as assuming that all his income is spent or that he has already decided how to allocate his income between saving and spending. For the present it does not matter which of these assumptions we make; the end result is the same. The individual has a certain amount of money which he spends on different commodities.

We make two assumptions about the consumer. Consumer means the individual purchasing goods or services for use or consumption, that is for immediate personal enjoyment and *not* to be used in production. We are therefore not considering here firms or entrepreneurs who may buy goods to be used as raw materials or inputs into their own production processes. The first asumption is that the consumer is rational. By this we mean that he always seeks to attain the objective we specify for him, and that he behaves in a consistent way. The second assumption is that the consumer seeks to maximise his utility. Utility is the satisfaction obtained from the consumption of goods and services.

By combining these two assumptions we conclude that the consumer must always behave in a way which will give him more and not less utility. This may sound reasonable enough but there is one absolutely crucial point to remember: *we cannot measure utility directly*. I cannot say I got six units of utility from consuming or purchasing a new shirt and three units of utility from a visit to the cinema. I can say that I got twice as much utility from the shirt than from the cinema, but that is not the same as being able to measure in consistent objective units the difference between the utility obtained from consumption of the two different items.

A second important feature of utility is that because it is essentially subjective – it is the satisfaction a particular individual derives from consumption – and there are no standard units of measurement of utility, we cannot make quantifiable comparisons or assessments of the utility obtained by different individuals. The fact that I get twice the utility from buying a particular shirt than I do from a cinema visit does not mean that anyone else has the same ratio of utilities from these two goods. You could get equal utility from them or the cinema visit could give you twice as much utility as the shirt.

Even if you tell me that you also get twice as much utility from purchasing the shirt than from going to the cinema, so that we have the same ratios of utilities, I cannot tell whether the *amount* or *level* of utility you get from the shirt is the same as the amount or level of utility I get from it. It is not possible to measure the level or amount of one person's utility and compare it in a quantifiable way with that received by another. This is exactly the same as recognising that we have or do not have any way of measuring the pain or pleasure received by two different individuals.

Strictly speaking we cannot make interpersonal comparisons of utility. As we shall see later, we often act as though we can, or we make certain economic policy decisions on the basis that while we may not, strictly speaking, be able to measure and compare the utilities of different individuals, we can nevertheless make certain generalisations. If we tax a very rich person and redistribute the income we have taxed away from him to a poor person, we are saying that the utility lost by the rich man losing £10 is less than the utility gained by the poor person receiving that £10. We are saying that total utility will be increased by such a transfer of income and consumption. We cannot actually prove this because we cannot directly measure the amount of utility lost and gained by the two individuals.

Diminishing marginal utility

It is universally assumed that in normal cases the amount of utility we derive from the consumption of each additional unit of the same commodity diminishes. As we consume additional units of the same commodity, marginal utility declines. Marginal utility is the extra utility obtained from an additional unit consumed. If I obtain one pair of shoes I will get a certain amount of utility. If I get a second pair I will still derive some utility but less than I did from the first pair because I already have one pair. A third pair will give me still less utility than the second pair, and so on. Strictly speaking, each pair of shoes should be identical in order for us to come to this conclusion, but even if they are not identical the general principle probably still holds.

For most goods every additional unit will provide *some* extra utility so that the marginal utility will be positive even though it is diminishing. However, there may be some special goods where the marginal utility is zero. I get utility from the first copy of today's issue of the *Guardian* newspaper that I buy. I would not obtain any additional utility from buying a second copy of today's *Guardian*. I would get some positive marginal utility from a copy of today's *Times*, and from a copy of tomorrow's *Guardian*, but a second copy of today's *Guardian* has zero marginal utility for me.

The concept that marginal utility diminishes has to be applied rather carefully. It applies, strictly speaking, only to additional units of the same commodity, and it is not always easy to decide when two items are additional units of the same commodity and when they are different commodities. Let us assume (and I certainly hope that it is a valid assumption) that a copy of this book has some positive marginal utility to a student of economics. Even I, as the author, would admit that a second copy is unlikely to have any positive marginal utility to that student. A copy of a different book on economics could have more or less utility than has this book, and a copy of a book on company administration could have high, or perhaps zero, marginal utility to that student, depending on whether he is studying that subject. It is quite difficult, therefore, for us to say whether all books have diminishing marginal utility. We can say something about the marginal utility of additional copies of the same book, but this is not all that helpful. If we are referring to books in general we might conclude that the principle of diminishing marginal utility applies but that there can be exceptions. The books needed to study for Part 3 of an examination might have as much utility as those needed to study for Part 1, so that marginal utility for these different books does not decline; indeed, it could actually increase since passing Part 3 becomes more important once the time and effort in passing the earlier parts have been incurred.

There may be other situations in which the general tendency for marginal utility to decline is inappropriate. Goods associated with addiction may be one example. Someone addicted to tobacco or a drug may obtain as much, or even more, satisfaction from additional units. A collector of stamps may gain more satisfaction from purchasing an extra copy of a very rare stamp; for example, if there are only three copies known to exist, the satisfaction obtained from purchasing the third, if he already owns the first two, may be much greater than that derived from his purchase of the first.

However, we should regard these as exceptions to the general rule and accept what is referred to as the law of diminishing marginal utility. We should remember that this 'law' is an assertion about people's general behaviour based on our reasoning of how most people seem to behave most of the time.

Demand and consumer choice

By applying the law of diminishing marginal utility to the assumption that an individual has a limited income which he must spend in a given time period, and the assumption that the consumer is seeking to maximise his utility, we can explain how he will decide how much of the various commodities to purchase. The amount purchased is the demand for a product. Demand means purchases; it does not mean the things we would like to have, but only those commodities which we actually purchase.

We will start by assuming that there are only two goods which the consumer can buy, butter and coffee. This is, of course, totally unrealistic, but it allows us to establish the principles of consumer choice. Both butter and coffee will have diminishing marginal utility. The consumer has a given amount of income to spend on the two commodities and is seeking to maximise his total utility by allocating his income between butter and coffee in an optimum way. Let us assume that the units of these two goods are measured in lb.

Each 1 lb of butter will give less utility than the previous 1 lb, and each 1 lb of coffee will similarly have diminishing marginal utility. Each additional 1 lb of butter and coffee will provide some additional utility. The consumer will decide between butter and coffee so that he gets more utility from each purchase. If 1 lb of butter costs 10p and 1 lb of coffee also costs 10p, his choice would be simple. He should buy butter and coffee in such a combination that the last 10p of his income that he spent would give him the same marginal utility whether he bought 1 lb of butter or 1 lb of coffee.

If he had bought 15 lb of butter and 20 lb of coffee, the marginal utility of 1 lb of butter should be the same as that of 1 lb of coffee. If it were not, he would not be maximising his utility. If the marginal utility of an extra 1 lb of coffee were higher than that of butter, he should not buy the fifteenth pound of butter but instead should buy 21 lb of coffee.   *sixteenth*

If the marginal utility of a twenty-second pound of coffee is higher than that of the fourteenth pound of butter he should continue buying coffee. When the marginal utility of 1 lb of butter is exactly the same to him as the marginal utility of an extra 1 lb of coffee, he is maximising his total utility by buying that combination of goods.

The utility-maximising principle is that the consumer should not be able to obtain more utility by giving up – not buying – the marginal unit of one good and buying an additional unit of another good. In the simple example we have just looked at, he must not be able to get more utility from buying an extra lb of coffee than he loses from forgoing the last 1 lb of butter. Because we assumed that the price of butter was exactly equal to the price of coffee, we concluded that the marginal utilities of the two goods should be equal if total utility were to be maximised. This is an unreal assumption since the prices of all the goods a consumer can buy are not equal. This means we have to make an important adjustment to our conclusion.

Let us assume that 1 lb of butter costs twice as much as 1 lb of coffee. If the marginal utility of 1 lb of butter were equal to that of 1 lb of coffee, the consumer would not buy the last 1 lb of butter, but with the money buy 2 lb of coffee, which would give him twice as much marginal utility. He will be maximising or in an optimal position only when the marginal utility lost by not buying the last, or marginal, 1 lb of butter is equal to the extra utility gained by spending the money which the last 1 lb of butter would have cost him, on coffee. If 1 lb of butter costs twice as much as 1 lb of coffee, he is maximising his utility when he gets twice as much marginal utility from the last 1 lb of butter as from the last 1 lb of coffee.

This is perhaps easier to see if we consider two different commodities. Assume I am choosing between buying a suit and a gramophone record. The suit costs 20 times as much as the record. If I got only the same additional or marginal utility from the suit as from the record, then obviously I should buy the record since I would then have the difference in their prices to spend on other goods. If the suit gives me 50 times as much marginal utility as the record then I obviously buy the suit. I am maximising my total utility when the suit gives me 20 times as much marginal utility as the record. Using this general principle allows us to move away from the simplified assumption that there are only two goods between which the consumer chooses. This utility-maximising rule applies no matter how many goods there are.

The general principle is that a consumer maximises his total utility when the ratio of price to marginal utility is equal for all goods and services bought.

A utility-maximising rational consumer will therefore allocate his income among different commodities in such a way as to equate the ratios of their marginal utilities and prices. He will make adjustments at the margin, i.e. switch from buying marginal units of one commodity to buying marginal units of another in order to bring their marginal utilities and prices into the same ratio. He *does not* buy goods until their marginal utilities are equal; if he did this he would not be maximising his total utility. If the prices of goods differ, so should the marginal utilities of the last units purchased. To obtain only the same additional marginal utility from two goods which cost different amounts of money cannot be a maximising choice.

Indifference curves

We can explain consumer choice by using a different concept. We still assume that marginal utility diminishes with the consumption of additional units of a commodity. We put this somewhat differently but the main notion is the same. Again for simplicity we start by assuming there are only two commodities. We can assume that an individual derives a certain level of satisfaction from the consumption of a certain combination of these two commodities. Initially the consumer has 15 lb of butter and 20 lb of coffee, and from this derives a certain level of satisfaction.

We could maintain that same level of total satisfaction if we take 1 lb of butter away from him by giving him some more coffee. Let us say he would be equally satisfied with 15 lb of butter and 20 lb of coffee or 14 lb of butter and 22 lb of coffee. If we then take a further 1 lb of butter away from him we would have to give him more coffee if he were to be equally satisfied. When we took away the fifteenth pound of butter he was satisfied to have an extra 2 lb of coffee. Now that he has only 14 lb of butter the loss of the next marginal pound of butter will mean more to him than did the loss of the fifteenth because he has less butter. Also, the extra satisfaction obtained from extra coffee will be less than it was because he now has more coffee. Taking away the fourteenth pound of butter and giving him only two extra pounds of coffee will not maintain his total satisfaction. We have to give him more than 2 lb of coffee to compensate him for the loss of the fourteenth pound of butter. It might take an extra 3 lb of coffee. If we then take away another 1 lb of butter so that he has only 12 lb we shall have to give him even more than 3 lb of coffee if he is to remain equally satisfied, since he will have even fewer pounds of butter so each will give him more satisfaction, and even more coffee, which gives him diminishing additional marginal satisfaction. This is exactly the same concept as diminishing marginal utility.

Table 4.1. Combination of two goods providing equal satisfaction or indifference

Butter (lb)	Coffee (lb)
10	48
11	38
12	30
13	25
14	22
15	20
16	19.2
17	18.6
18	18.1
19	17.7
20	17.4

Table 4.1 shows the different combinations of butter and coffee that give this consumer the same level of total satisfaction. They are combinations of these two goods among which the individual is indifferent. This means that if we put each combination shown in the table into a separate box, spread all the boxes on the floor and asked the individual to choose the one which he preferred, or which gave him most satisfaction, he would be unable to do so. He would say that they each gave the same satisfaction, that he did not have a preference for one over the others; he would be truly indifferent as to which box we gave him.

In Fig. 4.1 we plot the various combinations from Table 4.1 into a curve IC_1. This is an *indifference curve* and represents the various combinations of goods which give identical satisfaction to this individual consumer. Note that the curve is convex to the origin. This is because as we reduce the quantity of one commodity we have to give increasing amounts of the other in order to maintain the same level of total satisfaction. It is the same as diminishing marginal utility.

Figure 4.1 also shows two other indifference curves, IC_2 which is above IC_1, and IC_0 which is below it. Indifference curve 2 is preferred to IC_1, which in turn is preferred to IC_0 since the higher the curve the greater the total level of satisfaction. IC_2 represents more goods than IC_1, and IC_0 less.

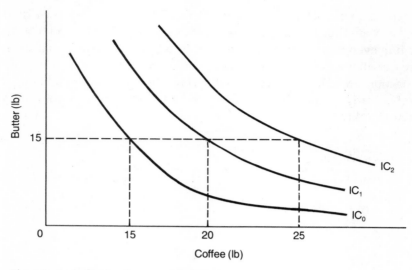

Fig. 4.1 An individual's map of indifference curves

As can be seen from Fig. 4.1, with IC_1 there is a combination of 15 lb of butter and 20 lb of coffee, whereas on IC_2 15 lb of butter are combined with 25 lb of coffee, and with 15 lb on IC_0. The individual is indifferent which combination of goods he has on any one indifference curve, but always prefers to be on a higher indifference curve.

Assume that an individual has an income of £30 and that 1 lb of butter costs £1 and 1 lb of coffee costs 50p. If he spent all his income on butter he could buy 30 lb, and if he spent it all on coffee he could buy 60 lb. The line Y_1 in Fig. 4.2 shows the various amounts of butter and coffee that the individual could buy with an income of £30. It is his *budget line*. It is determined by the amount of his money income and the prices of the two products. This line is tangential to IC_1 in Fig. 4.1. The highest level of satisfaction that he can obtain, given his income and given the price of butter and coffee, is the combination of goods at the point where his budget line is tangential to the highest indifference curve, so in order to maximise his satisfaction he would buy 18 lb of butter and 24 lb of coffee.

With indifference curve analysis the assumption that an individual seeks to maximise his utility, or satisfaction, means that he will move to the highest indifference curve available to him given his income and the price of goods. (If he does not spend all his income, but saves some of it, he will seek to move to the highest indifference curve that he can, given the amount of his income that he has decided to spend.) The individual is

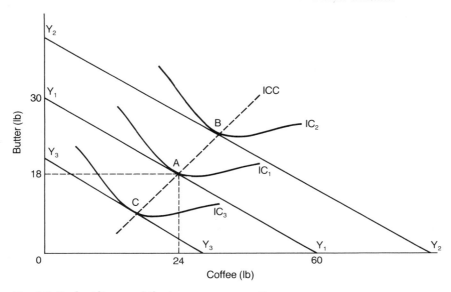

Fig. 4.2 Budget lines and the income consumption curve

therefore maximising his satisfaction by buying 18 lb of butter and 24 lb of coffee since this enables him to move to the highest indifference curve available to him.

The actual amount of the two goods that he buys is shown by the point of tangency of the budget line and the highest indifference curve it touches. This is shown as point A in Fig. 4.2. At that point the slope of the budget line is equal to the slope of the indifference curve. The slope of the indifference curve – the shape that it is at different parts of the curve – is known as the *marginal rate of substitution* (MRS). This is the rate at which one good can be substituted for another without affecting the total level of satisfaction.

Remember, an indifference curve shows the various combinations of goods which provide the same satisfaction, or among which the individual is indifferent. It therefore shows us the rate at which we have to give this individual more butter as we take away coffee if he is to remain equally satisfied with the new combinations of the two goods. Similarly, it shows the rate at which we have to give more coffee, or substitute coffee for butter, if we reduce the amount of butter he has.

At point A the slope of the budget line is equal to the slope of the indifference curve so that it is equal to the marginal rate of substitution. At this point of tangency, therefore, the ratio of prices of the two goods, shown by the budget line, is equal to the marginal rate of substitution. This is a universal condition for maximising satisfaction. A consumer will allocate his income among goods (and this is true whether there are two or many more goods) in such a way that the ratios of their prices are equal to the ratios of their marginal rate of substitution. This is the same principle as we found when we used marginal utility rather than indifference curve analysis to explain consumer choice, except that then it was the ratios of marginal utilities rather than of the MRS that equalled the ratios of prices.

Income and price changes

So far we have assumed that the consumer's income remains fixed and that the prices of the two goods remain constant. We can now relax, or drop, these two assumptions and see how the demand for two goods is affected. We will continue to equate a change in income with a change in consumption by assuming that all the extra income is spent on consumption goods.

Income changes Let us assume that the consumer's income increases to Y_2, as shown in Fig. 4.2. Because we are assuming that the prices of butter and coffee remain constant, the higher income provides a new budget line, Y_2, which is parallel to Y_1. The consumer can buy additional amounts of both commodities according to the amount by which his income has increased. The higher income allows him to reach a higher indifference curve, IC_2, and his new position of equilibrium has moved from point A on indifference curve IC_1 to point B on IC_2. If his income were to fall to budget line Y_3, his new equilibrium position would be point C on IC_3.

If we draw a line through the various equilibrium positions A, B, C, we obtain an *income-consumption curve* (ICC). This shows us how the demand for a commodity will vary as income changes and prices remain constant. In the examples used here the consumer buys more of both goods as his income rises, and both these goods are therefore said to be *normal goods*. A normal good is defined as one for which demand increases as income increases, the prices of all goods remaining constant. With normal goods the income-consumption curve is positively sloped, which is another way of saying that the demand rises as income rises. We can actually measure the rate of change of demand for a good in response to changes in income by dividing the percentage change in the quantity demanded by the percentage change in income. This is the *income elasticity of demand* (YeD), so that $YeD = \%dD/\%dY$, where %d is the percentage change, D is demand, and Y is income. A normal good has a positive income elasticity of demand.

There may be some goods where demand falls as income rises.

In Fig. 4.3 we look at a consumer's response to a rise in income where the two goods are mutton and lentils. As income rises from Y_1 to Y_2 the consumer buys fewer lentils and more mutton, so that the income-consumption curve for lentils slopes back on itself, or is negatively sloped. As income rises the demand for lentils shown on the bottom, or horizontal, axis declines from 10 lb to 6 lb, and the amount of mutton rises from 3 lb to 7 lb. A commodity with a negative income elasticity of demand is referred to as an *inferior* good.

Inferior does not mean that it is shoddy or not as well made as some other commodity; it means that it has a negative YeD. It does not necessarily mean that the YeD is negative all the time. In Fig. 4.3, at lower income levels lentils are a normal good, with a positive YeD at income levels below Y_1. As can be seen, the income-consumption curve is positively sloped up to point A and only becomes negatively sloped at income levels higher than Y_1.

The income elasticity of demand for a product can change with the level of income. As our income rises we may buy more of a particular good. As

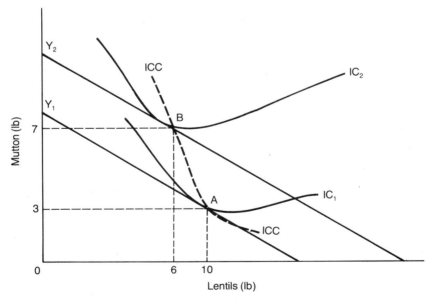

Fig. 4.3 Income consumption curve for an inferior good

our income rises again we may buy a little less of it, and if our income rises again we may buy substantially less of it until a point may be reached when with a particular level of income we do not buy that commodity at all. The fact that we may know the YeD for a commodity at a particular level of income does not mean that the YeD will be the same at other levels of income. When we measure the YeD we should do so for only a small change in income.

Price changes In Fig. 4.4 we show a budget line, Y_1, and its point of tangency with the highest indifference curve, IC_1, when the consumer has an income of £30 and butter costs £1 for 1 lb and coffee costs 50p for 1 lb. The consumer is maximising his satisfaction at point A, where he buys 18 lb of butter and 24 lb of coffee. If the price of butter changes to 75p a lb he can now buy either 40 lb of butter or 60 lb of coffee. He now has a new budget line, Y_2, and this allows him to move to a new indifference curve, IC_2, and a new position of maximum satisfaction at point B. He will buy more butter.

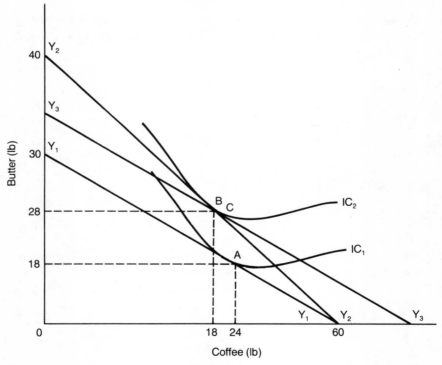

Fig. 4.4 Income and substitution effects of a price change

The consumer will substitute butter for coffee as a result of the change in relative prices. Butter has become relatively cheaper, i.e. cheaper in relation to the price of coffee. The same result would be obtained if the price of coffee had risen; butter would then also become relatively cheaper than coffee and so the consumer would substitute butter for coffee. This tendency to buy more of a good when its price becomes lower, *relative to other goods*, is known as the *substitution* effect. If the price of both butter and coffee had risen, but by different proportions, the consumer would still tend to substitute the relatively cheaper commodity, the one whose price had risen relatively less, although he would, of course, be able to buy less of both commodities in total.

The reduction in the price of butter can be seen as equivalent to an increase in the consumer's *real income*. Real income means money income adjusted for changes in the prices of goods which the consumer buys. Even though his money income remains the same at £30, he can buy more goods because the price of butter has fallen from £1 to 75p for 1 lb, so his real income has increased. It is possible that this consumer could have reached IC_2 as a result of his money income rising to budget line Y_3 with the price of butter and coffee remaining the same. Budget line Y_3 would then be parallel to budget line Y_1 and the new position of maximum satisfaction would be point C in Fig. 4.4. The consumer is equally satisfied with position B or position C, since they are both on IC_2. He is indifferent between them, and they are both equally preferred to position A on IC_1.

We can distinguish the income and substitution effects of a change in relative prices. The income effect is represented by the increase in consumption of butter indicated by the movement from A to C on IC_2 in Fig. 4.4, and the substitution effect by the movement from C to B. Because indifference curves are convex to the origin the substitution effect will always be positive: it will always lead to an increase in demand for the good which is now relatively cheaper.

If the good is a normal good and has a positive income elasticity of demand (YeD=0), the income effect will also lead to an increase in demand for that good. However, if the good has a negative income elasticity of demand, the positive substitution effect which increases demand for the relatively cheaper good will be offset by the negative income effect which reduces demand for that good as real income increases. Whether demand for the relatively cheaper good will rise, and by how much, will depend on the comparative strengths of the income and substitution effects.

Giffen goods

There is a special kind of good where the negative income effect is so strong that it outweighs the positive substitution effect, so that a reduction in the price of the good leads to a fall in the amount demanded. In the nineteenth century Sir Robert Giffen observed that when the price of bread rose, poor people bought more of it rather than less, and similarly if the price of potatoes fell poor people might buy fewer potatoes and more meat. If incomes are low, and one commodity, such as bread or potatoes, accounts for a large proportion of total expenditure, an increase in the price of that commodity leads people to buy more of it because they cannot afford to substitute other goods, even though they are now relatively cheaper. Similarly, if its price falls, they buy less since they substitute some preferred, but more expensive, item. A Giffen good will be a major item of poor people's consumption and one which they buy in order to obtain enough food for subsistence, but one which they would prefer to have less of if they could afford to buy other foods. However, while Giffen goods are interesting exceptions to the general rule that consumers tend to buy more of commodities as their relative prices fall, they are not widespread. We may still find Giffen goods in less-developed economies where incomes are low.

All Giffen goods are inferior goods since they have a negative income elasticity of demand. Not all inferior goods are Giffen goods, because the negative income elasticity of demand is generally swamped by a positive substitution effect.

Price elasticity of demand

We have seen that if the price of a good changes, we would expect, *ceteris paribus*, a change in the demand for that good. If all other prices and the consumer's income remain constant we would expect to see demand rise when the price of a good fell and demand fall when its price increased. The relationship between a change in price and the resulting change in demand is called the *price elasticity of demand* for the product. We measure it by dividing the percentage change in quantity demanded by the percentage change in price, so that the price elasticity of demand is %dQ/%dP. If the price elasticity is greater than 1 so that there is a proportionately greater change in the quantity demanded than there is in the price, we say that the demand for the commodity is *price-elastic*. If the price elasticity is less than 1 we say that the demand is *price-inelastic*, and if it is exactly 1 we say that the product has unitary price elasticity of demand.

Clearly, the price elasticity of demand of a product is very important. If the product is price-inelastic so that the quantity demanded falls by less than the percentage increase in its price, an increase in price leads to an increase in the total amount of money spent on the commodity. Conversely, if the price falls the total amount spent on that commodity will also fall: although demand will rise, it will not rise proportionately as much as price has fallen. With price-elastic commodities the demand will fall proportionately more than the price increases, but if price falls there will be a relatively larger increase in demand so that total expenditure on that commodity will increase. Commodities with unitary price elasticity of demand will have changes in the quantity demanded exactly equal to the proportionate change in price but, of course, in the opposite direction to the price change. Total expenditure on these commodities will remain constant, no matter what happens to the price.

Income elasticity of demand

In considering price elasticity of demand we assumed that income remained constant and that all income was spent. We can now assume that all prices remain constant but that income changes. This is represented by the movement from Y_1 to Y_2 in Fig. 4.2. As we have seen, the relative demand for different commodities may change as income rises. There are some goods which we do not consume if our incomes are low but which we start to buy as our incomes rise. Similarly, there are some goods which we stop buying as we get more income. We might consume less bread and more meat as we get more income, even though the prices of bread and meat remain unaltered.

We measure the response of changes in income to changes in the demand for a product by calculating the *income* elasticity of demand. This is the percentage change in quantity demand divided by the percentage change in income, or, %dQ/%dY. As with price elasticity of demand, if the result is less than 1 we say that the demand for the product is income-inelastic, and income-elastic if it is greater than 1.

Sometimes we refer to commodities with an income elasticity of demand greater than 1 as luxuries; if it is less than 1, or income-inelastic, we consider them necessities.

It must always be remembered that there are two quite distinct types of elasticity of demand – income elasticity and price elasticity of demand. To refer only to the elasticity of demand is wrong and confusing. Some people do this and usually refer to price elasticity of demand, but it is never totally clear that this is the one they are using. Always refer to either price elasticity of demand or income elasticity of demand. You should add 'demand' because, as we shall see later, there is also a price elasticity of supply which is quite different. The two sorts of demand elasticities can be shortened so that PeD refers to price elasticity of demand and YeD refers to income elasticity of demand, but always specify whether it is price or income elasticity of demand to which you are referring.

Cross-elasticities of demand

There is one further sort of elasticity of demand. The demand for some commodities is closely linked to the demand for others. The demand for blank video tapes is related to the demand for video recorders, and the demand for typewriter ribbons is related to the demand for typewriters. We would expect the demand for tapes and ribbons to move with the demand for recorders and typewriters. Where this happens we say that the goods are complementary; they are used together or one complements the other. In these cases changes in the price of tapes or ribbons might be less important in influencing demand for them than changes in the price of recorders and typewriters, which influences the demand for the main good.

There can be opposite relationships. As the demand for one good rises the demand for another may fall. In some countries the demand for beef and mutton may behave in this way, but in others this may not be the case due to dietary or religious practices. There may be inverse relationships between the demand for tea and coffee, so that if the price of one rises the demand for the other goes up to a much more marked extent than we would expect to happen for other goods. We refer to such goods as *substitutes* since the consumer substitutes one for the other as their relative prices change. We know from earlier discussion of the price effect that there will be some substitution away from the good whose price has risen, but with goods which are substitutes this will be a much stronger relationship. In one sense all goods are substitutes for each other, but we are using the term substitutes here to mean that the goods are close substitutes and the consumer easily and readily moves from one to another in response to changes in their relative prices.

CHAPTER 5

Industry demand and supply

We have considered how consumers determine their demand for particular products and seen how a firm's costs of production are determined. We will now bring together some of the conclusions we are able to make about demand and supply. In this chapter we confine ourselves to the industry, and by an industry we shall mean the total suppliers of a single product. We are therefore looking at the behaviour of all the producers of a product, and for simplicity we shall assume that all these suppliers produce only the one product. Consumers, who provide the demand side, are able to demand many products but we shall look only at the demand for the single product produced by the industry concerned. We are, in effect, assuming that there is a product or commodity which is sufficiently distinct and separate from other products to allow us to consider it as a completely separate good.

In the real world it is often very difficult to define a product, commodity or good in a completely satisfactory way. In an earlier example we took coffee as a commodity and considered how a consumer decided between buying coffee and butter. In practice there are different types of coffee, made from beans grown in different countries, which provide different flavours. Or consumers might buy a particular brand of coffee produced by a manufacturer, such as Nescafe or Maxwell House. It may be that to some consumers these two brands are identical, since they do not care which brand they drink and would change from one brand to the other if there were the slightest difference in their prices. Other consumers may believe there is a great difference between them, and it might take a significant price difference before they would switch from one brand to the other. For the first group we might say that the two brands are a single product, but for the second group of consumers they are two separate products and might be regarded as different from each other as each is from tea or cocoa.

There is no really satisfactory general definition of what we mean by a product, good or commodity. The best approach will depend on the purpose for which we wish to define 'product', and will always involve some consideration of the price elasticity of demand and cross-price elasticities of demand for it and other products. In the end it is the consumer who decides whether two things are the same or different products. If the consumer believes they are different, even though objectively they are identical in their physical components, then to that consumer they are different products. Some bakeries sell the same bread under different brand names. Loaves from the same batch of dough baked in the same oven may be put in different packaging and sold under different brand names. To some consumers these are different products. They will buy one brand of bread but if it is not available they would not choose to buy the other as they believe it is a different product. In this situation it *is* a different product because these consumers say so and act accordingly.

Aggregate demand

We have seen in Chapter 4 that a consumer will, *ceteris paribus*, substitute towards a commodity when its price falls and substitute away from it when its price rises. The consumer will, therefore, if his income and all other prices remain constant, buy more of a good at a lower price and less of it at a higher price. The demand curve for a good will therefore take the general slope of the line D–D in Fig. 5.1. It will slope downward from left to right so that as the price falls, more is demanded. The steepness of the slope, for any given axis, is determined by the price elasticity of demand. The steeper the slope of the curve, the more price-inelastic the demand. Curve D_1–D_1 shows a perfectly price-inelastic demand curve. The amount demanded remains constant no matter what the price is. Curve D_2–D_2 shows a perfectly price-inelastic demand curve. If the price rises at all, by no matter how small an amount, all the demand disappears. This is likely to happen only if there is some other product which all consumers regard as almost identical to this one, so that they are not prepared to pay anything more than the present price for it. If income or the price of any other product changes it will be necessary to calculate a new demand curve for the product.

We assume that we are able to draw the full demand curve over various price levels, but in practice this is often not possible. We simply do not

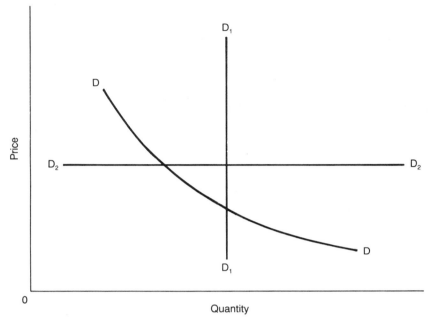

Fig. 5.1 Types of demand curve

know how all the various consumers will behave if the price were to rise or fall by all the possible amounts indicated by the price levels on the vertical axis. Nor do we know how many additional consumers who do not now demand the product will begin to do so if the price falls. A product demand curve is composed of two separate elements: changes in demand of existing consumers, and the entry of new consumers.

Shifts in a demand curve

Firms would often like to know the shape of the demand curve for their products and may spend large amounts on market research to obtain more information about consumer behaviour. While it may be possible to obtain some information, there will always be some uncertainties. One problem is that income and all other prices do not remain constant so that we are not sure whether changes in demand are reflecting the price-elasticity of demand for this product, or the effects of the price-elasticities of demand for other products whose prices have changed, or income effects.

Equally important may be changes in consumers' tastes and preferences. We all have certain tastes and preferences. We may prefer tea to coffee, apples to oranges, new fashionable clothes to expensive holidays, books to gramophone records, and so on. These tastes and preferences determine the utility we place on the consumption of particular commodities and the satisfaction we obtain from their consumption. They are the basis on which marginal utility analysis and indifference curve analysis are built. It is possible, and indeed highly likely, that our tastes change through time. We may like one sort of food when we are young, and different kinds of food as we get older. We may have a taste for pop music and records when we are young, which changes into a preference for a television set, visits to the theatre, or bottles of whisky as we get older. In addition, our tastes may be influenced by marketing and advertising campaigns by manufacturers. Indeed, for many new products there probably needs to be some advertising before the product can enter our demand schedules. If we do not know that a new product has been designed, produced and marketed, we are unable to demand it.

If there are changes in tastes or preferences we should expect to see a shift in the demand curve. In Fig. 5.2 the original demand curve D–D is shown as shifting to D_1–D_1 as a result of a change in tastes. At each price more of the product is demanded. This could be the result of an advertising campaign, or because the population is older and this commodity has a greater attraction to, and so is bought more by, older people, or it could be the result of increases in prices of other products.

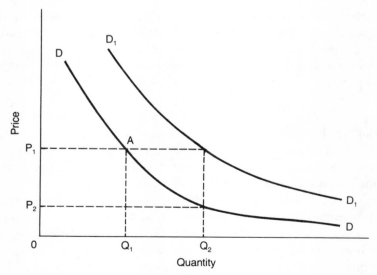

Fig. 5.2 Effects of a shift in a demand curve

It is important to understand the difference between the movement *along* a demand curve, and a *shift* in the demand curve. In Fig. 5.2 we will assume an initial equilibrium at point A where the price is P_1 and aggregate demand is Q_1. If for some reason prices were to fall to P_2, demand would increase to Q_2. We see this by moving along the same demand curve from price P_1 to price P_2. Remember, a single demand curve shows us what happens to demand as a result of changes in the price of that commodity with income and all other prices remaining constant. However, instead of a price reduction there could have been a change in tastes which shifted the demand curve to D_1–D_1. If this had happened, demand at price P_1 would have risen to Q_2. It could have increased by more or less than this (Q_2–Q_1) according to the extent of the shift of the demand curve and the shape of the new or revised demand curve. We have shown it as leading to the same increase in and so the same new level of demand, Q_2, in order to make an extra point. A given increase in demand, in this example from Q_1 to Q_2, can occur as a result of a reduction in price from P_1 to P_2, given the same demand curve (according to the price elasticity of demand), or can result from a shift in the total demand curve.

Aggregate supply

We will make some comments about aggregate or industry supply, although a full treatment will have to wait until we have considered how individual firms determine their output levels, since the industry supply is merely the aggregate of the supply of all the individual firms in the industry making the product concerned.

As we saw in Chapter 3, a firm is faced with a set of short-run costs which first fall and then rise with the level of output. The firm's short-run cost curves are U-shaped, although the U may have either a pointed or flat bottom. A firm will not wish to stop production when it is on the downward-sloping part of its cost curves since it can reduce both average and marginal costs per unit of output by expanding production. It will, therefore, seek to expand production at least to the level where its costs are falling. If it then increases output it will face rising costs and so, because we are assuming profit-maximising firms, it will increase output only if the price is rising. We will consider this in more detail in Chapter 6, but for the present we can safely assume that, *ceteris paribus*, a firm will increase its supply, given its short-run cost curves, only if there is an increase in the price at which it can sell the product. The supply curve of the firm will therefore slope upward from left to right, as shown by curve S–S in Fig. 5.3.

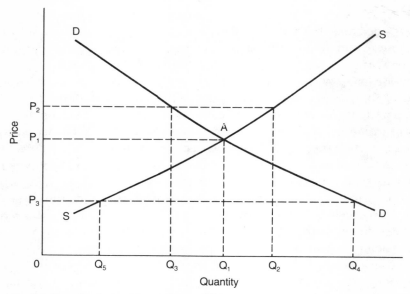

Fig. 5.3 Supply, demand and the equilibrium price

The supply curve of the industry will slope in the same way since it is merely the aggregate of all the supply curves of the firms in this industry; curve S–S can thus be regarded as the short-run supply curve for the industry. The slope of the line will be determined by the price elasticity of supply, and as with the demand curves, a supply curve can be perfectly price-inelastic or perfectly price-elastic. With a perfectly inelastic supply curve, no more can be supplied in the short run no matter how high the price goes. This might be the supply curve for seats for a football match in a particular stadium. There is a fixed number of seats, no matter how high the price. In the long run it might be possible to build an extension, but that is the long-run supply position. Or it could be the supply of fish at the dockside when a boat has landed. The catch is the total supply. Tomorrow there may be greater supply, for if the price is very high more boats may go fishing in response to today's high prices.

In Fig. 5.3 we show both the demand curve, D–D, and the supply curve, S–S, for a product. The two curves intersect at point A, so that at price P_1 supply and demand are the same at quantity Q_1. At P_1 every consumer is able to buy the amount he wishes at that price, and every producer can sell the amount he wishes to produce at price P_1.

At price P_2, producers wish to supply quantity Q_2 but consumers are prepared to buy only quantity Q_3 at that price. There would thus be an excess supply of (Q_2-Q_3). At price P_3 consumers demand quantity Q_4 but producers are willing to supply only quantity Q_5. At the price P_3 there would therefore be excess demand of (Q_4-Q_5). Neither of these two prices, P_2 and P_3, are equilibrium prices. In the one case there are unsatisfied sellers and in the other unsatisfied buyers. If the price were at P_2 we would expect suppliers to reduce their supplies since they would be unable to sell (Q_2-Q_3) and they would not wish to continue to produce goods which they could not sell. They would be incurring costs merely in order to accumulate extra stocks of unsold goods. We would expect them to reduce their price and output. As they did so, demand would increase. They would continue reducing the price until it fell to P_1, where the amount they wished to produce would be equal to the amount consumers wished to buy.

If the price were P_3 there would be a number of unsatisfied consumers (Q_4-Q_5). Some of these would be willing to pay a higher price for this commodity, as shown by the demand curve D–D. Those who were willing to pay a higher price in order to obtain as much of the commodity as they wanted at the higher prices would bid up the price. This would lead producers to supply more according to their price elasticity of supply. Ultimately the price would be bid up to price P_1, where demand and supply would be equal or in equilibrium.

With given consumer tastes, income and the price of all other goods, and with a given set of short-run cost curves, any disequilibrium between supply and demand will lead to producers and consumers moving along their short-run supply and demand curves until equilibrium is reached at the point of intersection between the two curves.

Long-run demand and supply

We have seen that a change in consumers' tastes or preferences leads to a shift in the demand curve. This can be in either direction, to the left or below the existing demand curve if there is a change which makes this product less desirable, or to the right, above the existing demand curve, if the change in tastes leads to a higher demand for it at all prices, e.g. as the result of an advertising campaign.

We can have shifts in the supply curve also. If the price of raw materials or some other factor input changes, we would expect the supply curve to shift. If the price of imported oil rises we would expect to see an upward movement to the left in the supply curve since the costs of production have risen, so that at each selling price a smaller quantity will be forthcoming. This is indicated by the movement of the aggregate supply curve from S_1-

S_1 to S_2–S_2 in Fig. 5.4. A reduction in the cost of a factor input would lead to an increase in supply at each price level and therefore a shift to curve S_3–S_3.

In the short run, changes in supply take place as a result of producers moving along a given supply curve. In the long run, supply can adjust by movement to a new supply curve. This can occur as a result of existing producers moving to a different short-run cost curve as they alter the size of their plant, adding additional capital equipment if they wish to expand production and cutting down their scale of production by not replacing some of their worn-out capital equipment if they wish to reduce output. This is the sort of movement discussed in Chapter 3 and illustrated in Fig. 3.3.

The supply curve may also shift as a result of new producers entering the industry. New firms may enter but will not be able to do so immediately. It will take time for them to obtain the appropriate capital equipment to produce the commodity, either because they will have to wait until new

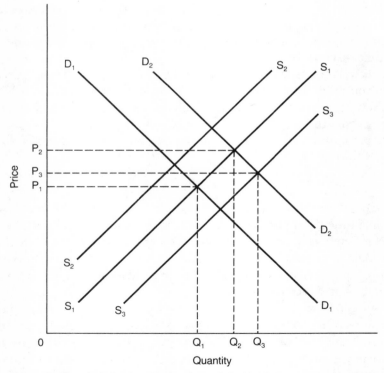

Fig. 5.4 Effects of changes in supply and demand curves on price and output

capital equipment can be produced and delivered to them, or because it will take time to adapt their existing capital equipment and resources in order to produce this product. For example, the supply of chairs in the short run depends on the output and costs of the existing furniture factories. In the long run new factories can be built, existing factories can be extended, and some factories currently producing other goods such as tables, doors or wooden packing crates can be adapted to produce chairs. As each of these additions to output takes place the supply curve will shift to the right, as shown by the move from S_1–S_1 to S_3–S_3 in Fig. 5.4.

It is possible that a shift in the demand curve will initiate a series of events which leads to a shift in the supply curve. In Fig. 5.4 the initial supply and demand are represented by curves S_1–S_1 and D_1–D_1, with a price P_1, and the quantity produced and demanded at that price is Q_1. This is an equilibrium position. All producers and consumers are satisfied with the amounts they are buying and selling at the prevailing price and there is no tendency for output, demand or price to alter. However, let us now assume a change in tastes so that demand increases to D_2–D_2. The new price level is P_2, and supply increases to Q_2 as producers increase their output by producing more from their existing fixed factors, i.e. they move along their existing short-run cost curves. Because the price has increased it may be that some new firms enter the industry. It might not have been profitable for them to produce at price P_1, but it is profitable for them to do so at price P_2. After they have installed capital equipment and begun production, the supply curve shifts to S_3–S_3 and a new price level is determined at P_3. This will always lead to a reduction in price from P_2 since there is now more supply at each price level. It may or may not lead to a lower price than the original one of P_1. The new equilibrium level of output, Q_3, is higher than the previous equilibrium level Q_2, which in turn was higher than the initial equilibrium output level of Q_1.

Whether P_3 will be below P_1, or between P_1 and P_2, will depend on exactly where the new supply curve S_3–S_3 comes. It will be determined by the *long-run* price elasticity of supply. The slope of any one short-run supply curve represents the price elasticity of supply in the short run and is determined by the cost curves on which each of the existing suppliers are operating. The location of the new long-run supply curve, which determines the long-run price elasticity of supply, will depend on the possibilities for obtaining economies of scale as existing firms expand and on the response of new firms when considering whether to enter this industry and start producing this product.

We will consider this in more detail in the next chapter. Here we emphasise that in the short run, supply can increase as existing firms alter their output given their existing cost curves – which will be determined by their fixed factors of production, the possibilities of obtaining constant or increasing returns to scale from their existing fixed factors, and the cost of their variable factors. In the long run the existing firms can alter the amount of fixed factors they use and so increase or decrease the size of their plant, and new firms can enter the industry.

We have therefore added an extra element to the notion of the long run when considering the industry as a whole. This is the possibility that output can change as a result of new firms entering. The long run for a firm is still the amount of time it takes it to change its fixed factors of production. The actual length of time which provides the long run for existing firms and for new entrants might differ and, indeed, might differ for individual firms within the two categories. Some existing firms might be able to change their fixed factors more quickly than others, and some new firms might be able to enter the industry more rapidly than others. It might therefore happen that the long-run supply curve S_3–S_3 arrives at the position it is shown at in Fig. 5.4 by a series of moves, each one representing the expansion of output by an increasing number of existing firms, and the entry, at different times, of various new firms.

CHAPTER 6

Perfect competition

We will now consider how a firm decides the level of output to produce. It is assumed that the firm is seeking to maximise profits. We are also going to assume that the firm is operating in a certain set of market conditions which are known as perfect competition.

Perfect competition is a set of conditions or assumptions made in economic analysis in order to discover how a profit-maximising firm makes its output decisions and to see how changes in supply and demand interact. The various assumptions or conditions which together provide the framework, or the rules within which our firm is operating, are not intended to describe how the world is, or how firms actually operate. Neither are they intended to represent a set of ideal conditions of how the world ought to operate or how markets ought to behave. They are merely a set of conditions specified in order to allow us to construct an explanation of how a profit-maximising firm would behave in the specified conditions. These conclusions might then help us understand some parts of economic behaviour of some economic agents in some conditions in the real world.

As noted, perfect competition requires that certain conditions exist. Each of these is specified in order to ensure that the behaviour of economic agents is in response to certain economic changes or stimuli, and only in response to them.

First, the industry consists of a very large number of firms, each of which produces only a very small part of the total output of a homogeneous product. This means that it is not possible for the actions of one firm to influence the price of the product. In the real world this condition frequently does not exist, so that if one firm stopped production the resulting fall in output could lead to an increase in the price. In perfect competition no one firm can be large enough for this to happen.

Second, each firm produces an identical product. The product is recognised as identical by all consumers and there is no brand loyalty. This means that the consumer is totally indifferent as to which producer he buys from and also that each individual firm must charge or accept the prevailing market price for the product. Further, because each firm produces only a very small amount of the total output of the product, it can sell as much of the product as it wishes at the prevailing market price. Consumers are assumed to be maximising their utility or satisfaction and will therefore not pay more than the prevailing market price for the product. No consumer is large enough to influence the price he pays for the product by obtaining discounts. All producers and consumers must accept the prevailing market price.

Third, all firms and all consumers are assumed to have perfect knowledge of the market conditions, so that everyone knows which products are homogeneous and also what the prevailing market prices of all commodities are.

From these assumptions we can conclude that every firm will charge the prevailing market price for its product. If it tried to charge even a fraction higher than the market price it would be unable to sell any output whatsoever. Consumers would not pay above the market price for a homogeneous product. They would simply buy from another firm. A profit-maximising firm would not charge less than the market price for there is nothing to be gained by doing so. It can sell as much as it wishes at the prevailing price. It would, therefore, lose revenue if it charged less than the market price. Each firm is therefore faced with a perfectly elastic demand curve for the product. It can sell unlimited amounts at the prevailing price, but will sell none at all if it raises the price above the prevailing market level. The industry faces the usual downward-sloping demand curve.

Fourth, new firms can enter the industry if they wish; there are no legal restrictions on entry nor are there any high costs or barriers to entry. Thus, we are assuming that the product does not require a very large amount of capital to produce it, for if this were the case it would not be easy for new firms to enter. We are also assuming that there are no patents preventing new firms from entering into production. Because all firms in the industry are producing a homogeneous product there are no advertising costs, and firms do not need to incur expenditure in establishing or promoting a brand image.

Fifth, every firm can obtain as much of each factor of production as it wishes at the prevailing price. If a firm wishes to employ more labour we assume that it is able to hire as many extra workers as it wishes at the prevailing wage level.

Each firm is therefore faced with a perfectly elastic supply curve of factors of production at the prevailing wage or price level. There are no discounts or lower prices for buying in bulk.

The firm's output decision

From the conditions we have just specified it is clear that the individual firm cannot determine the price at which it will sell its output. It must accept the prevailing market price. Firms which are unable to fix their price for their product are referred to as *price-takers*. In the pursuit of profit-maximisation they must take whatever price the market determines. They are, however, free to determine their level of output.

In perfect competition the price of the product will be determined by the interaction of the forces of demand and supply for the product at the industry level. We will assume that the product is a normal good so that the demand curve slopes downward from left to right. More will be demanded as the price falls. The industry supply curve will slope upward from left to right, since more will be produced as the price rises. The equilibrium price will be determined where the demand and supply curves intersect.

For the individual firm the price is given; it must accept whatever price emerges from the interaction of supply and demand at the industry level. It can choose whether to produce the good at all, and if so, how much to produce. This decision will depend on the firm's costs of production and the market-determined price of the product. In Fig. 6.1 we show the marginal (MC) and average (AC) short-run costs of a firm. The price of the product is shown as P_1. Price is the amount received from the sale of each item of production which is sold. Because we have assumed that each firm is faced with a perfectly elastic demand curve at the prevailing price, the firm will receive the same price for each unit sold. The marginal revenue (MR) obtained from each unit sold will be exactly the same as the marginal revenue received from the sale of the previous unit. Marginal revenue is the increase in total revenue, or receipts from sale, resulting from the sale of one extra unit of output. In perfect competition marginal revenue is the same as the price because the firm can sell as many units as it wishes at the prevailing price. In other market conditions marginal revenue may be less than the price. If the firm can sell an additional unit of output only by

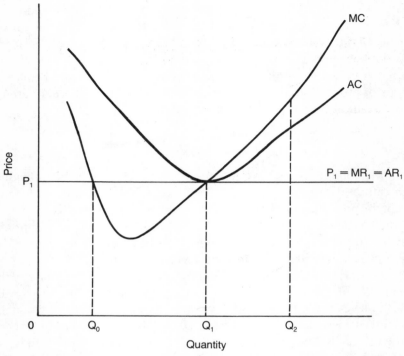

Fig. 6.1 Equilibrium output for the firm in perfect competition

lowering the price at which it sells all its output, marginal revenue will be less than the price.

This can be seen from a simple formula:

$$MR_x = (P_x \cdot Q_x) - (P_{x-1} \cdot Q_{x-1})$$

The marginal revenue from selling the extra unit of output x is obtained by subtracting the total revenue obtained from selling output (Q_{x-1}), i.e. the previous level of output, multiplied by the price obtained for each of those units, from the total revenue obtained from selling that output plus unit x. If the price remains the same, marginal revenue is the same as the price received for selling x, the marginal unit. If, however, the price at which the marginal unit can be sold is lower than the previous price, and the lower price is received for all units of output sold, total revenue received after selling the extra unit at a lower price may be lower than the total revenue received from selling the smaller level of output at a higher price per unit. In this case marginal revenue would be negative, since total revenue would be lower than in the previous situation.

In perfect competition, however, because of the assumptions we have made, or the conditions we have specified as necessary for the existence of perfect competition, marginal revenue remains constant and equals the price. The price is also the same as average revenue (AR). It is assumed that each unit sold is sold at the same price and therefore the average price received for each unit sold will be the same as the selling price of each unit. *Perfect competition therefore always provides conditions in which price equals average revenue which equals marginal revenue.* This is shown in Fig. 6.1 by the horizontal line P_1, where $P_1 = MR_1 = AE_1$.

In Fig. 6.1 the firm has the usual cost curves. Marginal and average costs first fall as the capital equipment is utilised more effectively; then costs rise as decreasing returns to scale occur. The price is P_1 and the firm has to decide how much to produce.

At all levels of output less than Q_0 the firm is making a loss since its average costs are higher than its average revenues. If AC exceed AR for a given level of output, then total costs must exceed total revenue since the totals are obtained simply by multiplying the average costs and revenues by the same level of output. If the firm produced the level of output Q_0 it would not be profit-maximising. If it expanded output beyond Q_0 the cost of each additional unit produced – the MC – would continue to fall and would be lower than the revenue received from the sale of that output. MR would be higher than MC and the firm would therefore receive more from the production and sale of these extra units than it would cost to produce them. A profit-maximising firm should therefore continue to expand production beyond the level of output Q_0.

As output expands beyond Q_0, the MR continues to be higher than MC until the level of output Q_1 is reached. Here, the MR is exactly equal to the MC. If the firm expanded output beyond Q_1, say to Q_2, the MC would be higher than the MR and so the firm would be making a loss on each of the units produced after the level of output Q_1. Moreover, the firm would be making an overall loss at Q_2 because AC are higher than AR at that level of output.

We therefore have two criteria for determining the output level of the firm. The first is the marginal production decision. Does the firm make one extra unit of output or not? As we have seen, this should be determined by the relationship of MR and MC. If the extra revenue obtained from producing and selling an extra unit is higher than the cost of producing that unit, i.e. MR exceeds MC, the firm should expand production and produce it. If MC would be higher than MR the firm should not expand production unless the MC curve is falling so that expanded output leads to lower marginal costs of production, as occurs to the left of output Q_0 in Fig. 6.1.

The second criterion is that AR should not be less than AC; otherwise the total costs of production would be higher than total revenue from sales and the firm would be making an overall loss. We shall later consider circumstances in which it might be in the firm's best interests to continue production even when its AC exceed its AR, but for the present we will conclude that the firm will seek to ensure that AR at least equals AC.

Normal profits

So far we have referred only to the firm covering its costs when deciding the level of output to produce, so that providing AR=AC the firm would remain in production in the long run and would be maximising its profits. However, if all that the firm was doing was covering its actual costs of production there would be no reason for it to remain in business since it would not be making any profits. We deal with this apparent paradox by assuming that the firm's cost curves include provision for profit. A certain level or rate of profit is therefore included in the firm's AC so that if AR=AC the firm is receiving the amount of profit included in its costs.

The amount of profit included in the firm's cost curves is referred to as *normal profits*. This is not expressed as a quantified amount or rate of return but instead as an equilibrium concept. Normal profits are the rate of profits such that if they are received there is no tendency for existing firms to leave the industry and no tendency for new firms to enter the industry. If firms were leaving the industry even though they were still making profits, and they might do this because they thought they could make higher profits elsewhere, we would conclude that the level of profits in that industry was below the normal level. Similarly, even if the rate of profit in an industry declined, if there were a tendency for new firms to enter we would conclude that the industry was making super-normal or excess profits.

Normal and super-normal profits should not therefore be seen as specific rates of return on capital but as relative rates of return which influence the leaving or entry of firms into the industry. They are relative in two ways: expectations of what can be earned in other industries can influence entry and leaving; and they may change in relation to some previous point in time. When we say, therefore, that a firm is making normal profits, we are not making any comment about whether the rate of profit is 'fair' or 'reasonable'. We are merely saying that the rate of return is not so low that existing firms are leaving the industry, nor is it so high that new firms are attracted into the industry by the rate of profit made by the existing firms. Normal profit is therefore a supply-side equilibrium concept.

In the same way 'super-normal' or 'excess' profits is not a value judgement that profits are too high in comparison with other forms of income or in comparison with some historical or past rate of return. It merely means that the rate of return is such that new firms are attracted into the industry. It is possible that they are attracted not because this industry's rate of profit has risen, but because the rate of profit elsewhere has fallen.

When AR=AC the firm is making normal profits. If AR is higher than AC the firm is making super-normal or excess profits, and if AR is less than AC the firm is making a loss in that it is not receiving normal profits and may actually not even be covering its fixed or variable costs of production.

Changes in price

In Fig. 6.1 we illustrated how a firm decided its output level given the price of the product and its short-run costs of production. In Fig. 6.2 we examine how production decisions are made if there is a change in the price of the product.

The left-hand side of the figure shows how the price of the product is determined at the industry level by the product supply and demand curves. We assume an initial equilibrium position where the market price is P_1. The

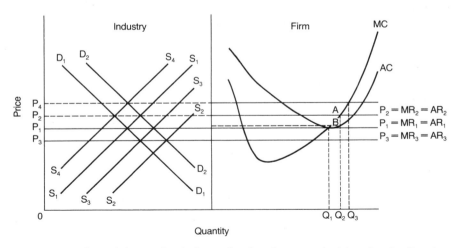

Fig. 6.2 Supply and demand at industry level and output decisions by the firm in perfect competition

right-hand side shows the effects on an individual firm. For the firm the price P_1 is the same as the industry price. We assume that the firm is maximising output by producing output Q_1, which is where the AC curve is at its lowest point, so that the firm is producing at an optimal level of output for its existing capital equipment.

We now assume that as a result of a change in tastes, demand for this product rises to D_2–D_2. This is shown in the industry part of the figure and will lead to an increase in price to P_2. Each firm in the industry will now receive price P_2 and thus AR_2 and MR_2 for its output and will still be faced with a perfectly elastic demand curve at the new higher price, so that it can sell as much of the product as it wishes at that price.

The firm will expand production to Q_2. Since it receives a higher MR for each unit sold it is profitable to produce beyond Q_1 even though both marginal and average costs are rising; the firm would not be profit-maximising if it remained at output level Q_1. For each unit produced up to the point Q_2, MR is higher than MC and so the firm should expand production. At Q_2, $MR_2=MC$; expansion beyond this point would not be profitable since MC are higher than MR_2 beyond output Q_2. At the level of output Q_2 the AR_2 is higher than AC by an amount equal to (A–B) in Fig. 6.2. This means that at the level of output Q_2 each unit produced has a higher AR than its AC. The amount of excess of AR over AC is shown by the difference between the AR_2 curve and the AC curve at the level of output Q_2. Since normal profits are included in the AC curve, this difference or excess of AR_2 over AC is the amount of super-normal profits. The total amount of super-normal profits is $(AR_2–AC)\cdot Q_2$. The excess profit $(AR_2–AC)$ is received on each unit of production and the total production is Q_2.

Firms have obtained the excess profits by expanding production from their existing equipment. They have moved along their existing supply curves. Only those already producing the product were able to benefit from the increase in price and so be able to reap the super-normal profits.

Long-run supply adjustments

The super-normal profits made in this industry can be expected to attract new entrants. Some firms producing other goods may decide to enter this industry by adapting their production processes, and some new firms which have not produced previously may decide to start up new production in response to the super-normal profits obtained by the existing suppliers. In addition, existing firms may decide to expand their production by moving to a different position on their long-run supply curve. They may buy additional capital equipment, and while this may result in a rise in their new short-run cost curves it is not regarded as undesirable, because the price of the product is now higher. Firms which might not have been profitable before might now be profitable.

The result of these various decisions to enter the industry or expand capital equipment is that the industry supply curve shifts to the right. This is shown in Fig. 6.2 as S_2–S_2.

The entry of new firms and the expansion of supply will lead to a downward adjustment of price as the industry-level forces of supply and demand interact to determine the market price. Let us assume that there is a large expansion of supply so that with D_2–D_2 and the new supply curve S_2–S_2 the market price is P_3. As we can see from the firm's section of Fig. 6.2, the price has fallen so low that it is not possible for this firm to cover its costs of production. At all levels of output AC are higher than AR. It is clear that this firm will not continue in production in the long run since it will be making a loss. However, it might continue production in the short run. It is possible that a firm, even one assumed to be profit-maximising, might continue in production in the short run even though it is not covering all its costs. This apparent contradiction can be understood if we remember the distinction made in Chapter 3 between fixed and variable costs.

The firm has to meet its fixed costs in the short run, i.e. for as long as those costs are fixed. It can, however, avoid its variable costs by dismissing or not employing the variable factors of production. The crucial question for the firm therefore is whether the new price, P_3, is sufficient to cover its variable costs. If P_3 is less than the variable costs of production of any level of output, the firm should dismiss its variable factors of production. To employ any of them would incur it in an avoidable loss. It will still have to meet its fixed costs, but by avoiding any loss on its variable factors it is minimising its losses. Minimising losses can be regarded as an extension of the assumption of profit-maximisation to a situation where no profits are possible.

If the firm can produce at a level of output where P_3 is higher than its variable costs, then even though the price is insufficient to cover total average costs (fixed plus variable), it should nevertheless continue in production. The excess of price over variable costs will help the firm pay its fixed costs. In the short run a firm should therefore continue to produce as long as it can cover its variable costs of production and make some contribution to its fixed costs. In the long run the firm should terminate its fixed costs and so avoid making any losses at all.

Thus if the price falls to P_3, some firms will leave the industry immediately because their variable costs will be higher than the price. Others will stay in since the price P_3 will permit them to make some contribution towards their fixed costs. In the long run, however, all firms whose total costs – fixed plus variable – are higher than the new price will leave. There will then be a new supply curve.

If the new supply curve is S_3–S_3, the new equilibrium price determined at the industry level will be the same as P_1. The firm will therefore again produce at the old level of output Q_1.

However, it will be a remarkable coincidence if the long-run adjustment in supply is exactly the amount shown by the shift to the new supply curve S_3–S_3. It is possible that the new supply curve will be less than S_2–S_2 and even less than S_1–S_1. Curve S_4–S_4 is an illustration of such a shift resulting from a large decrease in supply following the period of loss-making by many firms. It can be seen that with demand remaining at D_2–D_2, this will lead to a rise in price to P_4. With this price level the firm expands production to Q_3, which is higher than Q_2, and makes still higher excess profits. It might be assumed that this will lead to even more firms deciding to enter the industry than when prices rose to P_2, since the super-normal profits are higher. If this occurs, the new shift in the supply curve resulting from the entry of many more new firms could be even greater than the shift to curve S_2–S_2, so that the price would then fall even lower than P_3. This would cause still more firms to make losses and so the supply curve would again shift to the left in the long run – perhaps declining so much that less than S_4–S_4 was forthcoming. If this occurred, the resulting increase in price, assuming demand remained at D_2–D_2, would be even greater, so that the price rose above P_4. A further round of super-normal profits would be made which would attract new entrants, with the consequence that a further shift of the supply curve to the right would take place. This would reduce the price and could lead to even more firms making losses, so that the next shift in the supply curve was even further to the left.

It is possible therefore that the resulting shifts in supply following a change in demand could lead to ever-increasing fluctuations as super-normal profits were made for a time, new entrants were attracted, supply was increased as long-run supply curves altered, leading to downward price movement which, in turn, would cause a decrease in the long-run supply as loss-making firms left the industry. This would then generate a further round of higher prices, excess profits and an inflow of new firms.

There would be a series of oscillations of long-run supply curves which, in the example just considered, would generate an explosive pattern. Each adjustment would be more extreme than that in the previous round of adjustments so that the price fluctuated between ever-widening limits.

However, it is also possible that the adjustment process would consist of a series of damped fluctuations rather than explosive ones. When supply shifts to S_2-S_2 as new firms enter the industry in response to the excess profits, it may be that so many enter that the price falls below P_1 to P_3. Some firms will then leave. In the long run a new supply curve will emerge to the left of S_2-S_2. This might, however, be above S_3-S_3 but below S_1-S_1. The new price could be higher than P_1 but less than P_2. Some excess profits would be made but these would be less than were made when the price was P_2. New firms would then enter the industry but perhaps not so many as when the price was P_2. There might still be such a number that the new supply curve would be between S_2-S_2 and S_3-S_3, so that some firms could not cover their costs and these would leave in the long run. A new price level would be set by the new supply curve intersecting with demand curve D_2-D_2 and this would be a little above P_1 so that some excess profits were made. This could lead to more firms entering the industry and a gradual adjustment process could be generated which led to a new stable equilibrium with a price equal to P_1.

The adjustment process might consist of damped oscillations if we believe that the number of new firms entering the industry will be influenced by the level of excess profits being made and that the exodus of firms from the industry is influenced by the extent of the reduction in price following the shift in the supply curve. Lower excess profits will then lead to a smaller shift in the supply curve since fewer new firms will be attracted, and a reduction in price which is less than the previous price reduction will cause a less dramatic shift in the supply curve since fewer firms will leave.

Alternatively, if firms can enter and leave at different times as they are able to expand or contract and get rid of their fixed costs at different times, the adjustment processes should be damped. As firms enter or leave, the combined effect of changes in aggregate supply will be felt at the industry level and the adjustment process will consist of gradual movements in the supply curve, upward or downward according to whether supply is declining or expanding, rather than in periodic large shifts in the curve. If there are gradual movements in the aggregate supply curve, firms and new entrants will be able to observe what is happening to the price level and therefore to their expected level of profits and make their decisions accordingly. This could help to smooth the adjustment process and avoid the explosive fluctuations considered earlier.

Do we find perfect competition in the real world?

We do not find all the conditions associated with perfect competition anywhere in the real world. It is sometimes suggested that The Stock Exchange is close to a perfect market but there are some serious objections to this. Buyers on The Stock Exchange are not purchasing for consumption in order to maximise utility or satisfaction. They may be buying in order to sell later at a higher price. Some buyers or sellers may be able to influence the market price as a result of their own actions. Merely knowing that a particular individual or institution is buying or selling could induce other people to buy or sell if they believe that the 'experts' know best or have some better information. The perfect information assumed in perfect competition is lacking in Stock Exchange transactions.

However, we may get near to perfect competition in some situations. It is often thought that this is most likely in agriculture, where there are many small producers. This is where the explosive adjustment process may also occur, especially if the production time is short and relatively little additional capital is needed to expand production. For example, if there are many small farmers deciding whether to breed pigs for sale, if the price of pigs is high so that super-normal profits are made, many farmers may anticipate that the super-normal profits will continue. They will all then breed pigs. This can lead to such a large increase in the supply of pigs that the price becomes very depressed and the expected super-normal profits turn out to be losses. Many farmers then stop breeding pigs so that the supply falls considerably. The price rises very significantly and large excess profits are made, which leads even more farmers to breed pigs, and so on. It might operate in this way because once the decision to breed pigs has been made the production process is started and it is difficult to adjust the supply gradually.

If a farmer works out that there is a cycle of pig prices and profits and decides to work against the general fashion so that he stops breeding when everyone else is doing so, thereby avoiding the losses when prices fall, and produces when others are leaving so that he increases his supply when the rest of the supply curve is reducing, he will make above-normal profits. However, the problem with this explanation is, why do all the other farmers not do the same? If they did, no one would succeed; they would merely have shifted the timing of the explosive fluctuations.

It is obvious from this discussion that a key element in long-run supply adjustments is the way in which firms make decisions about entering the industry or expanding their production by moving to a new short-run cost curve. We have assumed that they are influenced by the current level of super-normal profits. However, because production takes place in anti-cipation of sales, these producers must expect the demand for the product to continue to remain at a level which, taking into account the future supply position, will lead to a price level which will allow the producer to make at least normal profits, and perhaps, he hopes, super-normal profits. There has to be some element of forecasting by producers. It is necessary for them to forecast both future demand and future supply in order to form a view of the future price level and so of the expected profitability of their investment in new capital equipment.

If there are many producers it is very difficult to forecast how they will react. Moreover, because there are no barriers to entry and new producers can enter the industry relatively easily and cheaply, it must be assumed that there are many potential suppliers able to enter the industry who may be attracted by the expected continuation of the super-normal profits.

We could conclude that the assumption of perfect knowledge includes knowledge about everyone else's investment plans, so that each producer is aware of what every other current and potential producer intends to do, and makes his own decision in the light of this knowledge. If a very large number of new firms intend to enter the industry as a result of the super-normal profits, the individual firm may decide not to do so since the expected increase in aggregate supply will drive down the price to the point where even normal profits will not be made. The difficulty with this type of explanation is that if each of the many other firms and potential new entrants had the same information, their own investment decisions would be affected so that none of them might expand or enter the industry.

We have to accept that if there are a large number of producers and potential producers of a product, it is very difficult indeed for any one of them to form reliable views of future supply levels in a free market. While each producer may supply only a minute proportion of total output, the combined effect of the decisions of many producers can be to generate large shifts in the aggregate supply curve with a consequential fluctuation in price.

It might be argued that profit is the reward for risk-taking and that the risk of expected future price levels being lower than anticipated is one of the risks that producers should take if they wish to earn profits. At the same time, if there are great fluctuations in prices so that there are periods when many producers make losses, the accepted level of normal profits might rise. Producers might be unwilling to enter a high-risk area of production unless they expect to earn profits which are higher than those obtained in less risky product markets.

A key element in understanding how output decisions are made in conditions of perfect competition is the psychology of producers. Their views of risk-taking and the way in which they decide whether to enter an industry in response to current super-normal profits will be influenced by their views of the future levels of profits – and this necessarily involves them in making judgements about how a very large number of other producers will behave. Economics cannot tell us how these producers will make up their minds, but it can help us to understand the consequences of their decisions and actions. Whether a change in demand leads to damped fluctuations in price and output which gradually move the industry back to a position of equilibrium, or to a series of explosive fluctuations which provide no stable long-run equilibrium position, depends on the long-run price elasticity of supply. This will be affected by what each potential individual supplier believes other potential suppliers will do.

Price stabilisation schemes

As we have seen, in conditions of perfect competition firms are price-takers and determine their output on the basis of their short- and long-run cost curves, producing to the point where MR=MC. If AR=AC the firm will be in a stable position of equilibrium. If AR is less than AC the firm will continue to produce in the short run, providing that AR is sufficient to cover its variable costs. If AR exceeds AC, super-normal profits will be made which will attract new entrants and induce the existing firms to expand production by moving along their long-run supply curve. Any change in demand resulting from a change in tastes, income or the prices of other commodities will cause the demand curve for the product to shift and this will initiate changes in output. Both price and output may be very unstable under conditions of perfect competition and there may be alternating periods of excess and subnormal profits.

In order to reduce the uncertainties and fluctuations in price and output accompanied by uncertain profits, producers may try to band together to stabilise demand for, and output of, the commodity. This may lead them to establish producers' associations which limit the amount each producer can produce, and also to enter the market to buy the commodity when demand is less than supply. The association may seek to establish buffer stocks, buying when supply exceeds demand and selling from the stocks when demand exceeds supply. This may provide some price stability to consumers and income stability to producers. If there are many small producers it may be very difficult to obtain the necessary agreement as well as the funds required to purchase output. If it is easy for new producers to enter the industry, then the more successful a price stabilisation scheme is, the greater the increase in supply as new entrants come in to obtain the guaranteed supported prices. Price stabilisation schemes therefore work most effectively when the government organises them and takes action to prevent new entrants increasing supply. Such schemes, of course, mean that the conditions of perfect competition no longer exist in the industry. Producers, however, frequently prefer not to be subject to the uncertainties of perfect competition. It may be that uncertainty – the presence of large risks which may lead to excess profits but which may also lead to losses and bankruptcies – is undesirable to producers. Even though profits may be seen as the reward for risk-taking, many producers may not want to be subject to too large a degree of uncertainty.

As a concept perfect competition is very useful to economic analysis. It helps us understand how output decisions might be made at the level of the firm when price is determined by supply and demand at the industry level and all firms are price-takers. It brings out the importance of excess profits in attracting new entrants and in expanding output. It also allows us to understand the profit-maximising price and output rules. A firm will produce to the point where $MR = MC$.

There is one further general point. In a position of equilibrium where $MR = MC = Price$, the firm is producing at the optimum level for its given short-run cost curves. With that set of cost curves production takes place at the level of output where costs are lowest, and price is equal to those costs. If we assume that there is a similar maximisation by consumers so that they are purchasing products to the point where the ratios of marginal utilities to prices are equal for all goods, or the ratios of the marginal rate of substitution are equal to the ratios of prices for all goods, then we can conclude that all resources are being used optimally, that is, in the way which leads to the greatest level of output and satisfaction. Consumers are obtaining the quantities of goods which they prefer at prevailing prices given their levels of income, and productive resources are being used in the way which maximises output and minimises costs given the existing capital equipment and short-run cost curves. The choice of short-run cost curves reflects the firms' optimising decisions in that they are free to move to a better or lower cost curve in the long run should they wish.

It can be said therefore that perfect competition leads to the optimum allocation of resources and maximisation of consumer welfare. We will consider this again after we have looked at other forms of market structure.

CHAPTER 7

Monopoly, oligopoly and monopolistic competition

We have looked at one form of market structure – that of perfect competition. There are, of course, many other types of market structures representing different forms of organisation with varying types and sizes of firms. In perfect competition the individual firm is a *price-taker* deciding the level of output it will produce on the basis of its cost curves, with price determined by the interplay of supply and demand at the level of the industry. In other forms of market structure the firm may be able to decide the price it will charge for its own product and will therefore be a *price-maker*. This freedom to determine the price it will charge for its product has an important implication. The firm will be unable to sell as much as it wishes. It will not be faced by a perfectly elastic demand curve at the prevailing market price as is the firm in perfect competition. If it chooses the price it charges for its product it must accept the level of output given by the demand curve facing it for that price level.

We drop the assumption that the firm cannot influence its own demand curve. In the various forms of imperfect competition we shall look at, the individual firm may be able to shift its demand curve by advertising and marketing campaigns. These will involve expenditure and so raise the firm's cost curves, but demand is not necessarily given by factors totally outside the control of the individual firm. In the short run, however, the demand curve will be given. Only in the long run will the firm be able to change it. In this context the long run is that period of time it takes for the firm to move its demand curve as a result of advertising or marketing. Also, as we shall see, a firm's demand curve may be influenced by the actions of other firms. If they expand their market share, one firm may lose some of its customers and so see its demand fall or its demand curve shift to the left.

Monopoly

Perfect competition is characterised by a very large number of producers. At the other extreme is monopoly, where there is only a single producer of the commodity. As with perfect competition it is necessary to define the product or commodity before we can decide whether there is but a single producer or a number of them. For example, there is only one producer of Ford automobiles so that the Ford company is a monopolist of their production. However, there are other makes of automobiles which may be regarded as very similar, if not identical, to Ford's, so that we would not claim that Ford had a monopoly of automobile production – only of Ford vehicles.

There is frequently some other commodity which can be substituted for a particular product, and it is the ease with which this can occur, and the willingness of consumers to switch from one product to another, which determine how strong a monopoly a producer may have. There may be only one supplier of electric power, but if there is some alternative product which can easily be substituted for electricity we might conclude that the electricity authority does not have a monopoly. If it is relatively easy to substitute oil for electricity as a source of heating but not for lighting, we might say that there was a monopoly in the supply of lighting but not in heating. There may be a monopoly in the supply of a particular product but there will always be some other commodities competing for the consumers' expenditures. Monopoly applies only to the supply of a particular product.

The demand curve facing a monopolist is therefore the demand for the product. If it is a normal good the demand curve will slope downward from left to right in the same way that the demand curve for the product facing the industry as a whole does in perfect competition. This has a very important consequence for a monopolist. With a given demand curve it is possible to sell more only if the price is lowered. The monopolist is not therefore faced by an infinitely elastic demand curve at any price. Because the demand curve for his product slopes downward the monopolist is not in a position where AR=MR.

We will continue to assume that Price=AR. This means that each unit is sold at the same price so that no customer is charged a higher or lower price than any other. However, because the demand curve is downward-sloping, MR is less than AR. An extra unit can be sold only if the price is lowered and this means that the price charged for each unit must be lowered. The marginal revenue for a monopolist is therefore determined by the price elasticity of demand for his product.

MR is the difference to total revenue resulting from the sale of an extra unit. Starting from sales of Q units at price P, the MR obtained from an extra unit Q_1 is $(Q_1 \cdot P_1)-(Q \cdot P)$. We know that P_1 must be less than P and the effect on total revenue will depend on how much reduction in price is necessary in order to sell an additional unit, i.e. on the price elasticity of demand for the product.

If the monopolist is operating on a part of his demand curve where it is price inelastic, a reduction in price will lead to a greater proportional reduction in total revenue than the growth in extra sales. A price reduction which takes a supplier down a price-inelastic demand curve will always lower total revenue and therefore MR will be negative. If demand is price-inelastic the MR curve in Fig. 7.1 would go below the bottom axis to show that it was a negative figure. Because MC are never negative – there is always some extra cost involved in producing an additional unit of output – MR must always be less than MC where the demand curve is price-inelastic. A monopolist will never determine his level of output on any part of his demand curve which is price-inelastic. He will therefore always produce on some part of his demand curve where he is faced with price-elastic demand.

With a given demand curve a monopolist can choose the level of output he will produce, but must then accept the price that the market will bear for that level of output so that the demand curve determines price once the monopolist has chosen the output level. Alternatively, he can choose the price at which he will sell but must then accept the level of output determined by the demand for the product at that price.

MR is always less than AR for a monopolist. This means that there are two important differences from perfect competition. Price and AR slope downward from left to right rather than being horizontal, since the monopolist can sell only a certain amount at any given price. Second, the MR curve always lies under the AR curve. This is illustrated in Fig. 7.1.

Unlike the firm in perfect competition, the monopolist can influence the level of demand for his product. He may advertise in order to change people's tastes and preferences by persuading them that they will get satisfaction by buying this product. If this occurs the demand curve, and so the MR and AR curves, shift to the right. It may also be possible to change the slope of the demand curve and the MR and AR curves by advertising.

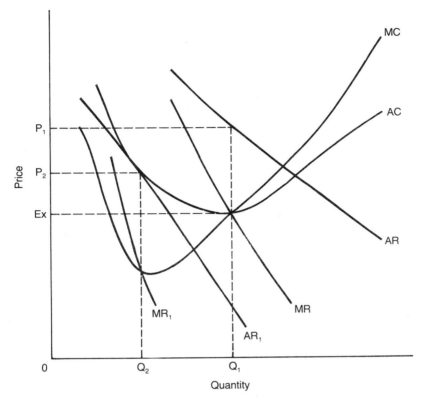

Fig. 7.1 Price and output under monopoly

This would have the effect of altering the price elasticity of demand.

The monopolist may also be able to discriminate among his customers, charging different consumers different prices for the same product. There are two essential conditions for price discrimination. First, it must not be possible for the product to be easily transferred from consumers in one market to those in another. If this were possible some people in the cheaper market would buy at the lower price and sell in the other market at a price lower than the monopolist was charging there. Price discrimination is often easier to practise when the product is a service which cannot be easily resold. Second, there must be different price elasticities of demand in the two markets. If they were the same there would be no advantage to the monopolist for he would produce to the point where MR=MC for each market and if the price elasticities were equal this would lead to the same production decisions and the same rate of profit.

We will assume that the monopolist has the usual-shaped cost curves so that costs fall and then rise as output is increased. The MR curve lies below the AR curve showing that as price is reduced in order to expand sales, the addition to total revenue is less than the price received for the extra unit sold, as all the intramarginal units have been sold at the lower price.

We will assume that the MR curve cuts the MC curve at its lowest point where $MC=AC$. The monopolist can be supposed to follow the same principles as the producer in perfect competition. He is seeking to maximise profits and does this by comparing the marginal cost and revenue of producing and selling an extra unit of output. He will therefore produce to the point where $MR=MC$ and his MC curve is rising. This is at a level of output Q_1. However, the price charged will be P_1, which is the level of the AR curve for output Q_1. The monopolist will therefore make excess or super-normal profits equal to $(P_1-Ex)\cdot Q_1$. This is calculated in the same way as the super-normal profits of producers in perfect competition and is the excess of AR over AC, multiplied by the number of units sold.

If his demand were represented by MR_1 and AR_1 and was therefore less than with MR and AR, output would be restricted to Q_2. The monopolist would not then make super-normal profits since at that level of output $AR_1=AC$. However, as can be seen, he would not be producing at the optimum level because his costs would be higher than if he were to produce Q_1. There is no reason to suppose that the monopolist will produce at the optimum level of output Q_1. This will depend on the location of his demand curve and so his AR and MR curves. However, if these are stable we might expect a monopolist to move to a set of cost curves which will allow him to produce the chosen level of output in the most efficient way.

Unless his AR curve is as shown by AR_1, or even further to the left of AR_1, in which case he would make a loss at all levels of production since AC would always be higher than AR, a monopolist will always make super-normal profits. Because AR is higher than MR there will always be some excess of AR over AC at whatever point the MR curve cuts the MC curve.

This gives rise to two criticisms of monopoly. First, the monopolist makes super-normal profits and therefore in some way 'exploits' the consumer in that prices are higher than they would be under conditions of perfect competition, with the same cost curves. Price is not set at the lowest point of the AC curve. Second, because the monopolist may not produce at the optimum point of his production curves there may be a misallocation of resources. Factors of production will not be used as efficiently as they might be. If the firm produced the level of output where average costs are lowest, efficiency would be maximised.

Replies can be made to these criticisms. It may be the case that the monopolist seldom produces at the point where AR=AC and so excess or monopoly profits will be made. Price will be higher than AC. However, this does not necessarily mean that prices will be higher than they would be in conditions of perfect competition; it means only that prices will be higher than they would be in conditions of perfect competition *with the same cost curves.* It is possible that the costs are lower under monopoly than they would be in perfect competition so that a monopolist might make excess or monopoly profits, with the consumer paying a lower price than he would in perfect competition. The crucial question is whether the monopolist and the producer in perfect competition have the same or different cost curves.

If there are significant economies of scale available to the monopolist he might be able to reduce his costs considerably. In perfect competition no single producer can produce such a large amount of the product that his actions can influence the price, and perfect competition is marked by a large number of small producers. This may mean that none of them are achieving economies of scale. This will depend on the nature of the productive process and the opportunities for economies of scale. The monopolist may be better placed to undertake research into new production methods which incorporate technological improvements, thereby increasing his efficiency. If there are economies of scale to be obtained from very large plants which use expensive capital equipment, the monopolist may be able to finance the purchase of the capital equipment much more easily than a producer in perfect competition. In perfect competition we assume that there is free entry into the industry so that there are no barriers to entry. This suggests that new firms should not be required to have large amounts of expensive capital equipment before they can enter the industry and produce the commodity. It would be difficult to imagine perfect competition among oil refineries. A monopoly may be able to finance and develop new methods of production which are more efficient and so have lower costs of production than firms in perfect competition.

This is illustrated in Fig. 7.2. The monopolist has lower cost curves, shown as MC_m and AC_m, since he is able to take advantage of large economies of scale. The firm in perfect competition produces a smaller amount of goods and has higher costs, shown as MC_p and AC_p. Even if the firm in perfect competition produces at the optimum level of output where AC is lowest, the price will be P_p. The monopolist will charge price P_m, and make excess profits of $(P_m - Ex) \cdot Q_m$. The price to the consumer will be lower even though excess profits are made.

There is more substance in the criticism that a monopoly results in the

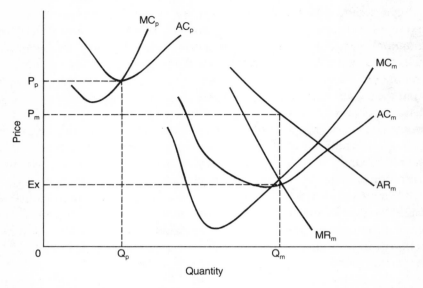

Fig. 7.2 Possible effects on price of economies of scale

misallocation of resources. If the monopolist's output was at level Q_m in Fig. 7.2, the production of an additional unit would lead to increased MC and this is the cost to the economy of producing that extra unit. Cost in this sense means the value of the resources which are required to produce the additional output. Those factors could have been used to produce a different commodity elsewhere, but because they have been utilised in the production of the monopolist's extra unit of output they cannot now produce the output elsewhere. It has, therefore, cost the economy the alternative output. This is the concept of *opportunity cost*, which is the level of output which is forgone as a result of using factors of production in a particular way. We can use the same concept when considering demand. The opportunity cost to me of a visit to the cinema is the consumption that I have to forgo in order to pay for the cinema ticket, so the opportunity cost might be a book or a new tie that I cannot now buy.

The consumer of the extra unit of output by the monopolist will have to pay a price which is higher than the monopolist's MC since AR_m exceeds MC_m. Thus, the consumer is required to forgo other goods worth AR_m but the monopolist is using resources which cost him only MC_m. If elsewhere in the economy those factors had been used to produce goods in conditions of perfect competition, the price which the consumers of that extra output would have paid would have been equal to the MC of their production. If these marginal costs had been the same as the monopolist's it would have been possible for the consumers to have obtained additional output of the products from perfect competition at a lower price and therefore their gains or benefits would have been higher than those they obtain from purchasing the extra output by the monopolist.

If, in all other areas of production and sales, MC=MR and there is perfect factor mobility, the existence of a monopoly will reduce society's total benefits by misallocating resources. However, we know that the rest of production does not take place in conditions of perfect competition and there is not perfect mobility of factors of production. Moreover, as we have seen, the monopolist may have lower cost curves than producers in perfect competition, and it may be that consumers and society gain more from the lower costs and prices of monopoly than they lose as a result of the misallocation of resources. We cannot tell from this conceptual analysis alone whether monopoly increases or decreases total benefits and well-being.

There are some circumstances in which we might expect a monopoly to emerge. If there are very high fixed costs it may be that once a firm has incurred those costs and attracted a high level of demand, it is able to operate at a point on its long-run cost curve which provides economies of scale so that it may be very difficult for a new firm to obtain a sufficient share of the market to be able to break even. In other words, the total demand for the product may be sufficient to justify only one large-scale producer, and once there is a firm in operation the market conditions determined by the total demand may effectively ensure that no competitor is able to enter and survive. The economies of scale may be such that there are very significant cost reductions but the total demand for the product is not sufficient to justify two large-scale producers.

There could be a waste of resources if a second producer enters. It is generally believed that there is no justification for more than one producer of electric lighting to individual houses. The cost of duplicating the installation of electric cables and the loss of economies of scale are thought to outweigh any potential gains from competition. In the same way a duplicate telephone company with telephone wires alongside the first one is thought to be undesirable.

Where the proportion of fixed to variable costs is high and it is thought that competition from additional producers would not be effective, due perhaps to the limited size of total demand, or because very large sales are needed to obtain the economies of scale, governments may intervene to ensure that consumers are provided with some protection against unduly high monopoly profits. One approach is to nationalise the monopoly so that it is publicly owned. This might be advocated on the grounds that a State-owned monopoly would not abuse its monopoly powers. Or, the excess profits could be used for other purposes, so that there would be benefits as well as losses from monopoly. It does not follow, however, that the gainers would be the same consumers or individuals who had paid the higher prices (higher meaning in excess of MC) for the monopolist's products.

An alternative approach is for the government to regulate the activities of the monopolist. This might take the form of controls on prices or could be aimed at preventing price discrimination. It could also involve attempting to improve the efficiency of the monopoly, say by examining its costs.

We have hitherto assumed that the monopolist behaves in the same way as a producer in perfect competition and is a profit-maximiser. However, it may be that the monopoly firm does not seek to maximise profits but rather to satisfy or obtain some satisfactory level of profits. This may be higher than the level of normal profits obtained elsewhere but still be less than the monopolist might possibly obtain given his demand curve. One of the advantages of being a monopolist is the possibility of obtaining excess profits. Another is the opportunity to enjoy a quieter life which is less subject to the pressure of competition.

We discussed earlier the possibility that by using some of his excess profits to finance research, a monopolist might have lower cost curves than a firm in perfect competition. This could lead to improvements in technology and production which lower costs and prices. Alternatively the monopolist may decide to spend little, if anything, on research. If he feels secure behind the protection of his monopoly against the entry of competitors he may not even keep up with technological improvements elsewhere, far less initiate and develop his own.

When we compare cost curves of different producers and seek to determine which is the most efficient, we usually assume either that each of them is faced with homogeneous factors of production as their inputs, or that each of them is seeking to use such factors of production as they employ in the most efficient way. Neither of these assumptions may be valid. A monopolist may decide to share some of his excess profits with labour. He may require a lower effort-input from his workforce. This will mean that efficiency will be lower than it could be and is equivalent to a reduction in the marginal physical productivity curve illustrated in Fig. 2.2. As a result, prices will be higher than they need or would be if the factor inputs were the same as in other areas of production.

The producers or managers of the firm may decide to take things rather easier than they would in a more competitive market. This is an accusation which has often been made against both privately owned and publicly owned monopolies. It may be difficult to test whether it is true in a particular case since there is no immediate basis for comparison.

In brief, we are unable to lay down a totally general rule as to whether monopolies are, in practice, good or bad. Such a decision can be made only after we have specified the alternative against which monopoly is to be compared. Perfect competition is sometimes suggested as the appropriate alternative but, as we have seen, we are unable to tell whether perfect competition will lead to faster or slower rates of technological improvements than monopoly, or whether a monopoly will have higher or lower prices than firms in perfect competition. Moreover, perfect competition can lead to undesirably wild fluctuations in prices and output. The consequences of bankruptcies as firms fail to make normal profits can have social considerations which might lead us to decide that intervention in a market structure of perfect competition might be desirable in order to provide a greater degree of stability, even though this leads to some distortions from the full model of perfect competition.

Oligopoly

Oligopoly is a different type of market structure, where we find a few firms producing the total output of the product. It is not necessary to specify exactly how many firms we mean by 'a few'; the important point is not the exact number of firms, but that each of them believes that its own actions will have important effects on the decisions and actions of the others. Each firm's price and output decisions are therefore influenced by its views or expectations about how the other firms will react to its decisions. Clearly, in perfect competition a single firm cannot influence price or total output and each firm must accept the prevailing market price. In monopoly there are no other firms producing the product, but a monopolist may make his price and output decisions in the light of how he thinks government may react. With oligopoly each firm expects the other firms in the industry to react to its decisions and therefore its decisions are influenced by the expected responses of the others.

The usual oligopolistic situation is a few large firms producing the same product. There may be slight product differentiation, which may be real or created in the minds of consumers by each firm's advertising and marketing campaigns. For example, there may be real differences among different brands of instant coffee or petrol, or they may be basically the same product but each producer has persuaded some consumers that its own product is different and preferable to the others. We shall assume that while there may be some product differentiation this is not strong enough to withstand much variation in price. The different firms are therefore producing a commodity which is regarded by the consumers as easily substitutable.

This leads to an important element in the analysis of behaviour in oligopolistic markets. Each firm believes that if it lowers its price in order to attract consumers away from its competitors, the other firms will follow suit. The demand curve for the firm below the prevailing price will therefore be determined by its share of the price elasticity of demand for the product or industry as a whole. Each firm can expect to increase its sales at a lower price only to the extent to which it obtains a share in the product price elasticity of demand.

However, if the firm increases its price it believes that other firms will not increase their prices but will maintain their current prices and attract consumers away from the firm which has raised its prices. If this is so, the demand for the firm's product at prices higher than the prevailing price will be much more price-elastic than the price elasticity of demand for the whole industry's products. Each firm believes that its demand curve is 'kinked'. Above the existing price the firm will lose considerably as consumers switch to competitors who have not raised their price, and below the existing price demand will increase only as a result of total demand for the product rising, since other firms will follow it in reducing their prices. The firm believes that the demand curve for its product is a mixture of two factors: its share of the total demand for the product as a whole, and the price elasticity of demand for the product as a whole.

Once prices have been established in the market each firm believes its own demand curve is kinked or hinged around the present price, as illustrated in Fig. 7.3. At price P_1 the firm will produce output Q_1. If it increases price its MR will decline as it loses sales to other firms. If it lowers its price and the others follow, its MR curve suddenly drops, as shown by the vertical part of the MR curve A–B. This follows from the change in the price elasticity of demand for the firm's product, shown by the bend in the AR curve. If the firm's cost curves are MC and AC, it will make super-normal profits of $(P_1-C) \cdot Q_1$. If there is any change in the firm's cost curves the price and output decisions will remain the same provided that the new MC cuts the MR curve between points A and B, for this will still be the profit-maximising position.

This explanation of oligopoly suggests that there will be stability in the

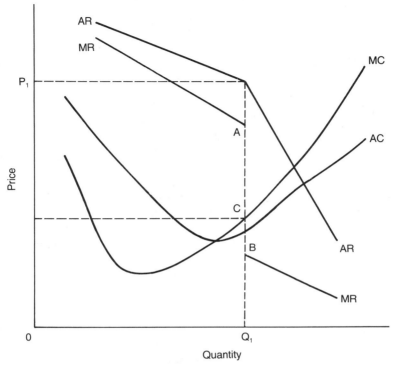

Fig. 7.3 Price and output in oligopoly – the kinked demand curve

relative prices of different firms in the industry. Each of them believes it has little to gain from a price reduction or price increase. However, this does not necessarily mean that prices will remain at their present level. If costs rise because of an increase in factor input prices which are common to all firms, each firm may conclude that the others will increase their price if it does so, since their costs will have risen also. This could be wrong. One firm could decide to absorb the higher costs and accept lower excess profits for a while, perhaps hoping that there will be a switch of consumers towards it when its prices are relatively lower than those of its competitors. If there are further economies of scale to be obtained from expanding production this could allow the firm to make higher excess profits in the future.

Generally, however, firms in an oligopolistic situation might be expected to maintain relative prices. Often one firm emerges as the price-leader. It increases its prices when costs rise and other firms follow suit as their costs have also risen. In some situations there may be formal agreements to establish price-leadership, or a price cartel. Government may intervene to prevent this, fearing that it will lead to unduly high excess profits and exploitation of consumers. However, as we have suggested, informal price-leadership and stability of relative prices with the absence of price-cutting competition may emerge from an oligopolistic situation without any collusion but as a result of each firm making its own profit-maximising decisions separately. The firm's expectations about how other firms will react to its price decisions may lead to the same price relationships as would emerge from a formal cartel.

This does not mean that oligopolistic firms do not compete. It may mean that they do not often indulge in price competition, but they may adopt other forms of competition. This will more usually take the form of advertising and marketing campaigns designed to attract consumers to their own products and to establish consumer loyalty, which might make it more difficult for other firms to attract their customers away.

New entrants may be attracted by the excess profits, but there will usually be some barriers to entry. Oligopolistic firms are often large and a new entrant will require large amounts of capital. Product differentiation and brand loyalty may mean that a new entrant will have to incur heavy advertising and marketing costs in order to establish its products and create its own brand loyalty. During this time the existing firms may lower their prices, being willing to accept what are seen as temporary reductions in profits in order to keep out a potential competitor. If it is thought that the total demand for the product is fixed, the entry of a new producer can only be at the expense of lost customers by existing producers. The new entrant's advertising and marketing campaign may lead to some additional demand but this will probably not be sufficient to allow each of the existing firms to maintain its present output level, since the new firm will require some of their customers to switch if it is to be viable. Price competition may occur therefore if a new entrant appears, and advertising and marketing expenditures by existing firms will probably also rise to try to counteract the effects of the new entrant's campaigns.

Monopolistic competition

The final market structure we consider is monopolistic competition, which has some of the features of perfect competition and some of those associated with oligopoly. There are a large number of producers each making a similar product, but one which is differentiated in some way from the others so that there is brand loyalty.

The products are close substitutes. There is relatively free and easy entry since there are few barriers to entry. Consumers believe that the various products differ in some ways from each other, but these differences are such that they will tolerate only relatively small differences in relative prices. Because there are no high entry costs or large barriers to entry, new firms can enter with their own slightly differentiated product; this will tend to reduce the market of each of the existing producers as the new entrant attracts some of their customers away from them. The total demand may increase as a result of the new entrant's differentiated products creating some new demand, or increasing the existing demand.

Each firm will be faced with a downward-sloping MR and AR curve. In the short run, demand can be increased only by reducing price. These curves will not be kinked since it is not thought that all the other firms will respond to a price reduction by any one producer. There will be various forms of non-price competition as firms seek to establish brand loyalty to reduce the substitutability of other products for theirs.

The individual firm will determine output and price in the same way as the monopolist. Output will be set at the point where MR=MC and price, or AR, will exceed AC as excess or super-normal profits are made. The short-run profit-maximising position will therefore be P_1 and Q_1 in Fig. 7.1. However, new entrants will be attracted by the excess profits and their entry will gradually reduce the demand for the output of the existing firms. Their demand curves, and so their AR and MR curves, will shift to the left as their demand falls. This reduction in demand for the product of the existing firms can continue until the AR curve is reduced to the position of AR_1 in Fig. 7.1. With a level of output Q_2, AR=AC and the firm is making only normal profits. Any further reduction in demand will mean that AR will be less than AC at all levels of output and the firm would then leave the industry.

The long-run position of the firm will therefore be either Q_2 and P_2, or some level of output greater than Q_2, such as Q_1. This will depend on the extent to which new firms are attracted into the industry and are successful in attracting consumers away from this firm. If the existing firm can build sufficient brand loyalty it will be able to prevent its demand curve from shifting as far as AR_1. However, creating brand loyalty will involve the firm in additional costs of advertising or marketing. This will have the effect of raising its cost curves above MC and AC in Fig. 7.1. The long-term equilibrium postion will therefore depend on where the new cost curves lie as well as on the ability of the firm to prevent a reduction in its revenue curves to AR_1 and MR_1.

There is some element of indeterminacy about the long-term price and output levels of firms in monopolistic competition. The product differenti-ation created by the various firms gives consumers greater choice. It may be that there is relatively little difference in the physical characteristics of the various products, but if consumers believe they are different, and are prepared to pay slightly higher for one than for another, or express a clear preference for one rather than another, those products are different to those consumers. It can be argued that consumers benefit from the choice available to them as a result of product differentiation even though the differences might be small. Consumers would not be able to test variations of products and so determine whether they preferred them if firms did not offer product differentiation.

The misallocation of resources, and the resources expended on advertis-ing and creating brand loyalty, are sometimes criticised as 'wastes'. However, they can also be seen as desirable in that they provide greater choice and may stimulate inventions and developments as firms seek new products and new ways of differentiating their products from those of other producers. Economic theory cannot really tell us whether the misallocation of resources and the failure to operate at the lowest point of the AC curve with prices equal to MR=MC, in monopolistic competition, oligopoly and monopoly, are preferable to the results of perfect com-petiton. Much may depend on what happens to the actual costs and prices, as illustrated in Fig. 7.2, and on whether consumers prefer a wide range of choice.

CHAPTER 8

Production costs, risks and uncertainty

We have seen that a firm combines factors of production in order to make goods or provide services for sale. We have considered the distinction between the short run in which one factor is fixed on supply, and the long run in which the amount of all factors used can be varied. We will now consider how the firm decides how much of the various factors to employ in order to produce its output. We will assume there are only two factors of production, capital and labour.

In Chapter 2 we saw that a firm will employ additional units of labour up to the point where the cost of an additional unit of labour is equal to the value of that unit's marginal revenue product. This is a general rule. Each factor should be used to the point where its marginal cost is equal to its MRP. If the firm is faced by a perfectly elastic supply of all factors, the MC of each factor is equal to the price. In this case the maximising rule can be expressed as, MRP of a factor = the price of that factor. Thus the two factors, labour and capital, would be used in the optimal combination where the MRP capital = price of capital and MRP labour = wage level.

This will be achieved where

$$\frac{\text{MRP capital}}{\text{price of capital}} = \frac{\text{MRP labour}}{\text{wages or price of labour}}.$$

If MRP/price of capital were lower than that for labour the firm could reduce its total costs of production by using more labour and less capital. For example, if MRP/cost of capital were 8/4 = 2, and that for labour were 6/2 = 3, it would mean that a firm could obtain 8 additional units of output by employing extra capital at a cost of £4, which would give a cost of production of 50p a unit of extra output. If it employed extra labour it would obtain 6 additional units of output at a cost of £2, or at a cost of 33p a unit. It would be to the firm's advantage to substitute labour for capital until the ratios of MRP/price of the factors were equal.

This is a long-run maximising position. In the short run the supply of one factor is fixed and therefore the firm will continue to employ additional units of that factor as long as its MRP is higher than or equal to its price.

Long-run factor combination

We have explained that the optimum combination is when the ratios of all factors' MRP/price are equal. We can explain this in a different way which will also help us to understand how a firm may change its capital–labour mix through time. This method of analysis is very similar in some regards to indifference curve analysis, but while the concepts and diagrammatic explanations have similarities, care must be taken not to confuse the two different explanations of two different activities.

We can draw an *isoquant* which shows the various combinations of the two factors of production, capital and labour, needed to produce a given amount of output. The term isoquant means equal product or output and therefore the curve Q_1 in Fig. 8.1 shows the various combinations of capital and labour which can produce amount Q_1 of this product. We assume that labour is homogeneous and that the amount of effort-input per unit of labour time is given. Similarly, for each unit of capital the state of technology is given. We are not therefore permitting some capital to be better or more advanced than some other, and the capital is appropriate for the production of the good in question. Thus we would consider a plough to be an appropriate unit of capital for agricultural production but not for making chairs.

The isoquant Q_1 is convex to the origin. This is because capital and labour are not perfectly substitutable. It is possible to replace one by the other but as we do so the factor of which we have additional units becomes less effective than that of which we have fewer. This is the same notion as diminishing marginal physical productivity and we are assuming it applies to both factors. If we use less capital to produce the given level of output we need proportionately more labour, and similarly if we use less labour we need proportionately more capital.

Thus, in Fig. 8.1, if we reduce the amount of capital from 30 units to 15, we need an extra 10 units of labour to produce the same output, but a further reduction of 5 units of capital also requires an additional 10 units of

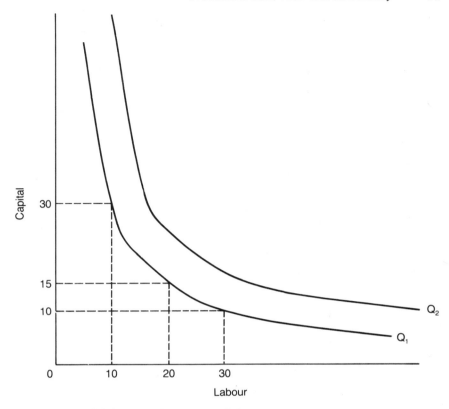

Fig. 8.1 Capital–labour production possibility curves

labour to produce the same output. Or, if we start from 30 units of labour and 10 units of capital, a reduction of 10 units of labour requires an extra 5 units of capital to replace it, but the next reduction of 10 units of labour, from 20 to 10, needs 15 units of capital to maintain the same level of output.

The slope of the isoquant gives us the marginal rate of substitution or the substitution ratio of the two factors. It tells us the rate at which one factor has to be substituted for the other if the level of output is to remain constant.

Isoquant Q_2 in Fig. 8.1 shows the combinations of factors which can produce a larger output, Q_2. We can draw a large number of isoquants, each one showing the various combinations of factors which can produce the level of output represented by that isoquant. Isoquants further away from the origin, or to the right, represent higher levels of output.

In Fig. 8.2 we have drawn an isoquant for output Q_1 and an *isocost*. An isocost shows the varying amounts of factors of production which can be employed, or bought, for the same amount of money. Thus IS_1 represents a given amount of money. If it were used to buy capital, OK units could be bought, and if it were spent on labour, OL units could be bought. Isocost line IS_2 shows the combination of factors of production which can be bought with less money than IS_1, and IS_3 the amounts which can be bought if more funds than represented by IS_1 are available. It is assumed that the price of capital and labour remains the same when drawing the different isocosts IS_1, IS_2 and IS_3.

The least cost combination of factors to produce a required output is shown at the point of tangency of an isocost with the appropriate isoquant. Level of output Q_1 can be produced most cheaply by using OX units of capital and OY units of labour on isocost curve IS_1. If the firm only has resources represented by IS_2 it is unable to afford to employ enough factors of production to produce output Q_1; the most it can produce is Q_2. This is the highest isoquant touched by isocost IS_2. The firm could produce output Q_1 at point B on isocost IS_3. This would be an unnecessarily expensive method of producing output Q_1, as this could be achieved at the lower cost of IS_1. However, if the firm wished to produce the level of output Q_3 it would have to incur costs of IS_3.

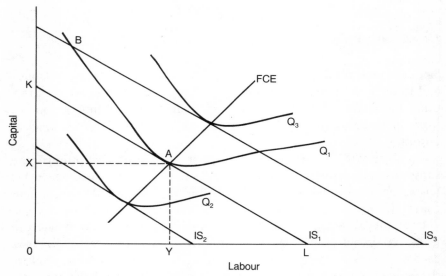

Fig. 8.2 Most efficient combination of factors of production by use of isoquants and isocosts

By combining isoquants and isocosts in the same figure we are able to determine two separate issues. First, we can discover the most effective combination of factors and lowest cost necessary to produce a given output. This is shown by the lowest isocost which is tangential to the isoquant of the desired output level. Second, we can discover the highest level of output possible from the best combination of factors which can be bought or employed for a given amount of money. Thus, the level of output Q_2 is the most that can be produced for a cost of IS_2.

At the point of tangency of the isoquant and the isocost line the marginal rate of substitution of the two factors is equal to the ratio of their prices. This is a general rule of the optimum use of factors.

If we join the various points of tangency of isocosts and isoquants we obtain the FCE line or the factor combination for expansion curve. This shows us the changing amounts of the two factors that will be used by the firm as it expands output.

If the price of one factor changes the firm will seek to substitute the now relatively cheaper factor. New isoquants will have to be drawn, and a new FCE line obtained. This is similar in approach to a change in relative prices in indifference curve analysis, but if the relative efficiency of the two factors remains constant, a change in price will always lead to substitution towards the relatively cheaper factor.

If technological improvement takes place so that each unit of capital becomes more efficient, it will be necessary to draw a new series of isoquants and isocosts. This could also be necessary if there were a change in the efficiency of labour due to more training or a change in effort-input.

Risk and uncertainty

Most production takes place in anticipation of demand. Exceptions are such activities as bespoke tailoring or products made to order. Producers believe that if they incur the costs of production they will be able to sell their output in the future in sufficient quantities and at prices such that they will recover the production costs incurred and make a profit. It is necessary for the producer to make a number of forecasts. These include the future level of demand at particular prices, and the costs which will be incurred during the production period. Future market conditions are uncertain and because the producer is required to undertake expenditure in anticipation of future sales it is necessary for him to take risks. His forecasts of future demand, or of his production costs, could be wrong.

Expected profits could turn out to be losses. This is why it is sometimes said that profit is the reward for risk-taking.

Producers face different sorts of risks. If they are price-takers the market price which prevails at the time they sell their finished product may be less than expected and less than the production costs they have incurred. Farmers may anticipate the price at which they will sell their crops and decide how much they can afford to pay the various factors of production. They will be required to pay the factors during the period of production. When the crops are harvested and sold the market price may be lower than expected and so losses rather than profits will be made. The longer the production period – the time between starting production (and incurring costs) and the time at which the products are completed and are ready for sale – the greater the risk of changes in selling price. Of course, prices may be higher than expected so that super-normal profits will be made.

There is a risk that production costs may rise during the production period. For example, a firm may anticipate a certain level of selling price and make its output decisions on that basis, given its current costs of fixed and variable factors. It will then determine output according to the relationships of its expected AR, MR, AC and MC curves. However, factor costs may rise. If wages increase *ceteris paribus* there will be an increase in the firm's costs so that, given the expected price, the firm will now revise its expectations and anticipate making lower profits, or a loss. If it expects that prices will rise proportionately to the increase in costs it will have to decide whether there will be a shift in the demand curve so that the same quantity can still be sold, or whether the higher price will lead to lower sales so that only a smaller quantity can be sold.

Again, the longer the production period the greater the risk of a rise in factor input prices. An important relationship therefore is the relative lengths of the production period and the period over which input prices are, or can be expected to be, stable. If, for example, wages are revised only once a year, either as a result of a collective agreement or a law, producers may be reasonably confident that their wage costs will be stable for some specific time ahead. However, as we have previously discussed, if there is a change in the effort-input from each unit of labour, labour costs may change even though wage levels have remained constant. An increase in effort-input per unit of labour time will increase MPP, and with constant wages will lead to lower unit labour costs per item produced; the converse will be true if effort-input per unit of labour time is reduced.

If raw material prices rise there will be a similar increase in costs. Firms may therefore prefer to enter into long-term fixed-price contracts with the suppliers of their raw materials if they expect these prices to rise. The suppliers of raw materials, if they hold the same expectations about future price movements, would be reluctant to make long-term fixed-price agreements at the current price level.

As we saw earlier, a firm may nevertheless continue with production in the short run, even though there has been a rise in costs or a reduction in the expected price of the finished products, if it is able to cover its variable costs and make some contribution to its fixed costs.

Price-makers such as monopolists and oligopolists may face smaller risks of fluctuations in the future selling prices of their products. They have some freedom to determine the price at which they will sell. This will mean that they must then accept the level of demand determined by the consumers' price elasticity of demand for those products. If consumers' incomes rise there may be changes in demand depending on the income elasticity of demand for the product, and these may result in higher or lower demand for the goods at each given price level. Luxury goods will have a positive income elasticity of demand and necessities a negative one.

These producers may also have competition from new entrants which was not foreseen at the time the production decisions were made. A monopolist may face competition from a different but related product, as with oil and electricity for heating. Competition may also come from different products. For example, a monopolist may be the sole supplier of, say, mink coats. His expected future sales may be less than anticipated as a result of competition from suppliers of diamonds if consumers change their tastes as fashions change. Oligopolists may have increased competition from new entrants, perhaps with slight product differentiation which is considered more attractive by consumers. Market structure may provide different opportunities to influence both demand and supply.

Consumers' tastes may change as a result of the appearance of new products. Fashions may be unstable and lead to constant shifts in the demand curves for some products. Medical opinion may affect the demand for products such as tobacco or sugar. Different types of products will be more or less susceptible to sudden changes in demand. However, both monopolists and oligopolists may be able to shift the demand curve facing them by advertising and marketing campaigns. This will increase their costs but may lead to a disproportionate increase in sales.

If demand is liable to fluctuate a producer may seek to reduce his risk of losses by choosing a combination of factors which gives him a flat-bottomed cost curve rather than one which is more sharply curved, even though this could mean that his costs are a little higher. For example, in Fig.

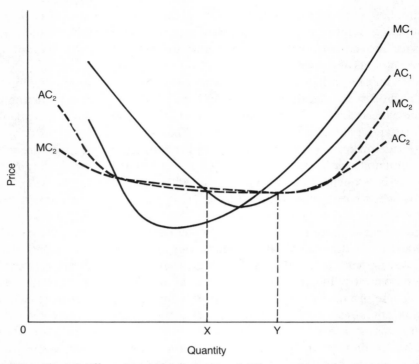

Fig. 8.3 Effects on production costs of different plant organisations

8.3, cost curves MC_1 and AC_1 are, at the optimum level of production, lower than cost curves MC_2 and AC_2. A level of output between OX and OY can be produced at lower costs by adopting cost curves MC_1 and AC_1. However, a different combination of factors which might involve different technology, represented by cost curves MC_2 and AC_2, would allow production outside the range of OX–OY to be produced more cheaply. If the firm is confident that its desired output levels will be between OX and OY it should select the first combination of factors and cost curves. If, however, there is much uncertainty, and the expected range of desired output, determined by demand and price levels, might vary much more widely than this, the firm could decide to select the second combination of factors and cost curves. This is more likely to occur if the firm is in imperfect competition when excess profits are expected, so that the higher costs associated with MC_2 and AC_2 can be borne. Although profits will be lower in the range of output OX–OY, this need not be so great as to prevent normal profits and some excess profits from being made, and will avoid losses at other levels of output.

If there are changes in factor costs, producers will change their factor mix, substituting towards the relatively cheaper factor. In the short run, they can change only their variable factors but, as we have seen, in the long run all factors are variable and the producer must then decide his appropriate combination of factors on the basis of expected future levels of demand and prices, and the expected costs and efficiencies of the different factors over the production period and the asset life. There may be greater risk involved in substituting capital for labour. This will increase the fixed costs and lengthen the short run so that the producer may have less flexibility in the future in changing the factor mix. The substitution of capital will also raise the burden of fixed obligations on the producer. However, there may be considerable advantages to be obtained from the substitution of capital for labour. Depending on the shape of the long-run cost curve and the gains from the specialisation of labour, the producer may be willing to take the risks associated with higher fixed costs.

In practice, labour costs may be less variable than we have so far assumed. It may not be possible to dismiss labour when product demand falls, or it may be possible to do so only by incurring costs such as redundancy payments. Legal provisions may have the effect of making labour a *quasi-fixed* factor of production. The more elements there are of fixed costs associated with both capital and labour, the more important is the producer's estimate of the stability of future demand.

Government policies may have considerable impact on the extent to which labour costs are variable and on the level of labour costs. We have assumed that wages are the same as labour costs. However, there are other costs involved in employing labour. Employers may be required to pay insurance or pension contributions, or some form of wages tax on behalf of their employees. This will mean that producers must estimate future changes in these items of cost just as they must forecast future wage and effort-input levels. Alternatively, governments may subsidise employment so that labour costs are less than wage levels.

There are many sources of uncertainty relevant to the producer's decision to undertake production. Some of them emanate from the market conditions. Future demand may be uncertain because of changes in prices of substitutes or changes in income. Future supply may be uncertain because of large changes in production as many new firms enter, thus greatly increasing future supply, or due to natural phenomena which cause a decrease in supply – as may happen if hurricanes destroy sugar crops in a number of countries or some other natural disaster occurs. As discussed earlier, conditions of perfect competition may create damped or

explosive fluctuations in prices and output according to the supply responses to an initial change in demand. Agriculture may be especially subject to
uncertainties because of the possibility of natural hazards which affect
output, the entry of new suppliers, and the production period, which
means that once decisions have been made to grow or produce a particular
crop, adjustments cannot take place until the next sowing season.

Risk reduction

Producers may be expected to take steps to minimise or reduce the risks
they face. Price support schemes and other forms of producer associations
may seek to stabilise price by controlling output, or the amount of output
which is released on the market via buffer stocks. Oligopolists may spend
money creating brand images and brand loyalty in order to make it more
difficult for new entrants to come in and attract away some of their
customers.

Governments may support various measures to stabilise supply or to
limit the effect of fluctuations in demand and/or supply on prices and
output. Severe fluctuations in the incomes of many small producers or the
workers employed by firms subject to considerable market fluctuations
may have undesirable political repercussions. This intervention may
involve a limitation on competition or restriction of new entrants, or lead
to production taking place at less than optimum levels of output for each
firm in that it does not produce at the lowest point of its current or possible
future long-term cost curve. While these may be departures from optimum
conditions of production in a model of perfect competition, we are unable
to conclude whether they are 'better' than the alternative. We should,
however, expect producers to seek to reduce the uncertainty and risks
associated with their production activities. We must then decide whether
the steps they have taken are better than the situation they are trying to
avoid; what may be better for the producers may not be better for
consumers, employees or society as a whole.

CHAPTER 9

Taxation

A tax is a payment that has to be made to central or local government. There are two main purposes of taxation: first, to raise revenue for the government, and second, to influence the behaviour of economic agents. Government needs to raise revenue in order to finance its expenditure, but need not levy taxes to cover all its expenditure since it can borrow funds. Government may seek to influence people's behaviour by imposing a tax which leads to a rise in price and therefore a reduction in demand, or which leads to the receipt of lower net, or after-tax, income from economic activity, thereby making that activity less attractive and rewarding in financial terms. Governments impose three types of taxes.

Direct taxes These are taxes on income. Different rates of tax can be levied on income from different sources, so that income from employment may be taxed at a lower rate than income from property such as dividends, rent or capital gains. Some forms of income may be excluded from tax, e.g. interest received from certain types of government investment, savings banks or loans. Low income levels may be excluded from liability to pay income tax.

Indirect taxes These are taxes on expenditure such as purchase tax, value added or a retail sales tax, and customs and excise duties. Again, different rates of tax can be levied on different types of expenditure so that food, or certain items which are considered essential, may attract no, or only low, rates of tax; other commodities may be taxed at a higher-than-average percentage rate, perhaps to discourage their consumption.

Wealth taxes These are taxes on assets. They can take the form of an annual tax on all assets above some specified minimum level held by an individual, or certain types of assets may be excluded from the wealth tax so that people are not taxed on the value of their home. Sometimes assets may be taxed only at certain times or if a specified event occurs. Death duties are a wealth tax, not levied until a person's death. A tax on realised capital gains – the difference between the price paid for an asset and the price for which it is sold – should be regarded as a tax on income and not on assets. No tax liability occurs until the gain is realised and the asset sold for a higher price. If a tax of, say, 1 per cent per annum is levied on *all* assets (or all assets above some specified minimum level), including assets which have increased in value since their purchase, that is a wealth tax. The difference can be illustrated by taking the case of someone who ten years ago bought two shares in a company for £5 each. Today the market value of each share might be £8. If he still owns them his assets have risen from £10 to £16 and a wealth tax would levy tax on the basis of assets worth £16. If there was a tax on realised capital gains, and the individual still owned both shares, he would have incurred no capital gains tax liabiity, but would be liable to pay income tax on the dividends from the shares. If he had sold one of the shares during the current year, a wealth tax would assess him on assets valued at £8. A realised capital gains tax would assess him on £3 (the difference between the purchase and selling price of the assets he had disposed of during the tax year).

A tax may be *progressive*, so that the average rate of taxation rises as a person's income rises. If the average tax rate is rising this will be because the marginal tax rate is rising. The marginal rate of taxation is the rate applied to the last unit of income. A *regressive* tax structure is one where the average rate of tax falls as income rises. A *proportional* tax structure takes a constant percentage of income in tax.

Usually direct taxes, such as income tax, are progressive, but indirect taxes on expenditure may be regressive. Even if the indirect tax is applied as a constant percentage, say 5 per cent on all prices, it will be regressive if the rich have lower average propensities to consume than the poor. Since they spend a smaller proportion of their incomes they will be paying the 5 per cent indirect tax on a smaller proportion of their incomes and so the effective rate of indirect tax on them will be less than that on poorer people.

Governments generally try to incorporate two features into their tax systems. They seek *efficiency*, so that a given amount of taxation is raised as easily as possible and with the fewest undesirable effects on economic activity. They also seek *equity*. Equity can have two dimensions. It requires that individuals in equal circumstances should be treated equally, but also that those who are considered more able to bear the burden of taxation should make a larger contribution, so that individuals in unequal circumstances should be treated unequally. Most tax systems seek to obtain a greater tax contribution from the rich and a smaller, or negative, tax contribution from the poor. A negative tax contribution means that government pays out to the individual more than it takes from him in taxes. Government payments consist of such items as welfare payments, old age pensions, rent subsidies, free medical treatment, or free education for children.

The pursuit of these two objectives by government may lead to considerable difficulties. It is not always easy to interpret the objectives into practical policies, and much will depend on the value judgements held by the policy-makers. For example, it might be thought that those who obtain most benefit from the provision of common government services should make the greater contribution towards payment of their costs. In earlier times the system of payment of tolls to use roads reflected this belief. Those who travelled on the roads most often paid the tolls most frequently. The same effect might be obtained today by imposing higher indirect taxes on petrol, motor cars and driving licences.

However, to require those who receive most benefit from welfare payments such as unemployment, or State-provided sickness benefits, to make the highest tax contribution, would negate the social equity objectives incorporated in the welfare payments. These payments are made to those who are considered to be most in need of income from the State and are, therefore, presumably least able to pay the most taxes.

It is possible, however, that the effect of the various taxes imposed by a government will result in a contradictory position. Indirect taxes may fall most severely, in percentage terms, on lower income groups, since they may pay a higher proportion of their low income in regressive indirect taxation.

Progressive taxation reflects the view that ability to pay should determine the relative tax contribution of an individual. Those with higher incomes, therefore, have higher marginal and average rates of taxation. It is believed that to take a marginal £10 of income by levying income tax on a person with £10,000 imposes less hardship, or loss of utility, on him than would the imposition of £10 direct tax on a person with an income of £1,000. This view, widely held, is a belief, and not something which is capable of demonstration by economic theory or analysis. We cannot compare the utility functions of two separate individuals. We may believe that for each of them, income has diminishing marginal utility; thus the last £10 of the person with £10,000 has less utility to him than the previous £10, and certainly less than the marginal utility of the £10 of income he has between £990 and £1,000. But this does not allow us to conclude that the marginal utility of the income between £9,990 and £10,000, to the person with £10,000, is less than the marginal utility of the income between £990 and £1,000, to the person with an income of only £1,000. Nevertheless, in practice, governments often make just such a judgement and impose a higher marginal rate of taxation on people with higher incomes.

Even with a progressive tax structure we cannot necessarily conclude that the effect of government intervention is to redistribute income. Taxation leads to the reduction of gross income so that net disposable income is less than gross or pre-tax income. We must also consider the other aspect of government intervention – government expenditure. It is the combination of taxation and government expenditure which determines whether the net effect is to redistribute income or to leave the distribution of net income plus receipt of government benefits unaffected. Moreover, if income is redistributed, it may be redistributed in either a more, or less, unequal way. The combination of taxation and government expenditure could redistribute in favour either of those who were initially, in terms of pre-tax income, the relatively lower, or of the relatively higher income groups. Usually the net effect of government intervention is to redistribute the original or initial income in a more equal way, so that those with relatively low pre-tax original incomes receive more as a result of taxation and government expenditure.

The incidence of taxes

There may be a difference between the apparent and the effective burden of a tax. Those on whom it appears to be levied may not be the ones who actually pay it. For example, a tax on the sales of cigarettes may appear to be paid, or borne, by the person who buys cigarettes, but the burden of the tax might in fact be borne by the producers and sellers of cigarettes. The *incidence* of a tax shows us where the burden of the tax is actually borne.

Incidence of an indirect tax   We can illustrate this by assuming an indirect tax of a specified amount on each unit sold, no matter what price is charged for each unit. An *ad valorum* tax is a percentage tax according to the price of each unit sold.

In Fig. 9.1, S–S is the supply curve and D–D the demand curve for the product, before the tax is levied. Price is P and the volume of sales is Q. Let us assume that government imposes a tax of PT per unit sold. This means that at each quantity sold the price will rise by PT. A new supply curve S_1–S_1 therefore applies. This will be parallel to the initial supply curve S–S, and is PT higher than S–S. The initial price is raised by the tax from P to T. However, the new equilibrium price, where supply (S_1–S_1) equals demand, is A, and the quantity demanded falls from Q to Q_1. The tax is AB, which is equal to PT.

Producers must pay a tax of PT on each unit sold, so the net revenue received by the producer is not OA but OB. The difference between the price charged to the consumer, OA, and the net price received after tax by the producer, OB, (A–B), is equal to PT, which is the level of tax per unit sold. The price paid by the consumer has risen from OP to OA, but this is

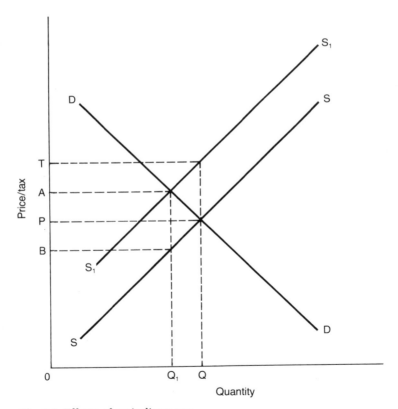

Fig. 9.1 Effects of an indirect tax

less than the price OT which would have resulted had demand and output remained at the initial level of OQ. The net price or marginal revenue received by the producer has fallen by PB, since the net-of-tax receipt per unit of sale has fallen from OP to OB. Government receives (O·Q_1 × AB) and the level of output falls from OQ to OQ_1. There will therefore be less employment in this industry because less output is produced. However, employment and output elsewhere might rise as a result of the government spending the tax revenue it has received.

The extent to which the price will rise after the tax will depend on the price elasticity of supply and the price elasticity of demand. The greater the price elasticity of supply, the larger the rise in price to the consumer. To put this a different way, the smaller the price elasticity of supply, the less will the consumer bear the incidence of the tax. The greater the price elasticity of demand, the smaller the rise in price to the consumer. The lower the price elasticity of demand, the more will the incidence of the tax fall on the consumer. The lower the fall in the net price received by the producer, the smaller will be the reduction in output following the imposition of the tax.

The more price-elastic are *both* supply and demand, the greater the reduction in the quantity demanded, so there will be a larger fall in output and employment, and the government will receive relatively little tax revenue. If both supply and demand are price-inelastic, there will be relatively little change in the quantity produced and demanded, and government tax revenue will therefore be relatively high. If the government wishes to raise a given amount of revenue from this form of indirect taxation it should, therefore, tax commodities with price-inelastic supply and demand curves.

If the government imposed an *ad valorum* tax, the analysis would be the same as shown in Fig. 9.1 except that the new supply curve S_1–S_1 would not be parallel to S–S. It would diverge more from S–S, and therefore be higher than S–S as the price rose. A 10 per cent tax means that the initial price plus tax will be higher, the higher the initial price on which the 10 per cent tax is imposed. With an *ad valorum* tax the vertical difference between S_1–S_1 and S–S increases as price rises.

Incidence of a direct tax We will now consider the incidence of an income tax imposed on earnings. In Fig. 9.2, curve D–D represents the demand for labour and curve S–S the supply of labour before a tax is imposed. Labour is measured as the number of hours demanded and supplied. In the absence of a tax, wages would be W, and the level of

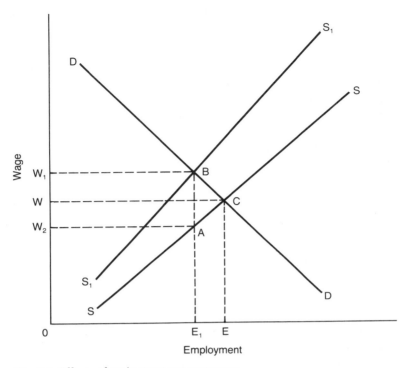

Fig. 9.2 Effects of an income tax on wages

employment, E. The gross wage paid by the employer would be the same as the net wage received by the workers.

If income tax is imposed on wages, the demand for labour will be unaltered. The gross wage, or cost to the employer, will remain the same, and so the amount of labour demanded at each gross wage level will be the same. The supply of labour curve S–S shows the supply of labour forthcoming at each gross wage level but, because there is no income tax on wages, the gross wage level is also the net wage level. Labour supply is assumed to be determined by the net wage. This is the amount workers receive for accepting the disutility and effort of work, and for surrendering their leisure. This means that we must draw a new supply curve S_1–S_1. S_1–S_1 is above S–S by the amount of tax levied on that wage level.

The gross wage paid by the employer is shown by S_1–S_1 and so the amount of labour demanded will be where D–D intersects S_1–S_1. This is at a level of employment E_1, with a gross wage level of W_1. Workers, however, receive only the net-of-tax wage W_2. The amount (W_1–W_2) is taken by income tax.

The gross wage paid by employers has risen from W to W_1, but the net wage received by workers has fallen from W to W_2. The incidence of the income tax has fallen on *both* workers and employers.

The same general rules will apply as with indirect taxes. The more price- or wage-inelastic the supply curve, and the more price- or wage-elastic the demand curve, the more will the incidence fall on the worker or seller, rather than on the employer or buyer of labour. If the labour supply curve were completely wage-inelastic, so that the same amount of labour was supplied no matter what the wage level was, the full incidence of the tax would fall on workers.

Except in the special case of a perfectly inelastic supply curve of labour, the imposition of a direct tax will lead to some reduction in the employers' demand for labour, and so to a fall in the level of employment. However, it is possible that employment will increase as a result of the government spending the tax receipts.

Distorting effect of taxes

When an income tax is imposed there is a difference between the price paid by (or cost to) the employer, and the wage received by the worker. In Fig. 9.2, this is equal to AB or (W_1-W_2). Before the tax was imposed the wage level was W, and this was both the amount received by the worker and the cost to the employer. If, before the tax was imposed, the amount the employer was willing to pay for labour was equal to the marginal revenue of product of labour, then W was the value that people were willing to pay for the output of the marginal worker employed when the demand for labour was E. Also, the wage level W was the amount necessary to induce the marginal worker to undertake the amount of work represented by OE in Fig. 9.2. The marginal cost and benefits from work at employment level OE were equal before the income tax was imposed.

After income tax is imposed, and employment falls to E_1, the marginal cost and marginal benefits are no longer equal. At the level of employment E_1, the marginal social benefit measured by the value of the output, or MRP, which determines the employers' demand curve D–D, is higher than the marginal social cost represented by the supply curve S–S, which is determined by the net wage level needed to induce workers to give up their leisure for work. The direct tax therefore introduces a distortion which prevents the labour market from operating most efficiently. It is no longer possible for resources to be allocated so that marginal social costs equal marginal social benefits.

The amount of 'loss' following the imposition of the income tax is represented by the triangle ABC in Fig. 9.2. The same effect follows the introduction of an indirect tax. In Fig. 9.1 the 'loss' is equal to the triangular area AB and the point of intersection of S–S and D–D.

If you draw various diagrams for yourself you will see that the 'loss' is smallest (the triangle smallest) when either the supply or demand curve is very inelastic. The least distortion to the most efficient allocation of resources will therefore occur when government imposes taxes on commodities or activities which are most inelastic in demand or supply. This is not surprising since the quantity consumed, or the amount of activity undertaken, will fall by less, the more inelastic the demand or supply. Revenue can be most easily raised by imposing indirect taxation on goods or services which have inelastic demand curves, such as tobacco or petrol. Of course, if government is seeking to discourage the consumption of a commodity, rather than raise a given amount of taxation, indirect taxes will have the greatest effect where the demand curve is very price-elastic.

Taxation and incentives

Income tax may act as a disincentive to work. If the marginal rate of return from work is reduced by income tax, the rate of trade-off between work and leisure will be affected. Work will be less attractive. People may therefore choose to work less. Alternatively, because the imposition of income tax has an income effect, people may work more in order to restore their net after-tax income to its former level. There will be two possibly contradictory pressures – a substitution effect and an income effect. People should substitute leisure for work, since the income tax is the same as a reduction in the cost of leisure. The net reward from work is less so the opportunity cost of extra leisure, or not working, is lower. The income effect occurs because the income tax will reduce people's income, and they may then decide to work more hours. As with the indifference curve analysis of the income and substitution effects following a change in the price of a commodity discussed in Chapter 4, we cannot say whether the income effect will be strong enough to swamp the substitution effect, but the substitution effect will always be positive.

Choice of taxes

Government can choose which taxes to introduce and the rate at which various taxes are levied. As we have seen, in addition to raising revenue, taxes will also affect the behaviour of economic agents, the level of output and employment and the amount of tax raised, and the person who bears the final incidence of the tax may not be the nominal taxpayer. Governments can choose between direct, indirect and asset taxes. They can also impose tax structures which are progressive, regressive or proportional. We have discussed some of the economic criteria or consequences which might influence the government's choice.

There are also administrative factors which governments take into account.

Cost of collection If governments are seeking to raise revenue they will prefer taxes which are relatively cheap to collect in relation to the amount of revenue raised. If the purpose is to discourage consumption of certain commodities, or certain activities, the relative cost of collection might be less important.

Certainty It is widely accepted that the taxpayer, or potential taxpayer, should have certainty, or prior knowledge, of the circumstances in which tax will be levied, and the amount of tax which will be charged. There should, therefore, be certainty as to the liability for and rate of tax. Governments also seek another sort of certainty. They prefer taxes which allow them to be certain, or make a reasonably accurate forecast, of the amount that will be collected in a year. This information is necessary for the preparation of budget estimates of expenditure, revenue collection and borrowing requirements.

Convenience It is thought that taxes should be easily or conveniently understood, assessed and collected.

A new tax is something of a gamble. The government might have little information about the amount of revenue it will raise, for it has no past experience of that specific tax. As we have seen, economic agents adapt their behaviour to the changed conditions which follow the imposition of a tax, and government may be unable to anticipate how economic agents will react to a new tax. It is because economic agents adapt their behaviour to a tax that it has sometimes been said that 'an old tax is no tax'. This is a way of saying that people have already taken the tax into consideration when making their output, pricing or labour supply decisions. It does not mean that an old or established tax has no effect, but rather that its effects are predictable and that, in this sense, economic agents do not feel its burden in the same way that they would a new tax.

The new tax would change relative prices – either the relative prices of different commodities, or the relative price of leisure, according to the type of tax – and so induce economic agents to alter their decisions and actions.

When selecting its combination of different taxes and tax rates, a government has to decide on its objectives. In particular it must decide whether a specific tax is intended to raise revenue or influence consumption or some other economic activity. It will be influenced by its views on equity and the effects of tax on incentives and disincentives. Once it introduces taxes a government cannot avoid interfering with the allocation of resources, and with decisions by factors of production. However, it may be believed that the benefits obtained from government expenditure – the provision of public services financed by taxation – outweigh any losses arising from its intervention. Certainly, all our societies expect certain services to be provided by government and this inevitably leads to the imposition of taxes.

Part three

Macro–economics

CHAPTER 10

Investment decisions

In economics, investment means either the purchase of capital goods to be used in the production of other goods or services, or the production of consumer goods to be held as stocks or inventories. It does not mean the purchase of financial assets or the depositing of money in a bank or building society. While in everyday usage we might refer to someone as investing in stocks and shares, in economics we would not call this investment. Investment would take place if the purchase of shares were from a new issue and the funds received by the company were used to buy new machinery or capital equipment, but it would be the purchase of the capital equipment by the company, and *not* the purchase of the shares by members of the public, which formed the investment. Similarly, if a company produced consumer goods such as cans of baked beans, motor cars or shirts to be held as stocks to meet future orders, we would regard that as investment. For the time being we will concentrate on investment in capital goods and leave stocks on one side.

Companies invest in capital goods in order to produce other goods or services for sale. They anticipate demand and decide to incur fixed costs of production in capital equipment to provide productive capacity. They may use their own funds to finance the acquisition of capital goods or they may borrow funds. Assuming that producers are profit-maximising, they will consider two important aspects of a proposed investment. They will wish to know what the investment will cost, and what receipts or revenues they can expect to receive from sales if they undertake the investment.

The cost of investment is the rate of interest on the funds involved. If a proposed investment costs £100,000 and the prevailing rate of interest is 5 per cent, the cost of the investment is £5,000 per annum. This is what it would cost the firm to borrow £100,000, and it is also the opportunity cost if the firm is using its own funds. If it had £100,000 of its own it could obtain £5,000 a year by lending it to someone else at the prevailing 5 per cent rate of interest. If it did this it would also receive back its £100,000 at the end of the loan; if it undertakes investment in productive activity it would also expect to recover the initial cost of the investment, the £100,000, as well as sufficient to earn or pay a rate of interest of £5,000 a year.

The rate of interest therefore can be an important factor in determining whether or not a company invests in new capital equipment, for two reasons. First, it represents the cost of obtaining the funds required to finance the investment and, second, it reflects the opportunity cost of the firm using its own funds.

The marginal efficiency of capital

However, it may be that for a large part of investment activity, the expected revenues or receipts are more important. Each possible investment project will have an estimated stream of receipts during each year of the expected productive life of the capital equipment. Let us assume that the proposed investment is in capital equipment to manufacture shirts and that it costs £100,000 to buy the equipment, which is estimated to last for ten years. In each year the firm expects to use the equipment in conjunction with variable factors of production to produce shirts. It will have some idea of the number of shirts it can produce and the prices at which it will be able to sell different quantities of shirts. To do this it will also have to estimate its other production costs such as wages, electricity charges, the cost of its raw materials and transport costs. It will be possible to estimate total expenditure and total revenue from sales for each of the ten years during the life of the equipment. By subtracting the costs from the revenues a figure of expected profits can be obtained for each year. (If profits tax is paid, the expected gross profit flows can be reduced to net profit flows for each year.)

The amount received in each year can then be discounted to a present value. It is necessary to do this because £10,000 net-of-tax profit received in year nine is not worth as much as £10,000 received this year. If the £10,000 were received this year the company could, if it wished, invest it for the nine years and receive compound interest. We can calculate the current discounted value of £10,000 in nine years' time by dividing it by the appropriate rate of interest compounded for the appropriate number of years. It is the same principle as calculating compound interest in reverse. Thus if we now have a given amount of money, Y, to invest for n years at a compound rate of interest of r per cent, the future value of the present sum is $Y(1+r)^n$. Similarly, the present value of Y which will not be received for n years is

$$\frac{Y}{(1+r)^n}.$$

The expected future annual profit flows need to be discounted back to a present value in order that they can be compared with the cost of the investment. If each year's net profits are converted into a current value the total of the current values can be expressed as a current rate of return on the cost of the investment, i.e. in this example, of £100,000. Clearly if this figure, the marginal efficiency of capital (mec), is less than 5 per cent, the firm should not undertake the investment. If it does it means that it is not expecting to earn enough to cover the cost of borrowing the funds, or not as much as it could earn by lending the funds to someone else at 5 per cent.

A firm will have a number of possible investment projects which it could undertake. Some of them will have higher expected rates of return or mec than others. We can rank these in descending order of expected rate of return and obtain a marginal efficiency of capital schedule. This is a list of possible investment projects ranked by their expected profitability. We can also indicate the marginal efficiency of capital schedule diagrammatically. Figure 10.1 shows mec_1. If the rate of interest is 5 per cent, the amount of investment will be I_1. However, if the rate of interest rises to 7 per cent, investment will be reduced to I_3. The firm will decide not to go ahead with projects (I_1-I_3).

Mec_2 represents a different mec schedule. It is much more steeply sloping. In this case a rise in the rate of interest from 5 per cent to 7 per cent has much less effect on the level of investment (I_4-I_5). With mec_2, investment is interest-inelastic, while mec_1 shows a position where investment is more interest-elastic. Keynes, who developed the concept of the mec, believed that much investment was interest-inelastic.

We have seen from the brief discussion of how the mec is calculated that the firm or entrepreneur has to estimate a range of variables in order to arrive at the mec for any particular investment project. There are many uncertainties surrounding these estimates. The wages of the workforce, and the effort-input which will influence their MPP over the next ten years, will not be known. Nor will the shape or position of the demand curve for shirts over the next ten years. This can be influenced by fashions,

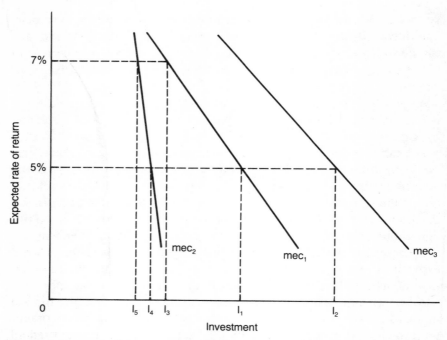

Fig. 10.1 The rate of interest, marginal efficiency of capital and level of investment

new entrants, competitors, the development of new materials and, if the firm exports, also by future exchange rates, import duties and import quotas at home and in overseas markets. Improvements in technology in three years' time might make existing capital equipment out of date. The new equipment might be much cheaper, thereby reducing the firm's competitiveness and future revenues. Given all these uncertainties and risks, a change in the rate of interest from 5 to 7 per cent might be thought to be relatively unimportant in determining whether or not the investment will take place.

It is obvious that the central elements are the firm's expectations of future demand – and therefore sales levels at certain prices – and the expected costs of production. If the firm is confident that there will be high demand in the future, it may be willing to invest even if the rate of interest rises. A rise in expectations which leads the firm to expect more sales or higher levels of demand in the future will lead to a revision of its mec schedule. In Fig. 10.1, mec_3 shows how more optimistic expectations lead to a revision of the mec schedule, which shifts to the right. Thus at a rate of interest of 5 per cent, investment will increase from I_1 to I_2. If firms are confident about future levels of demand, we expect them to increase investment in order to have the capacity to produce extra output to meet this demand. Conversely, if firms become pessimistic about the future and expect demand to fall, they will revise their mec schedules downward by shifting them to the left, as with a move from mec_3 to mec_1.

Marginal efficiency of capital schedules which represent a firm's assessment of the expected profitability of investment activity might be expected to be volatile if there are changes in any of the factors taken into consideration by firms when assessing future prospects. Mec schedules will also keep shifting even when all firms are optimistic. If their optimism continues to grow they might continually shift their mec schedules to the right as they constantly revise upward their assessments of future demand and profitability. It is because he believed that shifts in the mec were much more important than movements in the rate of interest that Keynes concluded that the optimism or pessimism of entrepreneurs and firms, reflected in changes in their mec schedules, were much more important than movements in the rate of interest.

However, there may be some kinds of investment activity where sizeable movements in the rate of interest can have more effect on the investment decision. If the investment project is in a capital-intensive production process so that the investment costs are a major part of total costs, and the investment is expected to last a long time so that the capital is tied up for many years and the annual flows of profits extend far into the future, the rate of interest will exert more influence over the expected relationship between costs and receipts. The current value of future receipts will be lower the further away the time that they are earned, so long-lived capital projects which are expected to provide revenues over 20 or 30 years will show relatively low current values of revenues since they will have to be discounted for a long period at a higher rate of interest.

Also, investment in stocks of goods for future sales may be affected by high interest rates because this will affect the cost of holding those goods as stocks.

Other investment appraisal methods

Firms may adopt different methods of appraising investment projects in order to decide whether they should be undertaken or not. There are various methods of doing this. Each has some advantages and disadvantages and there is no absolutely best way of deciding whether to undertake a particular investment project. Different firms will face different situations.

Some may have an abundance of cash resources while others may face a cash shortage, either currently or in the future. Some may find it easier and cheaper to borrow than others. Some may be facing, or anticipating, fiercer competition from home or abroad.

Discounted cash flow The mec approach is essentially a discounted cash flow technique. Future flows of cash or receipts are discounted back to a present value. If the expected receipts in each year of the investment asset's life are estimated as R_1 to R_n and the cost of the investment is K, the rate of return on the investment is:

$$K = \frac{R_1}{1+r} + \frac{R_2}{(1+r)^2} + \frac{R_3}{(1+r)^3} \cdots \frac{R_n}{(1+r)^n}$$

If the firm estimates the $R_1...R_n$ and the cost of the investment K, it can calculate the rate of return, r, necessary to ensure that the discounted expected future cash flows will at least equal the current cost K. It can then compare this rate of return, r, often referred to as the internal rate of return, with the rate of interest, or with any other minimum rate of return which the company has specified as necessary before investment will be undertaken.

Accounting rate of return This is the average annual profit or rate of return in relation to the cost of the investment. This simple approach ignores the fact that later receipts are worth less than the same amount received earlier.

Payback period Some firms may calculate the length of time before the investment will have paid for itself. The expected receipts minus running costs are aggregated until the cost of the investment has been recouped. This gives some indication of the period over which the company will have a net outflow of investment funds and also of the length of time over which it is taking a capital risk. It ignores receipts after the payback period.

In practice firms may use various methods of appraising investment projects. All of them involve uncertainties and estimates. What they seek to do is to apply a certain set of criteria in a consistent way. Some form of discounted cash flow analysis, such as the mec, provides the most useful. The discounted expected returns should be higher than the rate of interest in order to provide some additional reward for risk-taking.

Aggregate investment

We can use the same concept of the marginal efficiency of capital to explain aggregate investment. We merely add together the mec schedules of all firms in the economy to obtain the aggregate mec schedule. The main difference is that if investment increases as the rate of interest falls, the additional investment may be due to some firms increasing the amount of their investment as well as other firms investing for the first time as a result of the lower interest rate.

Replacement investment

It is sometimes useful to distinguish two types of investment. Replacement investment is investment undertaken in order to replace existing capital equipment which has become worn out. If a machine has an effective operating life of ten years the firm will need to replace it every ten years if it is to continue to produce the same level of output. If it has 20 machines it will, on average, replace two of them every year. This assumes that the firm grew to its present size of 20 machines by adding two additional machines each year. Of course, in reality it may have started with all 20 machines or with ten and added the other ten after two or three years. For an individual firm, therefore, the amount of replacement investment necessary to maintain its productive capacity each year will be determined by the amount of capital equipment it has, the length of life of each item of capital equipment, and the purchase date of each item of capital equipment. For the economy as a whole it might be reasonable to assume that the amount of replacement investment needed to maintain productive capacity will be equal to the amount of capital equipment, K, divided by the average life or number of years of productive capacity of that capital, l.

If the economy maintains the level of its productive capacity of capital equipment, its yearly replacement investment will therefore be $I = K/l$.

We are assuming that the total level of output remains constant and that there are no improvements in technology so that the technical or productive efficiency of the capital equipment remains the same. All that is happening in this simple explanation is that firms are replacing worn-out capital equipment and that they need the same amount of capital equipment to produce a given level of output as they did in the past. Of course, if there are technological advances, or if there is a substitution of capital for labour, we might expect the amount of capital used to produce a given level of output to change. Technological improvement would mean that less capital was needed to produce the same output, or that the same amount of capital could produce a larger amount of output. The substitution of capital for labour would mean that more capital was used to produce a given level of output.

The relationship between the amount of capital needed to produce a given level of output, or the amount of output which can be produced by a given amount of capital, is known as the *capital–output ratio*. If O is output and K is capital, the capital–output ratio is K/O. If £3 million of capital is required to produce £1 million of output, the capital–output ratio is 3. Calculation of the capital–output ratio assumes that the capital equipment is fully utilised so that there is no spare capacity or capital lying idle.

If firms believe that the present demand for their goods will continue in the future at exactly the same level, and if there is no techological change in the productivity of capital or substitution of capital for labour, the amount of replacement investment will be given by the capital–output ratio and the average length of life of capital equipment.

The average length of life of capital equipment, *l*, gives us the rate of capital consumption, or depreciation. Capital consumption means the rate at which capital is consumed or used up each year in the production of goods and services. Depreciation means the same thing, but it is important to note that to an economist, depreciation is the rate at which the capital equipment is used up and is not necessarily the same as the rate at which the firm provides depreciation funds out of its gross profits to finance the replacement investment. The firm may set aside part of its revenues to finance the purchase of the replacement equipment at a rate which differs from the yearly rate of capital consumption. Depreciation in a financial sense is not the same as capital consumption, which refers to the physical depreciation of the capital equipment. Tax regulations applicable to profits tax may provide yet another basis of calculation of depreciation allowances for tax purposes. This is the rate at which the tax authorities may permit deductions to be made from gross profits before tax is assessed in order to provide after-tax funds to finance the replacement investment. It does not follow that the funds will be used to finance replacement investment.

Changes in investment

A firm may decide not to replace its worn-out capital equipment, or it may decide to replace it and add extra capacity.

We have seen that expected future market conditions are very important in influencing firms' current investment decisions. The longer the time period before the investment can be completed, the further ahead the firm has to forecast and the more uncertainty there will be. The future is always uncertain and we all, whether entrepreneurs, investors, consumers or workers, have to make some estimates of future conditions sometimes. One of the factors which is likely to exert considerable influence on our estimates of the future is our recent experience. If the economy has been doing well and demand has been increasing year after year we might well expect it to continue to do so. If total income in the economy has been rising and the level of demand for goods and services has been growing, firms may well expect future demand to be higher than the current level.

This leads to an expected relationship between changes in the current level of income and changes in current investment. For example, if income has been growing at, say, 5 per cent a year, we would expect investment to have been growing. Demand would have been rising and companies would have expanded their productive capacity to meet rising demand and expected future higher levels of demand.

A very simple model might take the form $I_{(t+1)} = Y_t - Y_{t-1}$. This suggests that investment (I), in period $(t+1)$ is determined by the growth in income (Y) in the two previous periods. It is convenient to think of each period (t) as one year, but it could be any period we chose such as three months or a half-year. This model or equation says two things. First, if income grows, investment will rise; or if income falls, so will investment. Second, in this particular formulation, the effect of a change in income on investment will be seen in the next period. We could accept the first point and modify the second so that $I_{(t+1)} = Y_{(t-2)}$. It is a question of observable fact, or data, as to which is the appropriate time-lag between the change in income and the change in investment.

This principle is known as the accelerator principle. It means that if income is rising the rate of growth of income will lead to, or induce, an accelerated increase in investment. The change in investment reflects the belief of producers that demand will continue to rise, and it is this expected growth in demand which induces them to invest by causing them to revise their mec upward. If income were falling, they would revise their mec downward and this would lead to lower investment.

The accelerator

We call the effect of changes in income on the rate of change of investment the accelerator because a change in income will lead to an accelerated or magnified effect on the rate of change of investment. Let us assume that the total capital stock is £100 million, the average life of capital equipment is ten years and the capital–output ratio is 5. Total output is therefore £20 million a year (the capital stock divided by the capital–output ratio). If firms expect demand for their products to rise by 10 per cent next year, i.e. by £2 million to £22 million, they will increase investment to provide the additional capital equipment to provide the output to meet the expected higher demand. In order to produce an extra £2 million of output they will have to invest in an additional £10 million of capital equipment (the amount of output required multiplied by the capital–output ratio). Investment this year will therefore consist of £10 million replacement capital plus £10 million additional investment. Output will rise by only 10 per cent but investment will double. There will be an accelerated increase in investment.

The amount of additional investment induced by a change in income will depend on two things: first, the relationship between the change in income and the expected change in demand for goods and services; second, the capital–output ratio.

If we assume that a 1 per cent change in income leads to an expected 0.8 per cent change in demand in the next period, then expected demand in period $(t+1) = 0.8(Y_t - Y_{t-1})$. If the capital–output ratio is 5 we can calculate that a 5 per cent change in income will lead to a rise of 4 per cent in expected demand, and this will lead to a 4 per cent rise in the capital stock. If the existing capital stock is £10 million, total investment this year will be £1 million replacement investment plus £400,000 additional investment, a total of £1.4 million.

In this case we could say that gross investment was £1.4 million, and net investment was £400,000. The difference between gross and net investment is that we subtract replacement investment, or depreciation, from gross investment to obtain the net change in capital stock. If some worn-out capital is not replaced so that the total capital stock decreases, net investment would be negative. On the assumption that there has been no change in the productivity of capital as a result of technological improvements, or a change in the MPP of labour, this would mean that productive capacity was less and therefore output would be less in the next period. If the capital–output ratio remains constant, a change in the stock of capital leads to a change in the output of goods and services. An expansion in capital stock, or positive net investment, leads to rising output; a reduction in capital stock leads to a reduction in output. Negative net investment, where gross investment is less than the rate of physical depreciation of capital equipment, is sometimes referred to as disinvestment. Existing capital equipment is not replaced as it wears out.

It is not claimed that the accelerator principle is immutable and always operates. It is possible that firms come to the view that the growth in income is going to flatten out or even be followed by a fall. In this case they will not increase their investment. The accelerator principle, which offers an explanation of the *change* in the level of investment, by reference to the *change* in the level of income, is a broad general hypothesis and not an absolutely unbreakable law. There are no unbreakable laws in economics.

The multiplier expresses the effects of a change in the level of investment on the level of income; the accelerator expresses the relationship between a change in the level of income, affecting the level of demand, and the change in the level of investment induced or undertaken in response to the changed demand conditions expected in the future as a result of the changes in income in the current or past periods.

CHAPTER 11

Consumption and savings

When we considered the theory of consumer demand in Chapter 4, we assumed that the consumer spent all his income. This was, of course, a simplifying and unreal assumption. Some people do not spend all of their income; they save part of it. Others may spend more than their income by borrowing, getting into debt or, as we sometimes call it, dis-saving, which can mean using past savings to finance current purchases of goods and services. We shall now look at some of the factors which may influence the level of consumption or consumer demand. By consumption we mean the purchase of goods and services for current use.

The distinction between spending – or consumption – and savings is very important in economics. We define the two terms in such a way that all income must either be spent on consumption or saved. This is all that can be done with income; it must be allocated to either consumption or savings. This means that $Y = C + S$ where Y is income, C is consumption and S is savings. Savings therefore means income which is not spent on consumption. It does not matter how we save that part of our income which is not spent on consumption. We can put it in a bank, buy stocks and shares, lend it to a friend or relative or hide it in the mattress or a hole in the ground. What matters is that it is not spent on consumption.

It is reasonable to start from the assumption that the level of consumption will be influenced by the level of income. The more income we have the more we can choose to spend on consumption goods. It does not necessarily follow, of course, that if we get more income we will spend it on more consumption, or that we will spend all of it on consumption goods, but it seems to fit in with common sense and experience that as our income rises so does our level of consumption.

However, while this might be an acceptable general rule, it leaves a number of important questions unanswered. For example, how does our consumption change with income? Do we consume the same proportion of our income irrespective of our income level, or do we change the relative proportions saved and consumed as our level of income changes? Over what period might we expect to vary our consumption with income? What is the appropriate definition of income and whose income and consumption should we consider? We will look at these issues in turn. They form an important part of modern economic analysis.

Propensity to consume

The relationship between changes in income and changes in consumption (and therefore in savings since $Y = C + S$) is known as the propensity to consume. If people consume nine-tenths of their income, and always consume nine-tenths of their income no matter what their level of income is, the marginal and the average propensity to consume would be 9/10 or 0.9. The marginal and average propensity to save would be 1/10 or 0.1. The marginal propensity to consume is the proportion of an additional unit of income that is consumed. Similarly, the marginal propensity to save (MPS) is the proportion of an additional unit of income that is saved. The average propensity to consume (APC) is the total amount of consumption as a fraction of total income. The average propensity to save (APS) is calculated in the same way. It follows that $MPC + MPS = 1$, and $APC + APS = 1$.

In Fig. 11.1, curve MPC_1 illustrates a constant MPC of 0.8. The 45° line represents equality between income on the horizontal axis and consumption or savings on the vertical axis. Thus the 45° line shows that with an income of 100, consumption plus savings must also total 100 since $Y = C + S$. If the MPC is constant at 0.8, then 80 per cent of income will be spent on consumption and 20 per cent or a fifth will be saved.

MPC_2 shows a different consumption function. A consumption function is merely the relationship between consumption and income; it expresses consumption as a function of income so that as income changes so does the level of consumption. In MPC_1 the MPC is constant at 0.8, but the level of consumption changes with the level of income so that with an income of 100, consumption is 80, and with an income of 300 consumption is 240. With MPC_2 we have assumed that consumption is 100 plus 0.5 of income. Thus $MPC = 100 + 0.5(Y)$. This means that even if no income is received the level of consumption will be 100. In order to finance this consumption the individual might have to borrow or use past savings. At a zero level of

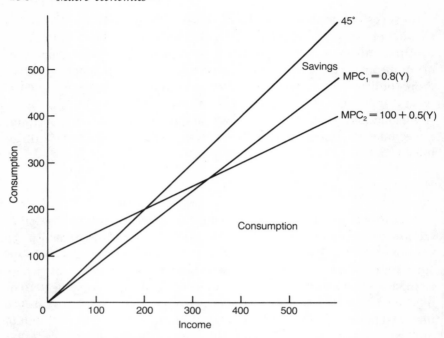

Fig. 11.1 Different consumption functions

income, consumption with MPC_2 will therefore be 100, while with a zero level of income MPC_1 implies that there will be no consumption.

As soon as any income is received the individual represented by MPC_2 will spend half of it as well as the basic constant consumption expenditure of 100. Thus with an income of 10, the level of consumption of MPC_2 will be $100 + 0.5(10) = 105$. With an income level of 200 the level of consumption will be 200, and with an income level of 300 consumption will be 250. If the two individuals each had an income of 500, MPC_1 would consume $0.8(500) = 400$, and MPC_2 would consume $100 + 0.5(500) = 350$. Thus with the two different consumption functions illustrated in Fig. 11.1, MPC_1 would consume less at lower income levels but more at higher income levels, while MPC_2 would consume more at lower income levels but save more than MPC_1 at higher income levels.

Different individuals may have different consumption functions reflecting differences in their tastes and preferences or in their desire to enjoy current consumption rather than to save for the future. Saving means that we can have a higher level of consumption in the future since we can receive interest on our savings. We might wish to save from current income so that we can have a level of consumption at some future date which will be higher than our future income. Many people save from their current earnings in order to provide income from which to finance future consumption when they retire and when their income will be lower.

Different societies and cultures may have different attitudes towards current consumption and savings. Some may encourage savings while others may regard current consumption as more important.

We may also change our consumption function, or our preference for consumption or saving out of current income, at different stages of our lives. It may be that initially we have a high propensity to consume, then we increase our propensity to save – perhaps when we get married and have family responsibilities. Indeed, we may even dis-save and have periods when our level of consumption is higher than our current level of income. Later, perhaps after our children have themselves married and we have fewer family responsibilities, we may increase our propensity to save in preparation for retirement and our old age.

Keynes believed that consumption was a positive function of income, i.e. that consumption rose as income rose, but that it did so at a diminishing rate. This means that the MPC decreases as income rises, so that as our income rises we increase our level of consumption but we spend a diminishing proportion of each additional unit of income on consumption. Alternatively, we can say that the marginal propensity to save increases with the level of income.

If this is correct it means that as our income increases so will our level of consumption, but the growth of consumption will be less than the growth in income since we will allocate an increasing proportion of additional income to saving.

We assumed that the MPCs illustrated in Fig. 11.1 referred to individuals. They could also refer to aggregate MPC functions. An aggregate MPC or consumption function is obtained by adding together the consumption functions of all individuals. If everyone has a diminishing MPC, the aggregate consumption function can change if there is a change in the distribution of income. If income is redistributed from those with higher incomes to those with lower incomes, there may be an increase in total consumption because the lower-income groups have higher MPCs than the higher-income groups. Thus redistribution of income could lead to a rise in total consumption and a fall in total saving even if the aggregate level of income remains constant.

Individuals or households

So far we have referred to the consumption functions of individuals and the aggregate consumption function of the whole economy. However, it may be that in the real world there is another important grouping – the household, or family unit. In many societies consumption decisions are not made individually, and the income of each individual is not necessarily the most important determinant of the level of his or her consumption. Often the income and consumption and savings decisions of people are made on a joint basis grouped on the family or household. In some societies the household may be confined to parents and their dependent children still at school. In other societies there may be an extended household which includes other relatives who pool or share their income, consumption and savings decisions.

If both husband and wife receive an income from work they may make joint decisions about consumption, and it is possible that the consumption–savings allocation from a jointly earned income will be different from the consumption–saving decision that would be made were the same aggregate income earned by only one member of the household.

Generally it is preferable to base analysis of consumption and saving decisions on some household unit rather than on individuals. There seems to be well-established evidence that the decisions are affected by the size and composition of households rather than being made on an individual basis.

Income

Acceptance of the view that consumption is a function of income still leaves unresolved exactly what we mean by income, and over what period the relationship between income and consumption is expected to hold. In the real world we can take two broad definitions of income. Gross income is the income we earn or are entitled to receive before any deductions are made. Net or disposable income is the amount of income we actually receive after deduction of taxes or other items such as compulsory insurance contributions for sickness benefit or a State pension fund, plus any receipts from the State. It is possible that gross income can rise without there being any change in net income.

The consumption–saving decision may be influenced by the reasons for differences in gross and net income. For example, if deductions are made in order to provide for a retirement pension, we may decide that we need not save as much ourselves on a voluntary basis. If there is a State-provided pension we may decide that we need not save as much for future consumption. If taxes increase to finance a free medical service we may decide to save less since we no longer need to have savings to provide for future medical expenses. A decrease in net income may therefore lead us to reduce the level of our voluntary savings. However, we could say that this was in some way offset by an increase in compulsory savings. Taxation or contributions to a State pension fund can be seen as a form of compulsory saving. When these compulsory deductions are taken from gross income we are left with net disposable income.

While, in general, it may be that net disposable income is the more relevant income figure for determination of the consumption function, it is possible that changes in net income will not always lead to a change in the level of consumption or savings. It may depend on the cause of the change in the relationship between gross and net income and our response to the expected future consequences of the change.

Time period relationship between income and consumption

If there is a relationship between income and consumption, and between changes in income and changes in consumption, we need to consider the time periods of the relationship. For example, we could suppose that the appropriate time period is the period in which income is received, so that if we are paid weekly we would base our consumption decision each week on the income received that week. If we were paid monthly we would determine our consumption and savings according to the amount of income we received each month. This does not seem to fit in with our experience. Certainly we know that in some periods our consumption is not a function of that period's income. We probably spend more in the holiday period than we usually do, and consumption expenditure rises during the Christmas period even though income may not have risen. Some people's income fluctuates from week to week or month to month, and while some of the fluctuations may lead to fluctuations in their level of consumption expenditure, there may also be some attempt to smooth out the income fluctuations into a more stable consumption expenditure pattern.

If we assume that consumption is a function of income, we must make some attempt to express a time period relationship between changes in income and changes in consumption, just as we sought to establish a relationship between the time periods of changes in income and demand

and changes in investment when considering the accelerator principle in Chapter 10.

One approach is to take the changes in income in some past periods as determining current consumption. We would then conclude that $C_t - C_{(t-1)} = Y_{(t-2)} - Y_{(t-1)}$. The precise length of the different periods of t could vary according to the evidence. This would say that changes in our current level of consumption, and therefore of savings, are determined by our past levels of income.

An alternative approach is what is sometimes referred to as the permanent income hypothesis. This says that we determine our current consumption and savings decisions on the basis of our expected future lifetime or permanent income. This implies that $C_t = Y_{p(t+1)} \; Y_{p(t+n)} \cdot Y_{p'}$ or permanent income differs from Y (income) as we have previously used the term in that it refers to expected regular income so that unexpected fluctuations in income are disregarded. It assumes that we estimate our income over the rest of our life and discount it back to a present value to get some sort of average lifetime income. We then base our regular consumption and savings decisions on the expected lifetime or permanent income. If there are unexpected fluctuations in our income we may adjust our consumption accordingly so that consumption is seen as having two elements: permanent consumption; and transient consumption, which is determined by transient or unexpected fluctuations in income. Transient consumption can be positive or negative.

The problem with the permanent income hypothesis is that it cannot really be tested in a predictive way. Consumption is held to be determined by the expected lifetime or permanent income, but we cannot measure what level of income people *expect* to receive over their lifetime. All we can do is conclude that if consumption rises, there must have been an increase in people's expectations of their permanent income.

It is therefore not a totally satisfactory explanation of consumption and savings decisions. However, it is useful in that it introduces the notion that expected future income may affect our current consumption and savings decisions. This appears sensible and reasonable. If we face uncertain future income we might reduce current consumption in order to provide savings for the future. Thus two individuals with the same level of income this year and the same family commitments may have different MPCs and APCs if one has expectations of the same or a rising annual income in the future, and the other faces considerable uncertainty about his future income level. They may of course have the same APC and MPC, or the individual facing uncertainty may have higher propensity to consume. He may decide that he would rather purchase the consumption goods and enjoy them now and let the future take care of itself. Different individuals will have different views about providing for the future and so react differently to the same circumstances.

It should by now be apparent that we really cannot draw any totally firm conclusion about the determinants of the actual level of consumption and savings either from a given income level or as a result of a change in income level. It may be that in broad terms we can conclude that as income rises we would expect the MPC and so the APC to fall, so that savings increase as income rises, but the MPC will still be positive. Some of the extra income will be spent, but a declining proportion of additional income will be devoted to consumption expenditure and a rising proportion to savings.

However, if there is uncertainty about the future there may be a shift in the APC and MPC as people change their behaviour in response to the uncertainty. Similarly, if changes in future income are expected we may alter our current consumption. If we are fairly confident that our future income will be higher we may increase current consumption and get into debt, choosing to enjoy higher current consumption which will be paid for out of future income. Or, if we expect our future income to be lower, we may reduce current consumption to even out current and planned future consumption levels.

Savings

We have emphasised the consumption function, although it should be obvious that every consumption decision is also a savings decision. Because all income must be either consumed or saved we cannot make one decision without making the other, and it is not always clear whether individuals or households are making what is primarily a consumption decision or a savings decision. In one sense they are always making both, but in another sense they may sometimes emphasise one rather than the other.

We may decide to increase our savings because we expect future income to be lower or because there is a risk or greater uncertainty surrounding our future income levels. This is the same as concluding that we prefer to defer current consumption for future consumption, but many of us would emphasise the savings rather than the deferred consumption element in our motivation. This might not matter so long as we remember that every consumption decision is also a savings decision, and every savings decision is a consumption decision.

If our preference for current rather than future consumption is greater than the rate of interest, it will increase our satisfaction if we borrow now and enjoy current consumption; our debt can be paid out of future income. The amount of future income we will have to give up – represented by the rate of interest – is less than the satisfaction we will get from having current rather than future consumption. When people decide to save for their retirement, they are concluding that the satisfaction they would obtain from higher current consumption they could otherwise obtain is less than the future satisfaction they will get from a higher level of consumption in the future.

This can be related to the concept of diminishing marginal utility in Chapter 4. If current income is high we might expect marginal utility to have diminished so that we get less satisfaction from current marginal units of consumption than we expect to get from our marginal income in the future when our income will be lower. Thus when we retire and our income falls, the marginal utility of the last unit of our income from our pension will be higher than the marginal utility currently obtained from the marginal unit of our employment income. We therefore decide to postpone some of our consumption to a time when we expect to receive higher marginal utility from it, both because our total level of utility might be lower in the future – since our pension income will be less than our employment income – and also because each unit of income saved will give us more consumption in the future as a result of earning interest. Of course if we do not lend the money to someone else but keep it in the mattress we shall not receive interest.

Wealth

Our past savings form our wealth assets. Wealth is a stock of assets from which a flow of income is derived, although there may be some forms of wealth which do not provide an income flow. Works of art, jewellery and similar assets may properly be regarded as wealth but do not generate income flows. However, many of our wealth assets might be regarded as providers of income. Owner-occupied houses or other property which we use ourselves rather than rent out to someone else do not provide an actual income to us, but it is conventional in economics to regard owner-occupied houses as providing *imputed rent*; we assume that there is an income equivalent to the rent which we would have to pay if we did not own the property. This will be considered again in Chapter 21.

We can regard wealth as a stock of assets which are worth a certain amount, or we can see it as equivalent to an annual flow of income. This annual flow is the amount we could spend and still keep the value of our wealth intact. Thus Friedman, who provided us with the permanent income hypothesis to explain consumption and savings decisions, prefers to regard all income, including income from employment, as expressions of the value of wealth assets. Income can therefore be converted into a figure of wealth. Earnings from current and future employment can be similarly converted into a single value of capital assets which may be envisaged as human wealth or capital assets. This single wealth figure can then be taken, with the rate of interest, to explain consumption–savings decisions. The rate of interest is relevant because it affects the terms on which we can exchange current for future consumption.

Even if we do not accept the permanent income explanation we may still wish to include wealth assets as something influencing our decisions to consume or save. The income we receive from our assets, such as dividends, interest and profits, will already be taken into account since they add to our level of income. However, the level of wealth assets, and changes in their value, may exert additional influence. For example, if the market value of stocks and shares falls, we may increase our savings in order to restore the real value of our wealth assets.

If we measure income as the flow of income or the amount of consumption we could undertake while still leaving the value of our wealth assets intact, a fall in the market value of stocks and shares would be equivalent to a reduction in income. We would subtract the amount of capital loss or fall in the market value of our shares from the total income received from dividends, employment, etc. If our income fell we would expect our MPC to rise; since we generally assume that MPC declines as income rises, it follows that MPC rises as income falls. Thus we would expect both the MPS and the amount of savings to fall when the market value of stocks and shares fell if we followed the definition of income just given. As we have said, however, the opposite may occur and the APS and MPS both rise in order to maintain the real value of wealth assets by increasing savings to buy more stocks and shares.

Whether the amount, type and changes in market value of wealth assets have much effect on savings is an empirical question to be determined by evidence appropriate to a particular society at a specific time. Very poor societies might not experience much effect because few people own stocks and shares and relatively few people may have many financial wealth assets of any sort. In some societies the assets owned by many people may be in the form of property and land which they – or the extended family – occupy, or wealth ownership may be in the form of animal livestock and jewellery. Only a relatively small part of total economic transactions may be through the medium of cash or money. Many developing economies have large subsistence farming sectors. This can influence the opportunity to save and the form in which wealth is kept.

The rate of interest

While the level of income, and perhaps the future expected level of income, might exert the greatest influence on the level of consumption, it is possible that other factors play some role. The rate of interest might be important in two regards. It is the rate at which current consumption can be exchanged for future consumption, and it is the rate at which current income can be converted into future income.

If we save some of our income we can obtain a higher income in the future by lending the savings at the prevailing rate of interest. Thus by forgoing current income (Y) we can obtain $Y(1+r)^n$ in the future. The higher the rate of interest the greater the rewards for postponing current consumption and increasing savings. At the same time, the higher the rate of interest, the more expensive it is to increase current consumption by borrowing. Also, the higher the rate of interest, the less do we need to save in order to have a given level of income in the future. There may therefore be two conflicting pressures following a rise in the rate of interest. If we increase our propensity to save we can enjoy a higher level of income and consumption in the future. This might lead us to increase our savings. If, however, we are saving in order to provide a given income level in the future, we can do so with a smaller amount of savings since interest rates are now higher and this can lead us to reduce our current savings and increase the level of current consumption.

The crucial factors will be our motives for saving and our rate of preference for current versus future consumption. Generally, we might expect an increase in the rate of interest to lead to a reduction in the propensity to consume and a rise in the propensity to save. We might therefore reformulate our original consumption function:

$$C_t = Y_{(t-1)} - Y_{(t-2)}, \; r, \; Y_{(t+n)}, \; A$$

This says that current consumption is determined by the change in income in some past period, the rate of interest, expected income in some future period and the level of wealth assets (A). Although less precise than the original formulation, this presentation might be more realistic. The real world does not necessarily provide either precision or stability in economic relationships.

CHAPTER 12

The level of income

In the two previous chapters we considered how decisions are made regarding the level of investment and the levels of consumption and savings. We will now bring these two areas of economic activity together and see how they interact to determine the level of income and changes in the level of income. It is clear from the earlier discussion that investment decisions and consumption–savings decisions are made by two separate groups of people. Investment decisions are made by firms or entrepreneurs, and consumption and saving decisions are made by households. Firms too may decide to save some of their income from profits, but for the present we will disregard this and concentrate on the savings decisions of households.

Income and consumption

When considering both investment and consumption decisions we saw that the actual and expected level of income played an important part. For present purposes we shall regard income as payment received for the performance of some economic activity. Thus wages, profits, interest and rent are forms of income because they are payments made to factors of production. Pocket money given by a father to his children is not regarded as income since no economic service has been performed and no production has taken place in return for the payment. Similarly, housekeeping money given by a husband to his wife is not regarded as income since there is no productive service performed. This is not to say that housewives do not perform a valuable service in looking after their family; it is merely that our economic definition does not count family activities and the transfer of money from one member to another as forms of economic activity and income. Of course, if a son were employed in his father's factory and received a wage like other employees, that would be economic activity and the payment would be counted as income. It may seem a little confusing and we shall consider it in more detail in Chapter 21, but the intention is to try to separate what we regard as economic activity from other aspects of our family and social behaviour so that we can seek to explain economic behaviour.

Income, then, is payment received for the performance of some economic activity. For the time being we will assume that the only forms of income are wages and profits, although this is a simplification and is used only to clarify the explanation. People obtain income from the performance of economic activity and economic activity takes place because firms believe that people will have income which they will use to purchase the goods and services the firms intend to produce. If, for the time being, we ignore the existence of government, all income comes from firms. They pay the factors of production for their services and this income is then used to purchase the goods and services which have been produced. There is a circular flow of incomes from firms to households as firms pay the factors of production, and back from households to firms as households purchase consumption goods and services from their income.

Not all the income received by households flows back to firms in the purchase of consumption goods. Households will save some of their income and this will diminish the flow of income back to firms. The larger the propensity to save, the less of a given level of household income will be spent on consumption goods and therefore the lower will be the level of demand for consumption goods. The quantity of consumption goods produced will therefore be less since firms produce only in response to their anticipated level of sales; if demand is falling, they will probably expect it to continue to fall, or at least to be less than it was previously. If firms decide to produce fewer consumption goods they will employ fewer factors of production and therefore household incomes will be reduced. This reduction in income can be expected to lead to a further reduction in the level of demand for consumption goods and accordingly to a further fall in production, employment and factor incomes.

This very simple account is intended to bring out an important point. Consumption decisions are made by a very large number of households on the basis of their levels of income and propensities to consume. Production decisions are made by a large number of producers or firms on the basis of their expectations of the future demand for their products. There is no reason to suppose that the quantity of consumer goods demanded by the very large number of households will be exactly the same as the quantity of consumer goods produced by the many producers. If producers wrongly estimate the future demand for their products they will take steps to adjust their output, and this will affect the incomes of the households and so lead to further changes in the level of demand for consumption goods.

We will now consider how the aggregate decision regarding the production of goods and services and the demand for them interact on each other.

Investment, as we have previously discussed, can be seen as the production of capital equipment to be used to produce other goods or services, or the production of goods for stocks. Consumption goods are goods which are produced for consumption *and are consumed*. It is necessary to add the qualification *and are consumed* in order to distinguish the production of goods for stocks from the production of goods for current consumption which are actually consumed. Goods made for stocks, even though they are consumable, are regarded as investment and not as the production of consumption goods and, as we shall see, there is a very important difference between the production of investment goods including stocks, and the production of consumption goods.

Income equals output

All output is either the output of investment goods or of consumption goods. All income must be either spent on consumption or saved. The total value of output is equal to the total amount of income received by the factors of production. This is an important relationship.

If a firm produces £100,000 worth of goods, that is the value of its output. The various factors of production employed by the firm, including profits paid to the providers of capital, must total £100,000. This is seen most clearly in a firm which does not buy any raw materials but only employs labour and capital in its production and therefore makes payment only to labour and capital in the form of wages and profits. For example, a mining company which owns the land which it works and which has no raw materials or other inputs except the capital equipment it has bought can be seen as producing a value of output which is exactly equal to the wages and profits which it pays to the factors labour and capital. If, in a year, it produces copper, zinc or whatever, which it sells for £100,000, and its wage bill is £80,000, its gross profits will be £20,000. If it had had a bad trading year it is possible that it sold its output for only £75,000 and its wage bill had still been £80,000. It would then have made a loss of £5,000, so that profits would have been a negative amount of £5,000 which, when subtracted from the wages of £80,000, would give us an income of £75,000 – which is equal to the value of the output.

The value of output over a period must equal the value of income received from the production of that output over the same period.

The calculations become a little more complicated if the firm buys raw materials. It is then necessary to calculate the net output or value added of the firm. For example, assume that a firm buys raw materials such as timber to make chairs for £10,000. It employs labour and capital to manufacture the chairs, paying total wages of £40,000. It sells the chairs for £70,000. The value of its output is *not* £70,000, since the total selling price includes the £10,000 of timber bought by the firm. The output of the chair factory is £60,000. This is the value added by the firm to the raw materials it bought in and is obtained by subtracting the total value of bought-in raw materials from the value of total sales or output. The output of the chair factory is £60,000, and the incomes received by the factors of production of the chair factory are £40,000 wages and £20,000 profits.

The output of the sawmill from which the timber was bought would be £10,000 because this was the value of its output when it was sold to the chair factory. Total output of the two firms, the sawmill and the chair factory together, would be £70,000. The use of added value as the basis for calculating the value of output of a firm is necessary if we are to avoid double counting. In the simple example of the sawmill and chair factory, if we added together the value of the sales of both firms, £10,000 plus £70,000, we would suppose that total output was £80,000. Yet we can see that this is not so; £10,000 of this is being counted twice, first as the output of the sawmill, and again in the output of the chair factory. The incomes received by all the factors of production in the two firms is only £70,000 and this is the *total value added* by both firms combined.

Investment equals savings

Some income will be received from the production of investment goods. People working in the investment goods sector producing equipment such as saws, hammers, chisels or large items of equipment like electric saws and trimming machines will receive incomes for their work. Thus all income is received from the production, or the output, of investment or consumption goods. As we have just seen, the value of output must equal the value of income and all income must either be spent on consumption goods or saved. This provides us with a simple but very important set of relation-ships which can be expressed in a simple equation:

$$C + I = O = Y = C + S$$

where C = the value of the output of consumption goods *and* the amount spent on consumption goods; this is referred to as consumption in short;

    I = the value of the output of investment goods, including consumable goods produced for stocks;

    O = the total value of output;

    Y = the total value of income;

    S = the total amount of savings.

Since C+I = C+S, and because we must define C in the same way in both parts of this equation, we can see that I = S. The value of investment goods produced and the amount of income received from the production of investment goods must equal the amount of savings that households make from their income. Given that investment decisions are made by firms and savings decisions by households, it may seem very surprising that the totals of the multitude of separate decisions made by these different groups should exactly balance and come to the same total.

Let us consider how the equality between investment and savings occurs. As is usual in economics it is easier to start from a position of equilibrium, where things have been continuing in the same way for some time, and then consider what would happen if something were to change. We will assume that the economy has been operating for a long time at a constant level of output and that everyone has been satisfied with their decisions. We assume that the level of output, and therefore income, is £1,000, made up of £100 of investment goods and £900 of consumption goods. Of the £1,000 income received, £900 is spent on consumption goods and £100 is saved. This is shown in Row 1 of Table 12.1, where it can be seen that I = S. The APC is 0.9 and the APS is 0.1. For simplicity of exposition we will assume that the MPC is the same as the APC so that the MPS is also the same as the APS.

Everyone is content with their decisions. Producers are content because they are producing £900 of consumption goods each period and are selling £900 of consumption goods. Households are content because they are allocating their income between consumption and savings in the way they wish.

Let us now assume that households change their APC and MPC. They decide they wish to save more and so decrease their consumption from £900 to £800. Their APS and MPS increase to 0.2. The effects of this are seen in Row 2a of Table 12.1. There is no change in the left-hand side of the equation. Firms paid out £900 to factors for the production of consumption goods and £100 to producers of investment goods because they intended to produce £900 of consumption goods. Their total output was £1,000 and this provided the total income of £1,000 of household. However, households decreased their purchases of consumption goods from £900 to £800. Clearly £900 does not equal £800, so the two values of C shown in the two sides of the equation in Row 2a differ. The same variable, C, cannot have two different values in the same equation. We cannot say that C is £900 and at the same time that C is £800. It must be one or the other.

Table 12.1. Effects of differences in planned savings and planned investment

| | | Changes in stocks | | |
		Planned	Actual	Total stocks
C + I = O = Y = C + S				
(1) 900 + 100 = 1,000 = 1,000 = 900 + 100				
(2a) 900 + 100 = 1,000 = 1,000 = 800 + 200				
(2b) 800 + 200 = 1,000 = 1,000 = 800 + 200			+100	+100
(3a) 800 + 100 = 900 = 900 = 720 + 180		−100		
(3b) 720 + 180 = 900 = 900 = 720 + 180			+ 80	+180
(3c) 700 + 0 = 700 = 700 = 560 + 140		−100	+140	+240

The correct value of C is £800, because C is the value of consumption goods and is therefore determined by the level of consumption that households incur. It is households that decide the level of consumption.

Firms thought they were producing £900 of consumption goods, and as firms do, they produced in anticipation of demand. However, after they had produced the goods they discovered that only £800 had been sold. They had produced £900 worth of goods but sold only £800. They were left with £100 of unsold goods, which were intended to be consumption goods but which were not in fact consumed. These goods became unplanned additions to stocks since firms were unable to sell them. Stocks are regarded as investment in this analysis so firms found they had undertaken £200 of investment. As planned, they had invested £100 in replacement investment to make good worn-out equipment, and they had also invested £100 in addition to stocks, which was unplanned. At the end of the period, after households had made their consumption and savings decisions, investment equalled savings as is seen in Row 2b of Table 12.1. However, this is at a level of I = S = £200 and not at the level which firms planned, £100.

Actual investment was equal to actual savings, as it must always be given the way we have defined the terms, at the end of the period, but planned investment was not equal to planned savings. Planned investment, the amount firms intended to do, was only £100, but planned savings was £200. In the earlier period represented by Row 1, both planned and actual investment were equal to planned and actual savings and this provided the equilibrium conditions.

Row 2b is not, however, an equilibrium position. Firms have been forced to undertake more investment than they intended. They have been compelled, given their earlier production decisions, to invest £100 in stocks – which they did not intend to do – and they have been compelled to do so by the decisions of households revising their savings and consumption decisions.

Firms must now make a new set of decisions regarding their production plans for the next period. In the past they had been content to replace £100 of worn-out capital equipment and produce £900 of consumption goods which they sold. However, in the previous period (2), they were unable to sell all their output of intended consumption goods and have £100 of intended consumption goods as unplanned additions to stock or as unplanned investment. They have to decide what to do in the current production period (3).

If you were responsible for making the decisions for the firms what would you do? You know that the sale of consumption goods was lower than the level you had anticipated and produced for in period 2. You may not be sure whether in period 3 households will revert to their previous consumption–saving decisions with an APC of 0.9 which, if their income remains at £1,000, will give a level of demand for consumption goods of £900, or whether they will keep with their revised APC of 0.8 which, if their income is £1,000, will lead to a demand for consumption goods of only £800. In either case you have an unplanned, and therefore presumably unwanted, addition to stocks of £100 of goods which you produced in the last period as intended consumption goods.

If you anticipate a demand for consumption goods of £900 in the current period, so that you expect households to revert to their previous expenditure patterns, and you expect them to have incomes of £1,000, you might well decide to produce only £800 of consumption goods this period, and sell off the £100 of unplanned increase in stocks from period 2. If this is the case you will make the output decisions in the left-hand side of Row 3a in Table 12.1. You will replace the worn-out capital equipment and invest £100; since you are expecting demand for consumption goods to revert to £900, you will need the previous capacity. However, you will produce only £800 of consumption goods in period 3, planning to sell off the stocks. The total output will now be only £900 instead of £1,000, so income will also fall to £900; but your decisions are based on an expected income of £1,000 and total consumption demand of £900.

This has important consequences for households. Their income has fallen from £1,000 to £900 because some of the people formerly employed in the production of consumption goods are no longer employed since firms have reduced the output of consumption goods. If households stick to their revised APC of 0.8 they will spend £720 on consumption goods and save £180. This will mean that not only have firms been unable to sell off the unwanted increase of £100 in stocks from the previous period, they have actually been forced to increase their stocks again because the level of consumption at £720 is less than the planned output of consumption goods of £800 in the current period. Firms will therefore have been compelled to invest an additional £80 in an unwanted increase in stocks, as shown in Row 3b.

However, let us now assume that at the start of this period you made a different decision from that set out in Row 3a. Let us assume that you anticipated a reduction in demand for consumption goods to £800 and that you planned to meet this by producing £700 of consumption goods in this period and selling off the unwanted accumulation of £100 of stocks from Row 2b. Since you believe that demand for consumption goods will now be lower than it has been in the past you also decide not to replace the worn-out capital equipment in this period; you intend to decrease your productive capacity to match the anticipated lower demand for consumption goods. The intended production plans of firms are therefore as set out in Row 3c of Table 12.1. They intend to produce £700 of consumption goods, reduce stocks by £100 and not invest in replacement of capital equipment. Output and income will therefore fall to £700. If households continue to maintain an APC of 0.8 they will allocate their income of £700 as shown in the right-hand side of Row 3c. Once again producers' expectations will not be met. Demand for consumption goods will be only £560 and instead of disposing of the accumulated stocks, they will find that they have actually been forced to increase their stocks by an additional £140. Their unplanned and unwanted stocks are now £240.

We can see that this imbalance between producers' planned and actual output decisions will continue until the level of planned or intended output of consumption goods plus stock adjustments is equal to the level of planned and actual expenditure on consumption by households. The actual levels of investment and savings will always be equal in any period because the actions of households in not buying some of the intended output of consumption goods converts those units of output from consumption goods into investment through stocks. *Actual investment* will always equal *actual savings* by adjustments in unplanned movements in stocks which are regarded as investment. This is an unstable or disequilibrium position since firms will seek to change their output decisions in response to their expectations of future demand for consumption goods. They will adjust their stocks to the desired level and adjust their output of consumption goods to the level of expected demand for consumption minus intended stock adjustments.

A position of equilibrium will be achieved only when *planned* investment equals *planned* savings, so that the planned output of consumption goods is also equal to the planned level of expenditure on consumption, offset by planned adjustments to stocks on the part of producers. Instability can arise if either group, firms or households, change their plans. The decisions of firms will then feed through and affect the level of income of households, and this will affect the level of demand for consumption goods unless there are perfectly compensating simultaneous changes in the APC and APS of consumers.

What would happen in the example illustrated in Table 12.1 is that households would have to change their APS and increase their demand for consumption goods, or firms would continue to cut back on both the production of consumption goods and replacement investment so that income would continue to fall. Ultimately households would become too poor to save large amounts, and planned investment and planned savings, with planned output of consumption goods and planned purchase of consumption goods, would move back into equilibrium. However, this might be at a very low level of income and employment.

The paradox of thrift

In the simplified example just presented the downward movement in output, income and employment resulted from an increase in the propensity to save. This has given rise to what is called the paradox of thrift. While we may believe that saving or thriftiness is a desirable virtue, we can see that if an increase in savings leads to a reduction in demand, the end result might be a reduction in income, output and employment until people are too poor to save as much as they planned. The levels of savings fell in Rows 3a, 3b and 3c in Table 12.1 because people sought to increase their savings, and the reduction in demand for consumption goods led firms to reduce their output and so the income of households.

There is a second paradox. An increase in the propensity to save, which means a reduction in the propensity to consume, leads initially to an increase in the level of investment. This seems peculiar and perverse because investment is expected to be a response to anticipated demand for goods and services. How then does a decrease in the demand for goods lead to an increase in investment?

As we have seen, it is because the decrease in consumption, resulting from an increase in the propensity to save, was not anticipated. It came as a surprise to producers and therefore led to an unplanned and unwanted increase in investment through unplanned accumulation of stocks. An unexpected increase in the propensity to save − unexpected by the producers of consumption goods − will therefore always lead to an increase in investment in the short run via the level of stocks. In the long run, however, investment will be reduced since the expected level of demand for consumption goods will be lower, and firms will not wish to replace their worn-out capital equipment when they anticipate a reduction in the level of demand for their products. The initial increase in investment, through an increase in the level of stocks, is, in a sense, forced on firms by the decisions of households which have increased their propensity to save.

To sum up again, actual investment will always equal actual savings in any period, but for a stable equilibrium position, planned investment must equal planned savings.

The multiplier

The above discussion might suggest that if there is an increase in the propensity to save, then output, income and employment will continue on a downward path until the economy comes to a new equilibrium position where planned investment equals planned savings but where income and employment are much lower. This may occur. However, it may be possible for government to intervene in order to increase income and employment. This was one of the new ideas put forward by Keynes and can be explained through his concept of the multiplier.

In addition to firms and households, let us now recognise the existence of government. We will assume that the economy is again in a stable equilibrium position where investment and consumption−output decisions and plans are exactly equal to the planned consumption and savings decisions of households. This is the same as the position indicated in Row 1 of Table 12.1. However, we will assume that at this position the level of output and employment is thought to be lower than it need be and that government seeks to increase output and employment.

If firms were to decide that the demand for their goods was going to increase they would employ more factors of production to increase their output, and by paying these factors of production there would be an increase in both output and income. The rise in income would lead to an increase in demand so that the higher output, or some of it, would be sold. However, there is no reason why firms should expect the demand for their goods to increase so they will continue with the production decisions of Row 1.

Let us assume that government decides to undertake some economic activity. This may be building a new road, a hospital, or even, as Keynes said, paying people to dig a hole in the ground and then paying them to fill it in again. What matters is that the government activity, which is regarded as investment, provides an income for people who were previously out of work. They are given an income some of which they will spend on consumption goods, so that other people will have to be employed to produce the consumption goods to meet the new demand. In turn they will spend part of their income and yet more people will be employed to produce consumption goods on which they can spend their income, and so on.

We can illustrate this in Table 12.2. Assume that the economy is stable as in Row 1 of Table 12.1, so that in Table 12.2 we are looking only at the *additional* activity which takes place as a result of the government decision to employ people in public works on an investment project. Row 1 of Table 12.2 shows that the government pays out £100 as wages to the people employed on its project and this appears as investment. Output is £100 since that is the value of the public works done and income is £100 since that is the amount received by those employed on the project. If they have

Table 12.2. Multiplier effects of an increase in investment

	C	+I	=	O =	Y	=	C	+	S
(1)		100 =		100 =	100 =		90 +		10
(2)	90		=	90 =	90 =		81 +		9
(3)	81		=	81 =	81 =		73 +		8
:									
Total									
(5)	900 +	100 =		1,000 =	1,000 =		900 +		100

an APC and MPC of 0.9 they will allocate their income of £100 as £90 spent on consumption, and they will save £10.

Because demand for consumption goods has increased by £90, additional people will be employed in the consumption goods industries to produce £90 of consumption goods. This is shown in Row 2. Those people will spend £81 on consumption goods and save £9. This in turn will lead to a further increase in demand for consumption goods of £81 so that further people will be employed in the consumption goods industries, as shown in Row 3. They will obtain an income of £81, and will in turn spend £73 on consumption goods. This will lead to further employment in the consumption goods industries, and so on. Ultimately, total income will rise as shown in Row 5 (Total), so that additional output of consumption goods will have been £900, expenditure on consumption goods will have been £900, investment and savings will both have increased by £100 and total income and output will have increased by £1,000.

The initial increase in investment will have had a *multliplier* effect on income, output and employment. The size of the multiplier effect will depend on the marginal propensity to consume. The larger the propensity to consume, the more is passed on in the form of increased demand for consumption goods, and so the larger the subsequent increase in output and income from the production of additional consumer goods. If, for example, those employed on the government project had spent only half of their income and had an MPS of 0.5, then only £50 would have gone to additional consumption and so there would have been fewer people employed in Row 2 of Table 12.2 to produce the £50 consumption goods for those employed on the government project. If they in turn had saved half of their new income there would have been only £25 instead of £81 passed on as additional demand in Row 3. The higher the MPC or the lower the MPS, the greater the multiplier effect.

We measure the multiplier effect as 1/MPS, so that in the example in Table 12.2 the multiplier is 1/0.1 or $1/\frac{1}{10}$, which is 10. You can check this from Table 12.2. If you calculate every row after Row 3 and total the columns of C, I, O, Y and S, you will find that they come to the figures shown in Row 5. Actually they will not come exactly to the totals, since the numbers never stop increasing. The rows could go on indefinitely as 0.9 of a very small amount of income was spent on consumption goods, but after a certain stage the additional increases in output and income become negligible.

The higher the MPC, the greater will be the increase in income or the multiplier effect resulting from an increase in investment. An increase in the propensity to save will therefore lead to a reduction in the level of income by decreasing the multiplier; we saw this effect expressed in a different way leading to the paradox of thrift.

The multiplier effect could have been prevented from operating if firms had met the increase in demand for consumption goods resulting from the injection of the extra £100 of income in Row 1 of Table 12.2 by releasing £90 of goods from their stocks. If that had happened, those working on the government project would have been able to obtain the £90 consumption goods they wished to buy without any further expansion of output and employment in the consumption goods industries. Row 2 of Table 12.2 would not have occurred.

However, if we assume that at the beginning of period 1 firms were holding the level of stocks they thought appropriate, an increase in demand for consumption goods of £90 might first be met by running down stocks, but firms would then wish to restore their stocks to the previous level. The expansion shown by Row 2 would then occur as firms replaced their run-down stocks. Indeed, because total demand for consumption goods was now higher than previously, firms might actually increase their level of stocks and this would itself generate further multiplier effects since increases in stocks are regarded as investment.

In practice, therefore, there might be a delay between Rows 1 and 2 of Table 12.2 as firms first respond to changes in the demand for consumption goods by adjustments in their levels of stocks. In an expansionary process, however, this merely delays the expansion and the multiplier effects and is the reverse of the contractionary process which occurred when there was an increase in the propensity to save.

While an increase in investment will lead to an additional increase in income and output through the multiplier, the effect will occur only as long as the higher investment takes place. If the government project lasted for only one week, those engaged on it would lose their income in week 2 and therefore their demand for consumption goods would disappear. If it is intended to raise and maintain total income by the £1,000 shown in Row 5 of Table 12.2, it is necessary for the additional investment to take place in each period.

If this happened it is likely that there would then be an increase in investment by firms. They would see demand for their consumption goods rising by a total of £900 in each period and would buy additional capital equipment in order to increase production to meet the higher demand. The accelerator would come into effect following the multiplier effects of the government investment.

We can see therefore that the multiplier and accelerator interact on each other so that an initial increase in investment leads to continuing expansion of income, output and investment. Similarly, a decrease in consumption demand or a fall in investment will generate contractionary multiplier and accelerator effects.

Investment with multiplier effects

We have seen that certain forms of economic activity have multiplier effects, and we sometimes refer to these, collectively, as investment, although they are not all necessarily investment in the sense of increases in capital equipment. Income generated by planned or unplanned additions to stocks have multiplier effects, as does government expenditure. It does not matter whether the government expenditure is an activity such as road-building or whether it is the distribution of income in the form of welfare payments or grants to students, or as payment of wages to civil servants. If people receive income without the production of consumption goods on which that income will be spent there will be multiplier effects, unless the higher demand is met by the release of consumption goods from stocks.

Similarly, if people are employed on the production of goods for export there will be a multiplier effect. If the £100 shown as investment in Row 1 of Table 12.2 had been received by workers producing consumption or consumable goods for export, when they spent £90 of their new income additional workers would have been employed to produce consumption goods for them as in Row 2.

Multiplier effects therefore result from investment, government expenditure and exports, no matter what sort of goods are exported.

However, things other than savings can affect the size of the multiplier. If government imposes taxation it will not be possible for that income to be passed on in the form of higher demand for consumption goods, so that taxation has the same effect as savings. It reduces the amount of additional demand for consumption and therefore reduces the expansion of output and income.

If those employed on the government project in Row 1 of Table 12.2 had spent all their £90 on the consumption of imported goods, there would have been no additional demand or employment and income expansion in Row 2, in this country. Those employed and the income received in Rows 2, 3 and so on would have been in the foreign country whose goods had been bought by the people in Row 1. Our imports would have been their exports and would have given them a multiplier effect.

Expenditure on imports therefore reduces the multiplier effect just as an increase in savings does. If you were one of the people hoping to get a job as a result of the expenditure on consumption goods of those employed in Row 1 of Table 12.2, you would be hoping to become one of those employed in Row 2. However, if the expenditure shown under C (£90) in Row 1 was on imported food there would be no job for you. Workers overseas would get jobs because the £90 of demand for their goods would to them be an increase in exports and generate multiplier effects.

We can make the simple statement I = S more realistic. Now we can see that I + G + X = S + T + M

$$\text{where } G = \text{government expenditure}$$
$$X = \text{exports}$$
$$T = \text{taxation}$$
$$M = \text{imports}$$

The crucial point to remember about multiplier effects is that they result from the generation of income which is not accompanied by the creation of consumption goods on which that income, or part of that income, will be spent, and will therefore lead to demand for consumption goods which creates additional income for other people. Leakages in the system of passing on demand for other people's output occur as a result of savings, taxation and the purchase of imports. These reduce the size of the multiplier and if all of the extra income is devoted to them, it means that there will be no expansion or creation of additional income.

Income and employment multipliers

In the examples in Tables 12.1 and 12.2 we assumed that when there was an initial increase in income which led to a rise in consumption, this resulted in a multiplied increase in both income and employment. When those in the investment industry (or producing for exports or in receipt of income from government) received their extra income and increased their demand for consumption goods, we assumed that this higher demand was met by the production of more goods which were sold at the same price as the previous goods. Thus when those employed on the government investment project in Row 1 of Table 12.2 spent £90 on consumption goods, we assumed that extra people were employed in the consumption goods industries to produce additional units of consumption goods.

It is possible that this did not occur. Let us take an extreme situation and assume that there is just one person unemployed, that it is not possible to import more goods and that there are no stocks of goods. If the government employs that one person on a project and pays him £100, he will spend £90 on consumption goods. However, there are no additional units of consumption goods for him to buy. All the consumption goods that are produced are being sold since planned output of consumption goods is equal to the actual demand for consumption goods before this last person is employed. When he tries to spend his £90 there is only the same amount of consumption goods as there was in the previous period. There is no one who can be employed to produce extra goods for him and there are no stocks from which he can buy £90 of consumption goods.

There are now only three possibilities. First, he must save all of his income and not buy any consumption goods. Second, some other households must decide to save an additional £90 of their income so that he can buy the £90 of consumption goods they had previously bought. Third, prices of consumption goods must rise so that the higher level of money demand for consumption goods – the previous level of C plus the £90 of C from this worker – is spent on the same physical amount of consumption goods as was purchased by the other households in the previous period.

It is not possible (because we have specified this through our assumptions) to increase the physical output of consumption goods. If we assume that before this person was employed the economy was in equilibrium at Row 1 of Table 12.1, his employment by government is equivalent to the addition to those figures at Row 1 of Table 12.1. If he spends £90 of his wage, as in Row 2 of Table 12.2, the total level of consumption will rise from £900 to £990 but there will be only the same amount of goods on which the £990 can be spent. Prices of consumption goods will therefore rise so that the same number of goods as could be bought previously for £900 will now cost, in total, £990. Prices will therefore rise by 990−900/900 × 100, or by 10 per cent.

The general rule is that the price increase will be $C_2/C_1 \times 100$.

This means that every household will be able to buy 10 per cent less for the same level of consumption expenditure. If they all accept this reduction in the real standard of living, the economy will settle at a new equilibrium level where prices are a little higher, the level of income is £100 higher and the real or physical level of output of consumption goods is the same as it was.

Because the same quantity of consumption goods is now selling for

£990, there will be a rise in the income of those producing consumer goods from £900 to £990. This will lead them to revise their consumption and savings plans and if they continue to have MPC = 0.9, this will lead to a further rise in the amount of income spent on consumption goods, a further rise in the price of consumption goods and a further rise in the income of those producing consumption goods. The multiplier will work itself through in terms of income so that ultimately income will rise from £1,000 to £2,000, total C will rise from £900 to £1,800, and I and S will rise from £100 to £200.

There will be no increase in employment because we specified that it is not possible to increase employment, but the income multiplier will nevertheless take place. The result will be a rise in prices, i.e. inflation.

If government had increased taxation by £100 and people reduced their APC accordingly so that they did not seek to maintain a level of consumption of £900 plus the extra £90 of C from the person employed on the government project, the prices of consumption goods could have remained constant. The £90 of consumption goods demanded by the additional worker could have been from the reduction in consumption demand following the increase in taxation. Similarly, if it had been possible to import £90 of consumable goods to meet the demand of the additional worker, there would have been no income multiplier effect and no inflation.

Let us relax some of the rigorous assumptions made in this example. We will assume that government employs the additional worker and pays him £100. He spends £90 on consumption goods so the aggregate demand for consumption goods rises from £900 to £990. We will still not permit imports to increase. However, there are some other unemployed workers. Firms in the production goods industries recruit one of these to produce the £90 of goods demanded by the extra man employed on the government project. To induce the unemployed worker to accept a job in the consumption goods industries, however, it is necessary to raise wages. He is not prepared to work at the existing wage level. Let us assume that instead of £100 a week he requires £120. This means that the costs of production in consumption goods will rise. If all workers in the industry are paid the same wage as the marginal or newly recruited worker, they will all receive a wage increase from £100 to £120. Costs will rise by 20 per cent.

If production costs have risen we would expect prices to rise. Let us assume that they also rise by 20 per cent. There will now be a restored equilibrium position in that planned output of consumption goods will equal planned demand for consumption goods, but prices have risen by 20 per cent. Incomes are 20 per cent higher because wages and profits have also risen. However, total output in real or physical terms has risen by less than total money income. There will thus have been a reduction in real incomes.

If households or workers are unwilling to accept a reduction in their real incomes they will press for an extra wage increase to compensate for the rise in prices. Unless someone is prepared to accept a lower real income, either workers/households or producers, there will be a self-perpetuating spiral of rising wages, costs and prices leading to further increases in wages, costs and prices.

Both employment and income may rise, but the rise in money incomes will be faster than the rise in employment. Inflation will occur.

It is possible that the multiplier effects on income and employment can be exactly the same. This will occur if wages and marginal productivity remain constant. Alternatively, there can be different multiplier effects on income and employment. There will always be an income multiplier determined by the MPC or MPS. There may or may not be an employment multiplier. This will depend on how producers respond to the increase in demand for consumption goods. If they seek to meet the higher demand for consumption goods by raising prices, there may be no employment effects, and in some cases they may be unable to increase output and employment and so be obliged to increase their prices. If imports can rise, or if savings increase or government increases taxation, there may be no employment multiplier.

As we approach full employment, we expect to see the employment multiplier become smaller as the increase in money incomes and in the demand for consumption goods leads to increases in prices and wages rather than to an increase in output and employment at constant prices and wages.

If there is an increase in productivity, it may be possible for an expansion in aggregate money demand resulting from an increase in money income to be accompanied by an increase in real or physical consumption without a rise in prices. The higher level of consumption demand can be met by an increase in the quantity of goods available as a result of the rise in productivity. This could occur if output per worker increases without an increase in wages, or if productivity rises faster than wages. This can result either from an increase in the effort-input of labour or as a result of technological improvement which increases the efficiency of capital equipment.

A government seeking to increase employment by stimulating demand through increased government expenditure or by lowering taxation must take account of the potential effect of an increase in aggregate demand on productivity and unit costs of production. If a higher level of demand and activity leads to an increase in unit production costs because of an increase in wages or a slowing down of the rate of growth of productivity, the main multiplier effects may be through the income multiplier and not through the employment and output multiplier. Obviously, the results of a purely income multiplier, with no employment multiplier effects, are inflationary.

However, if government believes that an increase in aggregate demand will not lead to an increase in wages or unit costs of production, so that at the higher level of aggregate demand prices will remain constant, it might well decide to inject additional demand into the economy so that the multiplier effects, reinforced by accelerator effects, will lead to higher output and employment. In the real world, the judgement of whether expansion will be in real terms, or merely inflationary with no growth in output and employment, is not only crucial but difficult. The end results will depend on how workers, their trade unions, households and producers respond, and this is uncertain.

CHAPTER 13

The supply of money

Athough we have on occasion considered the difference between real and monetary effects of economic actions, we have not so far discussed money. In this and the next chapter we will look at the supply of and demand for money.

Meaning and functions of money

Although we all have a general idea of what we mean by money in everyday activities, it is necessary for us to be more precise when discussing money in an economic context. There are different forms of money such as notes and coins, but what is accepted as money in one society may not be accepted as money in another. For example, sterling is accepted as money in the United Kingdom, so that £1 notes and 10p coins are money. This currency may not be acceptable in another country, so that it is necessary to exchange sterling for some other currency, such as rupees or dollars, which is acceptable in that economy.

In a similar way, what is acceptable as money in parts of one economy or for certain purposes may not be acceptable in other parts or for other purposes. I may be able to write a cheque which someone will accept as money, particularly if I have a banker's card or some other form of identification or guarantee. However, there may be some people who will not accept a cheque for some transaction purposes. I doubt if I could buy an evening newspaper from a newspaper seller with a cheque, and the bus driver will not accept it as payment for my bus ticket, although the booking clerk at British Rail will.

At different times in history, societies have used different commodities as money, such as salt, gold or sea shells. These have all had one feature in common. They were acceptable as a means of settling debts and this is an essential characteristic of money. We can get a better idea of what money is by looking at what money does. There are three main functions of money.

Means of exchange If there is no common commodity which is accepted as a means of exchange or method of settling debts, it is necessary for people to barter, i.e. to exchange the goods or services which they have for those which they want but which someone else has. If I have bags of wheat and wish to obtain cloth and tea, I have to search for people with cloth and tea who wish to exchange it for wheat. This is a very time-consuming, inconvenient and inefficient way of conducting exchange or trade. If there is a common commodity which all of us will accept as an intermediary commodity, so that we will exchange our goods for it, knowing that other people will accept it in exchange for their goods which we wish to obtain, that commodity acts as a means or medium of exchange. The more sophisticated the production and distribution of goods, and the wider the range of commodities or goods and services which people wish to exchange, the more important it is that there is some common commodity or money to act as an intermediary facilitating the exchange of goods and services.

The key element in the acceptability of anything as money is the certainty that people have that if they exchange their goods or services for it, they, in turn, will be able to exchange it for the things they want. I accept UK sterling in exchange for my services as an employee because I am confident that other people, shopkeepers, bus drivers, newspaper sellers and so on, will accept it from me. If I thought that other people would not accept the commodity from me, I would not accept it from them and this commodity would no longer be an acceptable means of exchange, and would no longer fulfil the function of money. In some countries there are laws which specify that certain notes and coins, perhaps up to specified limits, are legal tender and must lawfully be accepted as a means of exchange or method of settling debt. The terms 'means of exchange' and 'method of settling debt' can be regarded as interchangeable. Each purchase or exchange incurs a debt, and if money is used as a means of exchange when purchasing something, it is also used to settle the debt incurred in buying that item.

In order to be a convenient means of exchange, money must have certain characteristics. It should be easy to carry, not heavy or bulky. It must be durable so that it does not disintegrate or diminish in use. It needs to be divisible so that it can be used for large- and small-value transactions. It should be difficult to copy or counterfeit. If it is not, we may be reluctant to accept it for fear of being stuck with counterfeit money which we cannot in our turn use.

Store of value   To be effective, money should be able to act as a store of value. This means that if I have a certain amount of money, which represents a claim to a certain amount of goods or services today, I need to be reasonably certain that the money will retain its value in the future. If I have £10 today I could exchange it for a shirt, or four paperback books, or eight pairs of socks, or two theatre tickets. If I believe that by tomorrow the value of the money will fall so that I will be able to buy only two paperbacks, four pairs of socks or one theatre ticket, I will be very unlikely to want to accept it in exchange for my goods or services. I may have little choice since my employer may say that he can pay me only in this money, and if I wish to work I have to accept payment in that form. In this case I would try to get rid of the money as soon as I could in order to obtain goods, and this could lead me to ask for my wages to be paid to me daily or even twice daily to allow me to exchange the money for goods before the value of money fell even more. Thus inflation, which is rising prices, is a measure of the extent to which money is losing its value. The greater the rate of inflation, the less is money acting as a store of value.

Inflation will also adversely affect the ability of money to act as a means or standard of deferred payment. We can arrange debts and deferred payments because we have expectations that if we agree to defer payment of debts owed to us now and receive payment in the future, the money we receive, plus any interest to compensate for the delay in receiving payment, will still have roughly the same value as the money currently has. If inflation is very high and rapid, creditors will either demand very high rates of interest to compensate them for expected or possible reductions in the value of money between the time at which the debt is incurred and payment made, or they will seek to index the amount of repayment to the change in prices through the Retail or Consumer Price Index. This is, of course, the same as indexing repayment to the fall in the value of money.

Unit of account   Money should be in a form that can be used as an accounting unit which can conveniently be applied to transactions of different amounts and values. This allows us to use money as the single unit in which all transactions can be measured. It allows us to compare the relative value of different items, so that something costing £5 is five times more valuable or expensive than something costing £1.

Acceptability

As we have seen, for any commodity or notes and coins to be used as money, there has to be acceptability. I will accept something as money only if I am confident that you in turn will accept it and that it will not lose much of its value during the time that I keep it. If I fear that it will lose value, I might accept it, indeed I may have little choice, but I will seek to exchange it for goods or assets which will better retain their value, and this means that the particular commodity or notes and coins are poor forms of money. Notes and coins are the forms of money which most of us see most often, but the largest proportion of the settlement of debts incurred in transactions may be financed by cheques rather than notes and coins. Bank account transfers from one person, or one firm, to another are a common way of settling debts, and cheques are a widespread means of exchange for large transactions. This leads to an important source of money. Bank accounts, or bank overdrafts, can act in exactly the same way as stocks of notes or coins.

The supply of money

When we refer here to the supply of money we are referring to a stock or given amount of money. The money stock, the quantity of money, and the money supply can all be regarded as the same thing, since we are looking at the amount of money at a particular point in time. In the next chapter we will consider the complications introduced when we try to measure the quantity of money during a period of time.

It is clear from the previous section that part of the supply of money is the notes and coins issued by the government or the central bank. In some countries the central bank acts in an independent manner, or according to statutory provisions; in others it is more closely linked to the economic policies of the government so that its actions are more the expression of government wishes than its own independent judgement. The term monetary authorities is used to refer to the combination of institutions and government responsible for making the decisions regarding money policy. However, the amount of notes and coins issued by the monetary authorities, or the notes and coins in circulation, is not in itself necessarily of great economic significance. Sometimes people want many more banknotes than at other times, for example when on holiday or just before a traditional season when presents are bought or celebrations take place. Most of the extra notes issued at these times will be returned to the banks quite quickly as people spend them and shopkeepers and stores pay them into their bank accounts.

Banks

A feature of all developing economies is the emergence of a banking system. Banks provide security for people's money. They may also provide a source of interest according to the type of bank account and the practices of the economy. More importantly, banks provide the means for transferring access to money for current use from depositors to borrowers. Perhaps even more importantly, banks can create money. This is something we can understand by considering a simple model of a banking system, which is a general account of how banks developed.

From the early days when they acted as safe places in which those with more cash or gold than they currently wished to use could safely deposit their extra resources, banks or goldsmiths discovered that they did not need to hold all the money deposited with them in order to be practically certain that they would be able to repay anyone who wanted repayment. This is vital. Each depositor is prepared and willing to deposit his money in a bank only if he is confident that he will be able to obtain his money back when he wishes to. If we thought that our bank might not be able to repay us our deposits tomorrow we would all go down and withdraw them today. It is essential that banks be able to meet all requests for withdrawals or repayments if they are to maintain the confidence of their depositors.

However, there is no need for banks to keep all the money deposited with them in their tills to repay depositors. Experience has taught banks that only a certain proportion of depositors will want their deposits back at any one time. When the main form of money was gold this meant that banks could lend out some of the gold deposited with them to other people and charge a rate of interest for doing so. The difference between this and the rate of interest, if any, which they paid to people who had deposited gold with them provided the banks with profits, and it must always be remembered that banks are profit-making institutions. However, banks recognised that they should never lend out so much that they would be unable to repay those depositors who wanted repayments. The more they lent out the greater their profits, but also the greater the risk that they would be unable to meet all demands for repayment.

There thus arose conflicting pressures from profitability and prudence. Profitability encouraged more lending, but prudence required the retention of sufficient money to repay all depositors' demands. This conflict of contradictory pressures still permeates banking. In some countries laws may prescribe various relationships which banks must keep between their liabilities to repay depositors and their lending to other people. In other countries, such as the United Kingdom, the balance is maintained primarily by conventions rather than by laws, although the Bank of England as the central bank may issue guidelines from time to time.

Bank creation of money

Let us assume that there is only one bank. For simplicity we will also assume that the bank has discovered that it need retain only 10 per cent of its deposits as money – notes and coins – in its tills to be able to meet all the expected demands for repayment by depositors.

A bank's activities can be easily understood in terms of double-entry bookkeeping. Every deposit made by a customer into his bank account thereby simultaneously creates a liability – the bank is liable to repay the customer when he wishes to withdraw his deposit – and an asset – the bank has the customer's deposit for the time for which it is deposited.

If customers deposit £1,000 in the bank, the bank's balance sheet would be as shown in Row 1 of Table 13.1. The bank could lend out £900 as overdrafts. The balance sheet would then look like Row 2a. The bank would have liabilities of £1,000 to the original depositors. Its assets would be £100 cash in tills plus £900 assets represented by the overdrafts it had advanced.

This assumes that the advances or overdrafts were made by the bank paying out the overdraft or advance in cash, and this is why its cash in tills

Table 13.1. Example of simple banking system with 10 per cent cash ratio

Liabilities			Assets	
(1) Deposits (initial)	1,000		Cash in tills	1,000
(2a) Deposits (initial)	1,000		Cash in tills	100
			Overdrafts	900
(2b) Deposits (initial)	1,000		Cash in tills	1,000
(secondary)	900		Overdrafts	900
		Then	Cash in tills	190
			Overdrafts	1,710
(3) Deposits	10,000		Cash in tills	1,000
			Overdrafts	9,000

fell to £100. If this happened, it is very likely that the £900 or most of it would be paid back into the bank as deposits by those who received it as payment from those obtaining the overdrafts. The balance sheet would then change to that shown in Row 2b. Because the bank now has £1,900 of deposits, it needs to retain £190 as cash in the tills to satisfy its rules of prudence. This allows it to have the cash resources to meet all demands for withdrawals. It could therefore grant *further* overdraft advances of £810 (the £1,000 cash it has minus the £190 it needs for prudence). The same cycle of events would occur; those receiving the cash from those who had been granted the overdrafts would pay it back into the bank through their bank accounts. The final position would be shown in Row 3. The initial cash deposits of £1,000 would provide the base on which advances or overdrafts of £9,000 could be made. Total deposits would be £10,000 and cash in the bank's tills £1,000.

If there is more than one bank the procedure is the same but the time-scale may be a little longer. Part of the initial overdraft would be returned to the bank making the overdraft. Some would go to other banks. This would depend on which banks were used by those receiving the payments from those obtaining the overdraft. The original bank could continue to expand its overdrafts according to how much of the initial outpayment flowed back to it. Payments to people with accounts at other banks would mean that the first bank lost some of the initial cash deposits, but the other banks would have increased their cash deposits so that they would start increasing their overdrafts. Some of the payments made from these overdrafts would flow back to the first bank and some of the other banks, which would then each begin a further round of expansion of overdrafts. At the end of the process the balance sheets of the banking system as a whole, i.e. all the banks together, would show an increase in assets equivalent to that in Row 3 of Table 13.1. We sometimes refer to these banks as clearing banks to distinguish them from the central bank.

In practice it is more likely that those receiving overdrafts would not actually withdraw the amount of their advance in cash but would use the overdraft to settle debts by writing cheques. As they did this the bank's assets would rise as the advances were utilised and their liabilities would increase as the cheques were in turn paid into the bank accounts of those receiving them from those with overdraft facilities. Again, the end result would be as in Row 3 of Table 13.1. If we assume that all the banks were receiving an increase in their initial deposits at about the same rate at the same time, they would all be expanding their deposits and liabilities in step. It is only if one bank has a less than proportionate number of its customers receiving payments from those to whom it has granted overdrafts that it will end up a net loser of cash. Generally, banks will expand together.

What is not yet very clear is how the initial expansion of deposits occurred, or where the original £1,000 came from. Obviously, if it was a result of someone taking £1,000 from his bank to settle a debt with someone who had an account at another bank, there would be no net increase in overdrafts or in the liabilities and assets of the banking system as a whole. There would merely be a transfer from one bank to another; one would expand and the other contract.

We can see how the banking system can generate an expansion in its liabilities and assets if we add a little more realism to the analysis. Instead of having only cash in tills and overdrafts as its assets, we will now recognise that a bank has a range of assets. Some of these must be cash, for this is the form in which depositors may expect to withdraw their deposits. In addition, it will have another form of assets which are equivalent to cash and which can be converted into cash immediately at no cost and with no risk. In the United Kingdom every bank has an account with the Bank of England. These are very useful for settling inter-bank transactions through the bank clearing system. Customers of different banks pay cheques to each other every day and banks do not need to hand over payment to each other for every single cheque. They need only transfer the net difference between themselves to each other to settle the inter-bank payments, and can then adjust each account within its own bank without transferring and receiving individual payments for each transaction. Each customer's account can be adjusted without movement of money for each item.

If the government buys or sells government securities, it does so by means of payment through its account at the Bank of England. This allows the net debt transactions to be settled by adjustment of the accounts of the banks at the Bank of England. Each bank then adjusts its individual customers' accounts as with the central clearing system. Thus if government buys securities from individuals, the cheque it issues for them, drawn on the Bank of England, is paid into the individuals' accounts at their banks and this leads to an increase in those banks' deposits with the Bank of England. This is equivalent to an increase in the banks' cash in tills and provides the base on which an expansion of overdrafts can take place.

The fact that the government uses the Bank of England as its bank, and that clearing banks are required to keep cash deposits with the central bank, provides the key elements in the ability of the banking system to create money.

We have assumed that banks have established a ratio of 10:1 between the amount of cash they need to hold for reasons of prudence, or safety, and the total amount of their liabilities. The total amount of liabilities that a bank can have is therefore determined by the cash ratio and the cash base of the banks. The cash ratio is the ratio between the amount of cash a bank has and its total liabilities. The cash base is the amount of cash to which the cash ratio is applied.

Banks, however, do not hold all their assets in cash and overdrafts or advances. Advances may be difficult to recall at short notice. Even if the overdraft is given subject to immediate repayment should the bank so decide, it is known that in practice some overdrafts cannot be repaid at instant notice. The individual or the firm may be perfectly able to repay in two or three months' time but might be totally unable to do so immediately. In many cases, if the recipient of the overdraft were able to repay at instant notice, it is not clear why he should wish to have the overdraft and pay the bank interest.

Liquidity

Banks spread their assets over a range of different types of securities. This provides extra protection against the danger of a sudden unexpected large increase in the withdrawal of deposits by their customers. There are different types of securities which banks can buy and different types of loans which banks can make. Buying a security is the same as making a loan. The bank provides money now in return for a claim to a larger amount of money in the future when the loan plus interest, or the nominal value of the security, is repaid.

In the United Kingdom, banks lend money overnight to the discount market. This type of asset (call money, because it can be called back each day) earns interest for the banks, and also provides a very reliable buffer against unexpected shortages of cash. If the banks suddenly find that there have been more cash withdrawals than expected, so that their cash base is lower than necessary to sustain the total level of liabilities, they can recall call money from the discount market, thereby increasing their cash base.

Banks can also purchase or invest in government and other securities which are due to mature in a few days' time. The government borrows money from the public and financial institutions by issuing Treasury bills which are repaid in 90 days. Since these are issued each week, there is a stock of Treasury bills maturing each week, so banks can buy appropriate amounts to ensure that each week a flow of cash is available to increase their cash base if they so wish, or to be used to buy a further amount of replacement Treasury bills.

Other securities have a longer maturity date. Some may not be repaid for six or 12 months and others for two or three years. Generally speaking, the longer the time before repayment the higher the rate of interest. This is to compensate for the extra risks that the lender or holder of the securities is taking. It is always possible to sell securities, especially government securities, so that if the holder, an individual or a bank, needs cash immediately, the securities can always be converted into cash. There is therefore, for all practical purposes, certainty that the asset, the securities, can be converted into cash. However, there is no certainty of the price at which they can be converted into cash, or sold on the open market. If they are held until the maturity date the holder will receive the nominal or face value of the security, but if they have to be sold before maturity there is a risk that they may have to be sold at a loss.

We use the concept of *liquidity* to express the speed, ease and certainty with which an asset can be converted into cash. Obviously, notes and coins of the country concerned are the most liquid of all assets since they are cash. They have perfect liquidity. Notes and coins of foreign countries may be liquid in another country, since they can be exchanged for the domestic currency, but the price or rate of exchange may be uncertain. Securities which mature in seven days' time are quite liquid because there is certainty that in one week the holder of them will receive a specified amount from the issuer. Long-term securities can be converted into cash, i.e. they can always be sold, but there is greater uncertainty as to the price that will be received if they are sold between today and the maturity date. Today's market price for them is known, and the nominal or repayment value is known, but there may be fluctuations in the market price between now and maturity.

The liquidity of an asset is its nearness to money. Every asset can be converted into money since it can be sold, but liquidity includes the degree of certainty of the amount of money or cash which can be obtained for it.

Banks have established customary liquidity ratios as well as a cash ratio. They maintain a certain proportion of their total assets in liquid form. In some countries there may be statutory requirements that banks maintain a certain proportion of their assets in specified liquid assets. A reserve ratio is the cash or liquidity ratio banks choose to establish. A required reserve ratio is one they are required to hold by law or order of the monetary authorities. Table 13.2 sets out an illustration of a bank's balance sheet showing the main categories of items.

Table 13.2. Banks' assets and liabilities (£000 million)

Liabilities			Assets		per cent
Sterling deposits			Notes	0.4	(0.2)
sight deposits	46.7		Balances at Bank of England	2.1	(1.2)
time deposits	60.4				
			Market loans	53.6	(30.4)
Other currency deposits	41.7				
			Bills	6.3	(3.6)
Items in transmission,					
etc.	27.6		Investments	12.5	(7.1)
			Advances	87.7	(49.7)
			Miscellaneous	13.8	(7.8)
Total	176.4		Total	176.4	(100.0)

Note: Market loans include loans to discount houses, local authorities, other UK loans and loans overseas.

On the Liabilities side, deposits are divided into 'sight' deposits and 'time' deposits. Sight deposits, on which interest might or might not be paid, are those which the customer or depositor can withdraw immediately or at sight. These are obviously the liabilities most susceptible to sudden withdrawals. Time deposits which attract interest are those on which the customer is required to give advance notice of withdrawal, although in practice banks may forgo the advance notice and deduct the equivalent amount of interest. Certificates of deposit are fixed-term deposits which earn a higher rate of interest.

The Assets side shows the different types of assets listed in descending order of liquidity. Bills and securities include both government and private sector securities. Generally speaking, the interest earned by banks varies inversely with the liquidity of an asset, so that cash in the tills earns no interest (and, indeed, banks have to incur costs to protect these assets). Advances or overdrafts earn the highest interest; they are the most risky and the least liquid. There is little opportunity for a bank to sell this asset on the open market, although it is conceivable that an overdraft could be converted into cash if the bank sold the loan or debt to someone else.

Control of the money stock

Banks as profit-making institutions face a continual conflict between prudence and profitability. They are very conscious of the overriding need to be able to repay all depositors whenever the depositors choose to make withdrawals. The crucial factor is confidence. Banks must always maintain the confidence of depositors that full repayment will be made.

As noted, advances or overdrafts are the most profitable of banks' loans.

There is therefore pressure to increase the proportion of assets which are allocated to advances, but this is tempered by the requirements of prudence so that banks maintain appropriate liquidity ratios and allocate their assets among different forms. However, if banks can increase their cash base, or their liquidity base as appropriate, they will be able to increase the amount of their advances and so earn higher profits without disturbing their cash and liquidity ratios. In this way they can expand, increase their earnings, and provide the necessary safeguards which prudence or the law requires.

If the government buys securities from members of the public there will be an increase in banks' deposits at the Bank of England, which increases both the cash and liquidity bases of the banks. This allows them to expand their other assets and still maintain their cash and liquidity ratios. Advances *can* be increased. Whether there *will* be a growth in advances depends on two factors.

The first is whether there is a *demand* for more advances. This will depend on the state of the economy, whether individuals and firms wish to borrow more, and this may depend on the rate of interest which has to be paid for advances. The second is whether the banks regard the applicants for more advances as creditworthy. Not everyone who applies for an advance is acceptable to the banks. Some may be regarded as unreliable and their applications too risky. If the economy is declining or growing at a slower rate so that business conditions are less favourable, banks may tighten up on their assessment of creditworthiness. It will be more difficult for businesses to make sufficient profits to repay the advances; and individuals will face more uncertain futures, thereby increasing the possibility that they will be unable to repay the loan.

Government action to increase the cash and liquidity bases of the banks can create conditions in which it is possible for banks to increase the quantity of money by expanding the number and level of overdrafts, but this will not lead to an actual expansion in the supply of money unless there is a demand for more overdrafts and that demand satisfies the banks' criteria of creditworthiness.

If government takes part in open-market operations, selling securities on the open market, there will be a reduction in the cash and liquidity bases of the banks as their deposits at the Bank of England are reduced. If the banks accepted this passively they would be required to reduce the total amount of their assets by a multiple (the cash ratio) of the reduction in their deposits at the Bank of England. This would, of course, lead to a reduction in banks' profitability as they cut down the level of overdrafts and other assets. We should therefore expect them to seek to restore their cash and liquidity bases wherever possible.

If they are operating only on a cash ratio this is not too difficult. They can recall call money from the discount houses. This will allow them in effect to transfer assets which are not counted as part of the cash base into assets which are so counted. If this happens the discount houses will find themselves short of cash to replace that recalled by the banks. They will have to borrow from elsewhere, and in the United Kingdom they are always able to borrow from the Bank of England by discounting approved securities. However, they may be required to pay a higher rate of interest to borrow or obtain this cash. This will lead them to increase the interest rates at which they lend, and in particular will lead to an increase in the interest rate in Treasury bills since the discount houses submit a weekly tender for every Treasury bill issued. The end result of an initial squeeze on the banks' cash base will be a rise in the rate of interest. This will feed through the market so that all interest rates will tend to rise – including that charged by banks on advances.

This rise in interest rates may deter some applicants so that the demand for advances declines, and the banks may conclude that some applicants who were creditworthy at the lower interest rate are not acceptable at the higher rate. There could therefore be a reduction in the level of advances following the decrease in the banks' deposits at the Bank of England, but this is more likely to occur as a result of the higher interest rates than directly from the reduction in the cash base. Banks can always restore their cash base by passing the pressure on to the discount houses.

Many other countries do not have discount houses. Banks can respond in the same way by calling in their overnight or very short loans, or by not renewing their take-up of maturing government or other securities. These measures have the same effect. They allow the banks to restore their cash base by passing the pressure on to some other part of the banking or financial system by obtaining funds from parts of the system which may have a surplus.

If banks are working to a liquidity ratio, a reduction in their cash will also reduce their liquid base. Banks may respond to this by selling non-liquid assets or transferring assets from one side of the liquidity ratio definition to the other. They convert non-liquid assets into assets which are included in their liquidity base. The selling of some assets will lead to a reduction in their price so that the rate of interest will rise. However, if they sell to the private sector, which pays by cheque, this merely shifts the same amount of cash and liquid resources around the system.

Public Sector Borrowing Requirement

Governments need to borrow large sums of money to finance their activities. This is known as the Public Sector Borrowing Requirement (PSBR). Even if they intend to finance all or most of these activities by taxation, they may need to borrow short-term to finance expenditure during the year before the taxes are received. A main form of borrowing is by issuing short-term debt such as Treasury bills. The government therefore injects liquid assets into the banking system, and the need for government to raise short-term loans means that it cannot necessarily limit the supply of liquid assets to the extent it might wish from the viewpoint of its monetary control policy. Moreover, it may not wish to see interest rates rise since this will increase the cost of public borrowing.

If government cannot sell the extra government securities to members of the public it will borrow from the banking system. Government cheques drawn on the Bank of England, when paid into commercial or clearing banks, lead to an increase in these banks' deposits at the Bank of England.

The Treasury triangle

The Treasury view of the working of the monetary system under the Thatcher Government is set out in their evidence to the House of Commons Treasury and Civil Service Committee. Briefly, they see a triangular relationship consisting of the money stock, the PSBR and the rate of interest. They believe there is a connection between the PSBR and the money stock, although other economists deny this. Control of the PSBR is considered necessary if the money supply is to be kept under control. If the money supply is limited and there is an increase in the PSBR so that government seeks to borrow more of this limited stock of money, it will be able to do so only by paying higher rates of interest. This may be politically unpopular and the higher interest rates may have an adverse effect on economic activity. This may lead to a lower level of demand, or a lower level of demand which is acceptable as creditworthy by banks, for advances, and so lead to a reduction in the money stock or in its rate of growth.

In some circumstances a higher rate of interest could have the apparently perverse effect of leading to a higher demand for advances. If firms or individuals have to pay a higher rate of interest on advances, but have no immediate resources of their own from which to do so, they may be compelled to borrow more in order to pay the higher interest on their existing debts. This effect can also be seen in some developing countries that have large amounts of foreign debt to service.

If the government wishes to maintain a given rate of interest and control the money stock, it might not be able to finance the level of PSBR that it wishes. Alternatively, if it wishes to run a given level of PSBR and maintain interest rates at a given level, it might have to increase the money stock to the level consistent with its PSBR and interest rate targets.

The Treasury triangle version of economic relationships concludes that the government may be able to control any two of the three variables, the money stock, the PSBR and the rate of interest. Once having chosen which two it seeks to control it must accept that the third will be outside its control and will be determined by market forces operating through the banking and financial institutions. Some governments may give greater importance to control of the money stock because they believe this is crucial in the control of inflation (this will be discussed in Chapter 14), and to the rate of interest since this affects the cost of borrowing and may influence economic activity. They will therefore seek to reduce the PSBR so that they can control the money stock at lower rates of interest. This leads them either to increase taxation, which may have disincentive effects on economic activity, risk-taking and effort, or to reduce government expenditure, which can be politically difficult as well as having contractionary effects on economic activity.

Governments may differ in the importance they attach to any triangular relationship between the money stock, PSBR and the rate of interest, but many of them will continue to be concerned about the effects of public borrowing on the money supply and the necessity to raise interest rates when they seek to persuade members of the public to lend them more money.

Rate of interest

The rate of interest is the price paid for obtaining, or received for surrendering, liquidity. It is the reward for giving up immediate access to cash in return for cash at some future date. Our demand for cash today will be influenced by the price we have to pay for it, i.e. the rate of interest. We have seen that the traditional methods by which the monetary authorities sought to control the stock of money actually relied heavily on the rate of interest. Often the banks were able to avoid the direct pressures on their cash or liquidity ratios, but the effects of the monetary authority's actions was to raise the rate of interest and this frequently led to a reduction in the demand for advances. Monetarists regard the rate of interest as being one of, if not the, most important determinants of the demand for money and therefore of the amount of money stock. They believe, as do some non-monetarists, that the open-market methods of controlling the money stock do not lead directly to reductions in the quantity of money because the banking system can always find ways of obtaining the cash or liquid assets needed to underpin a given money stock if it chooses to do so. Whether it chooses to do so will depend on the demand for advances at different rates of interest.

Thus the supply of money is determined by whatever the system demands and the main influence on the demand for money is the rate of interest. In this view, therefore, the appropriate policy for the supply of money is a passive one on the supply side but active on the demand side. Measures to influence the rate of interest and the PSBR, which reflects the government's own demand for borrowing, are regarded as the prime determinants of the demand for money and therefore of the supply also.

The PSBR influences interest rates directly by influencing the demand for cash or loans. In order to borrow more money the government issues more Treasury bills or other securities. In order to sell these it will probably be necessary to reduce the price at which they are sold and this is equivalent to raising the rate of interest. With other securities it may be necessary to offer a higher rate of interest directly.

Interest rates and the price of fixed-interest securities

Higher interest rates for new issues or for other loans currently being made have the effect of raising interest rates on other existing fixed-interest securities by leading to a fall in their price. This is best illustrated by the example of Consols, or Government Consolidated Stocks. These are government securities which have no fixed redemption date. The government can choose when, or even whether, to redeem them by repaying the nominal value of the securities. They are therefore the nearest approach to an indefinite loan that there is. The holder of a $2\frac{1}{2}$ per cent Consol receives £2.50 for each *nominal* £100 Consol stock held. If the interest rate on assets of similar security is 5 per cent, the $2\frac{1}{2}$ per cent Consol can be expected to have a market price of £50 even though the nominal value of the stock is £100. This is because no one seeking to maximise his income from interest would buy the stock for more than £50. If £50 were invested at the prevailing rate of interest it would earn £2.50 a year; since the $2\frac{1}{2}$ per cent Consol pays only £2.50 a year in interest no one would pay more than £50 for it. If it were bought for £100 the new purchaser would be receiving only 2½ per cent interest rather than the 5 per cent that can be obtained elsewhere. If rates were to rise to 10 per cent the market price of the 2½ per cent Consol would fall to £25.

The exception to this strict rule for determining the market price of undated fixed-interest stocks is if there are expectations of changes in the rate of interest. If I believe that interest rates are going to fall in the future then I also anticipate that the market price of Consols is going to rise. I might then be willing to pay more than the current market price determined by the application of the above rule in order to receive the capital gain that will occur if the market price of the share rises. However, if everyone else believes that interest rates are going to fall, the current holders of the Consols will be unwilling to sell at the old price since they too anticipate a future rise in prices. However, while most or even all people might expect interest rates to fall and stock prices to rise, they might not all expect them to change by the same amount, so that there could still be room for differences in expected future prices; thus purchases and sales could take place as different people had different expectations.

There will probably be similar effects with dated stocks where the redemption date is a long time ahead. We would not expect such large fluctuations in the market price of short-dated stocks or those near to their maturity date. If a stock is due for redemption in 12 months' time, the holder of it knows that in a year he will receive the full nominal value. Thus if it is a 2½ per cent stock, everyone knows that in 12 months it will be worth £100. Even if the current interest rate is 10 per cent, the price will not fall to £25, for if it did the purchaser would receive £2.50 interest plus £75 capital gain in 12 months. This would be equivalent to a rate of interest of 310 per cent. The market price would be about £93. The holder would then receive £2.50 interest plus £7 capital gain or 10.2 per cent. If interest and capital gains are taxed at different rates and this is taken into account by the market so that market prices of stock are determined by net-of-tax yields, the market price would be affected by the relative contribution to the total net yield coming from interest and capital gain. The central point however is that fixed-interest stocks with approaching maturity dates will have market prices much closer to their nominal values than will undated stocks such as Consols.

Interest rates then affect not only the demand for cash or money but also the price or market value of existing stocks. The extent of the effects of interest rate changes on the prices of stocks will also be influenced by the market's views of future rates of interest. If all the market, or a large part of it, expects interest rates to fall, stock prices will begin to rise in anticipation of the rise in the market price of stocks, and this will itself have the effect of reducing interest rates on existing fixed-interest securities.

We have seen that the traditional open-market operations may not lead to a reduction in the money supply or may do so only through the demand mechanism following an increase in interest rates. Because higher interest rates may not be desired, governments and monetary authorities may seek other ways of controlling the stock of money.

Variable cash and liquidity ratios

In our exposition at the beginning of this chapter we assumed that banks were required to maintain a 10 per cent cash ratio. If this were increased to 12 per cent it would be necessary for the banks to convert some of their non-cash assets into cash or to restrict their loans and advances to a level consistent with the new cash ratio. It is probable that banks would seek to convert non-cash assets into cash in order to maintain their profitable loans and advances. There would then be great pressure on other parts of the monetary system as banks called in their very short-term loans. Interest rates would rise as those affected sought other sources of cash and were compelled to pay higher interest rates.

If the banks follow a liquidity ratio regime the same attempts and similar results would follow an increase in the liquidity ratio. Some countries have variable liquidity ratios and in the United Kingdom at certain times the Bank of England has required banks to deposit a certain percentage of their assets with the Bank. These took the form of liquid assets but could not be counted as part of the liquidity base. Generally this led to higher interest rates, moves by banks to convert some of their non-liquid assets into liquid assets thereby restoring or increasing their liquidity base, and to the development of new forms of liquid assets, or an expansion of existing ones which were less amenable to control by the monetary authorities. Thus if the authorities seek to control the issue of Treasury bills to deny the banks the opportunity to gain access to liquid assets with which to replenish their liquidity base, banks can encourage the development of private sector trade bills which serve the same purpose.

Sometimes the monetary authorities introduce sanctions against banks that increase their lending, particularly advances, above a specified level. This tends to lead to the development of additional financial institutions outside the definition of banks which is used to exercise the control. It also encourages the development of new kinds of banking activity outside the control. One result of this can be that new forms of money, instruments which serve the functions of money but are not included in the official definitions and statistics of money, and therefore do not appear in the official statistics of the controlled money stock, may emerge. This can mean that while the official definition and measurement of money appear to be under control, the effective stock of what is *now* accepted as money is not being controlled in the way or to the extent the monetary authorities desire. Banks and the financial sector can display considerable ingenuity and inventiveness in adapting to controls which appear irksome and restrict their opportunity to make profits.

This has led some authorities to impose direct controls. This too leads to avoidance and the development of new institutions and forms of money outside the controls. Appeals to banks to limit voluntarily their advances create problems for banks which might be required to discriminate between equally creditworthy applicants. Moreover, in a competitive banking system, there is no guarantee that other banks will observe the restraints, so that one bank might lose valuable customers to its less strict competitors.

It has to be recognised that a private enterprise banking system will seek to expand loans and advances subject to its concern to maintain prudence and exercise due banking caution regarding the creditworthiness of applicants for loans. A State-owned banking system might be able to impose its control of the money stock more easily but if the rate of interest and market forces are not used to allocate the available credit, some administrative criteria will have to be developed. A market-based economy believes that the market provides the best mechanisms for allocating resources, including credit. The imposition of administratively determined criteria for allocating credit could lead to a misallocation and prevent the other market mechanisms from functioning efficiently. It is only if the market system is abandoned and replaced by some other administratively determined mechanism for allocating resources and making production and distribution decisions, that an administered banking system can avoid creating inconsistencies. Even then it might result in a less efficient allocation of resources and lower levels of economic activity and output.

System of control of the UK money stock

The Bank of England no longer requires commercial clearing banks to hold specified cash or liquidity ratios. These are left to the banks' judgement of prudence. The Bank of England continues to act as 'lender of last resort'. This means that the banking system can always borrow from the Bank of England. It does this by discounting bills at the central bank. An approved short-term security such as a bill is sold to the Bank of England for a price below its nominal value or the amount which will be received on maturity. The difference between this selling price and the maturity price, expressed as a percentage of the selling price, is the rate of interest charged by the Bank of England for the loan represented by the selling price. Previously the Bank of England announced in advance the Discount Rate or Minimum Lending Rate (MLR). Commercial banks and discount houses therefore knew the rate of interest they would have to pay if their cash shortage, resulting from a reduction in the cash base needed to support a given level of deposits, led them to borrow from the Bank of England. They could arrange their affairs so that even if they paid a slight penalty when discounting at the Bank of England, they recovered this on the rest of their activities.

The Bank of England does not now announce the MLR in advance. Banks do not know how much they will have to pay if they are obliged to borrow from the central bank. As the penalty may be significantly higher than the rate at which they lend, the fear of incurring the penalty rate of borrowing may deter them from lending to the limit of their self-determined cash and liquidity ratios. They may therefore respond to reductions in their cash base, resulting from open-market operations by the monetary authorities, by cutting back on their total deposits, and particularly on advances. In addition, the government now announces target paths for the PSBR and for various measurements of the money stock for the next few years. This is intended to indicate to the banks and all economic agents the government's future intentions or desires. However, since the main instrument for influencing the money stock is the rate of interest, government will be able to achieve its target growth paths for the monetary indicators only if it is prepared to allow interest rates to rise sufficiently to lead to a reduction in demand. Penalty rates of interest financed by banks in borrowing from the Bank of England may have to rise considerably and be sustained for some time before the cost of borrowing marginal amounts from the central bank induces the banks to reduce their level of advances.

The UK system in the mid-1980s is therefore based on controlling the demand for money through its price – the rate of interest. By seeking to inject uncertainty into future interest rates at which the Bank of England will lend to the banking system, the monetary authorities hope that the suppliers of credit will contain their credit expansion to the government's announced targets. This will be backed up by action to raise interest rates where necessary, and the PSBR is subject to control in order to reduce the total demand for the limited amount of money.

CHAPTER 14

The demand for money

There are two main reasons for demanding or requiring money. The first is to finance our level of transactions, and the second is that money is one of the wide range of assets in which we can hold our wealth.

Transactions

In a modern economy we finance our transactions with money or credit. As we have seen, bank credit functions just as effectively and in the same way as cash provided that the person with whom we wish to settle our debt, to pay for our purchases, is willing to accept our cheque. Bank credit is in effect equivalent to cash, for most purposes. In many societies other forms of credit, such as credit cards, are increasingly accepted as equivalent to or identical with cash and are widely accepted as means of settling debts and permitting purchases to take place.

The amount of money which we demand for transactions purposes will be determined in the main by the level of transactions we undertake and the prevailing practices and conventions regarding the timing and method of payment. For example, if all transactions take place for cash with immediate payment on purchase, there will be a direct relationship between our level of transactions and our demand for money, and for money in a particular form – cash. If it is customary that purchases are paid for within 30 days of purchase, our demand for money will be lagged – it will occur 30 days after our transactions. If we can use credit cards and are not required to repay anything to the credit card company for, say, six months, *our* demand for money may not actually occur for six months, but if the credit card company has to pay the companies from which we have made purchases within 30 days, *their* demand for money will be lagged 30 days on our purchases.

If, as we have previously discussed, the level of our transactions is related to our level of income, then there will be a relationship between the level of income and the demand for money. As we saw in Chapter 11, the relationship between consumption, or our level of transactions, and income is not necessarily straightforward. There are different possible definitions and measurements of income which might provide the key variable to which consumption is related. The transaction demand for money will be determined by the income–consumption relationship, and whichever relationship we believe best explains the level of consumption is the one we should adopt to determine the transaction demand for money. However, we must also recognise that changes in financial provisions, the use of credit and so on, may change past relationships.

There is a relationship therefore between the level of transactions and the amount of money we need to finance them. The demand for money and the amount of money which people have may therefore influence the level of aggregate demand. This is the main reason why governments try to control the amount of money in an economy. If they can reduce the stock of money they may be able to reduce the level of aggregate demand, and if the amount of money is increased there may be an expansion in aggregate demand.

Asset demand for money

We can choose to hold our assets in many forms ranging from cash through stocks and shares to works of art or property. Sometimes we may decide to switch a considerable proportion of our assets into money because we believe there will be a change in the rate of interest or in share prices. If we expect these to fall we may decide to sell our existing assets and hold cash to avoid a capital loss, and also perhaps to enable us to buy stocks and shares when the price has fallen. This will be a stronger motive when we expect these prices to rise in the future. We will want to buy before the price rise takes place and to sell before the price fall occurs.

We may also wish to hold some of our assets in money merely in order to have a desired spread of our assets over a range of different forms. This is often referred to as the portfolio effect. We decide how we wish to spread our portfolio or collection of assets among the various possible assets available to us. Some will offer higher rates of return but will be more risky.

Even people with relatively small amounts of assets may spread them among different forms. They may have some in cash and some on current account with a bank, which may not earn any interest. They may also have some on deposit account which earns some interest, and some of their savings may earn higher interest in a different sort of account or with a different institution but may not be available to them until they have given a specified period of notice of withdrawal. This is a more risky form of asset for them, for they may find that they need access to the assets more quickly than expected, and if they are unable to convert them into cash immediately they may have to borrow at an even higher rate of interest.

Liquidity preference

Keynes developed the concept of liquidity preference to explain the demand for money. As we saw in Chapter 13, liquidity is the nearness to money of an asset or the ease and certainty with which it can be converted into cash. He believed that there are three main motives for preferring to hold one's assets in liquid form:

1. Transactions motive: this is the same as the transaction demand discussed above and is a function of the level of income.
2. Precautionary motive: this is the desire to hold money for precautionary reasons to cover unexpected emergencies; Keynes thought this also was a function of the level of income.
3. Speculative motive: this is the desire to take advantage of changes in the rate of interest as they affect the price of stocks and is a function of the rate of interest and the expected rate of interest.

Keynes grouped the first two together as L_1, as a function of the level of income, with the third, or L_2, as a function of the rate of interest in relation to the expected future rate of interest. The speculative demand for money is essentially the result of the switching of assets between fixed-interest securities and cash. If L_2, or the speculative demand for cash, is a function of the rate of interest, the demand for money in total is sensitive to changes in the rate of interest and not only to changes in the level of income or the volume of transactions. This means that the interest elasticity of demand for money is positive.

Keynes believed that at a certain low level of interest the demand for money, rather than for long-term or undated fixed-interest securities, would become infinite as everyone would prefer to hold all their assets in liquid form rather than in securities. If the rate of interest were very low in relation to the normal or expected rates of interest, the prices of fixed-interest securities would be high following the general rule of the inverse relationship between the price of fixed-interest securities and the rate of interest. Any rise in the rate of interest, even a relatively small one, will then lead to a fall in the market price of the securities. If everyone believes that interest rates are much lower than normal and that they are very unlikely to fall any further but are much more likely to rise, the risk of a reduction in the market price of the shares, and thus a capital loss, is far greater than the possibility of an appreciation in the market price. This will lead to an absence of buyers and a tendency to sell the stocks before the price falls. The excess of sellers will tend to reduce the price and increase interest rates.

In addition, financial institutions operate by having a margin between the rates at which they borrow and lend. If interest rates are too low there will be insufficient margin for them to obtain a profitable or working difference between lending and borrowing rates, so for institutional reasons there is probably some minimum level of interest which the market can tolerate.

Keynes believed therefore that there was a minimum level below which the rate of interest could not fall. This was referred to as the liquidity trap.

We can combine the two types of liquidity preference into a demand for money which relates the demand for money to the rate of interest for a given income level. This is shown in Fig. 14.1. The line L_1 shows the amount of cash balances demanded for level of income Y_1 in order to satisfy the transactions and precautionary motives. The level of income is given as Y_1, L_1 is a vertical line, and for this level of income, OL_1 amount of money will be demanded. Demand for the speculative motive will depend on the rate of interest. If the interest rate is r_1, amount L_2-L_1 will be demanded for speculative purposes and total demand for money will be OL_2.

If the quantity of money is M_1 the rate of interest will be r_0 and the quantity of money demanded OL_0. At this rate of interest the demand for money shown by the LP curve exactly equals the supply of money M_1. If the monetary authorities can control the quantity of money and decide to supply amount M_1, the rate of interest will remain at r_0 as long as the level of income remains given and there is no change in liquidity preference. If the quantity of money is increased to M_2 the rate of interest will fall to r_2. However, further increases in the supply of money will have no effect on the rate of interest since this is the point at which the liquidity trap operates. Similarly, if the quantity of money is reduced from M_2 to M_1 the rate of interest will rise from r_2 to r_0.

If the level of income increases to Y_2, L_1 will increase and the total

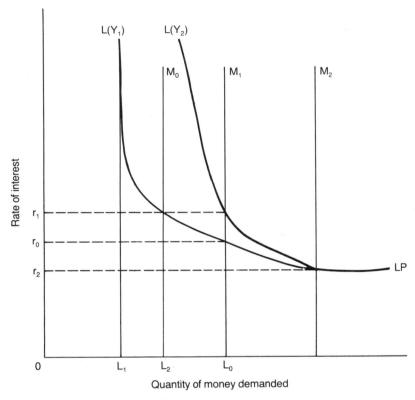

Fig. 14.1 The rate of interest, liquidity preference and demand for money

demand for money will shift from $L(Y_1)$ to $L(Y_2)$. If the quantity of money was M_1, the increase in the demand for money following the increase in income from Y_1 to Y_2 will lead to an increase in the rate of interest from r_0 to r_1.

Monetarist view

Monetarists do not accept the somewhat limited range of assets between which decisions regarding portfolio preferences are expressed in the Keynesian explanation. Rather than concentrating on money and fixed-interest long-term securities, monetarists believe that people choose their portfolio spread from the whole range of assets available to them, including property and investment in human capital through expenditure on education and training. The demand for money is seen as a function of one's total wealth assets; money is merely one of the many forms in which assets can be kept. However, Milton Friedman, the best-known advocate of the current monetarist revival, believes that people will hold a greater proportion of their assets in money the larger is the proportion of human to non-human capital. What this means is that if the only form of wealth you have is the expected future earnings from your human capital, i.e. employment income obtained by working and receiving wages which are related to the value of the education and training you have acquired, you will have a higher demand for cash than if your wealth assets of an equal total value consisted of securities or property. This can be seen as a different formulation of the transaction demand for cash balances. If our wealth assets consist of expected earnings it means that we have only our wages as wealth. Our income from work provides our income, and if our consumption is determined by income, and our demand for money by the level of transactions or consumption, then our human wealth can be said to determine our demand for money. It is necessary to express it in this complicated way because Friedman wishes to make all the demand for money a function of wealth and the rate of interest.

The rate of interest is relevant because this indicates the returns to be obtained from holding non-monetary assets and also the opportunity costs – the interest forgone – of holding money. The higher the rate of interest, the greater the inducement to reduce the amount of money we hold.

Keynes would accept that the rate of interest could have some effect on L_1. If interest rates were high people might adjust their behaviour and reduce the amount of money they held to finance their transactions. We might switch some of our money from current to deposit accounts if the rate of interest is high enough to induce us to accept the inconvenience of operating with lower current account balances.

The demand for money is a demand for one particular form of asset. As we have seen, there is no clear dividing line between money and some other assets. There is a gradual movement along a spectrum of liquidity, and additional new forms of assets may be developed to increase the spectrum. We demand, or require, money in order to finance our transactions, and as one of the forms in which to hold our wealth assets. Our level of transactions will therefore influence the amount of money we need, although the precise relationship can change as the economy alters its financial practices or develops new methods of payment. In the next section we will discuss whether changes in the money stock also affect the level of our transactions. Exactly which definition of income should be taken as providing the transaction demand for money is a matter of disagreement among economists, and the empirical evidence so far available does not provide a conclusive answer.

The demand for money for portfolio, asset distribution or speculative purposes is influenced by our level of wealth, the ease and cost of obtaining credit for speculative purposes, and the rate of interest, which not only affects the cost of credit and provides the opportunity cost of holding money but also affects the market price of some assets. Keynes may have concentrated on too narrow a range of assets when presenting the liquidity preference theory in terms only of money and fixed-interest securities. Shifting the emphasis to the whole range of possible assets may be to broaden the area of consideration too far.

The quantity theory of money

We have noted that in Keynesian analysis, the quantity of money is seen as exerting a direct influence on the rate of interest. However, other economic analysis may give more importance to the quantity of money and changes in it than merely its effect on interest rates. The simplest and best-known version of the quantity theory of money is known as the Fisher equation after Irvin Fisher who first formulated it. It is not really an equation but an identity in that it must be true. It takes the form $MV = PT$ where

M = the money stock
V = the velocity of circulation
P = the average level of prices
T = the number of transactions for which money is used.

We have already considered the money stock or money supply. The velocity of circulation is the average number of times each unit of money is used or circulates in a given time period. For example, if there are 10,000 £1 notes issued, or in circulation, each one may be used five times a year as they are passed on from customer to buyer in a whole series of transactions. V would then be 5. It is obvious that if there are 10,000 £1 notes and each one is used five times, the total value of transactions that they have financed in the year must be £50,000. The total value of transactions is the number of transactions multiplied by the average value or price of each transaction, i.e. PT. It follows therefore that MV and PT must come to the same aggregate value. Indeed, because we cannot actually measure V, we have no way of knowing how often each £1 note is used; thus we are unable to calculate V except to divide PT by M. The quantity of money includes bank credit as well as notes and coins. The exact definition of M will be discussed later in this chapter.

The Fisher equation does not in itself tell us very much about the economy except that the total value of all transactions in a period will equal the total value of the money paid to finance those transactions, and that is not very surprising. It is also not very helpful. However, if it is assumed, or established, that V is constant, so that it always remains at 5, then we may have a very important mechanism for influencing what happens in the economy. If V is constant and we increase the quantity of money from £10,000 to £11,000, we know that the total value of all transactions will rise from £50,000 to £55,000. It is true that we do not know whether P or T – or both of them – will rise, but we can conclude that PT will increase. If we make the further assumption that the economy always operates at full employment then we can conclude that T will remain the same. For if the economy is operating at full employment, so that there is a constant level of output, the level of employment and output will not change, and if the level of output does not change there is no reason to suppose that the number of transactions will change. Transactions involve the buying and selling of goods and services and if the total quantity of goods and services is fixed at the full employment level, it is unlikely that there will be either more or fewer transactions to buy and sell the same amount of goods and services.

If V is a constant we can rewrite the Fisher equation as $M = 1/V \cdot PT$ or as $P = MV/T$, and if T is constant there is a direct connection between changes in M and changes in P. If this reasoning is correct we conclude that changes in the stock of money, M, have a direct and proportional effect on the general level of prices. If the money stock is increased, prices will rise – there will be inflation; and if it is decreased, prices will fall. If it is increased, but at a slower rate than previously, prices will rise but at a slower rate than previously, so that while there will still be inflation because prices will be rising, the *rate of inflation* will decrease since prices will rise by less than they did previously.

Before considering the various assumptions made in this discussion of the quantity theory, it is useful to make one improvement to the Fisher equation. T, the level of transactions, includes all transactions financed by money. It therefore includes the buying of stocks and shares, and accordingly their prices have to be included in P, the average level of prices. In economic analysis we often wish to exclude transactions in financial assets from the price level and from the level of output or activity measured by T.

By doing this we get a measurement of the output of goods and services which provides an indicator of the standard of living, which is more likely to be related to the level of employment needed to produce the goods and services than is a measure of T which includes stock exchange and similar transactions. It is true that if there is a large increase in the number of stock exchange transactions and more stocks and shares are bought, there will be an increase in output by stockbrokers and their clerks, and there may be an increase in employment of stockbrokers' clerks. However, this will be much less than the increase in the value and number of transactions measured by counting each purchase and sale of the shares.

It is preferable therefore to exclude financial transactions and limit the analysis to those transactions which involve the purchases and sales, including intermediate purchases and sales, of goods and services. In this case we are including the sort of double counting we deliberately excluded in Chapter 12, since each of the intermediate transactions required payment and money was used to pay for the transactions. We are therefore now concentrating on those transactions which provide economic activity or the production of goods and services. Instead of T, which includes all transactions, we define and measure these as Y, or the level of output or income. We then obtain the equation $MV = PY$. V is now the income-velocity circulation of money and relates only to that part of the money supply which is used to finance transactions included in Y.

Effects on employment and wages

We can expand this revised version of the quantity theory to include the effects on employment and wages. If E is the level of employment and W the level of average wages, then $MV = PY = EW$. This says that the level of aggregate money demand will equal the total value of all transactions (PY), and this will equal the total wage bill. Even though we know that not all the proceeds of the transactions (PY) will go to labour, some will form the income of companies and entrepreneurs through profits; the relation will hold as long as the share of total income from production and sales which goes to labour remains constant. Thus we could write $(1 \cdot a)(EW)$ where a is the total income from production minus the proportion of income represented by EW as a percentage of EW. As long as a remains constant we can ignore it and for simplicity assume that EW is the same as total income from transactions so that $EW = PY$.

If wages and prices move together so that prices are always a constant percentage mark-up on wages, a change in P following a change in M will lead to a similar change in W. A change in Y will lead to a change in E. Thus whether a change in the money supply leads to a change in prices or output affects not only the rate of inflation but also the level of employment. This also follows from the assumption that changes in Y represent changes in output and that if output rises so will employment, and if output decreases employment will fall. If there is a rise in productivity it is possible for Y to rise without E rising or for Y to remain constant and E to fall.

If V is constant and M is fixed, an increase in W must lead to a fall in E, just as any increase in P must lead to a fall in output or Y. There will be a fall in output and employment if W and P rise while V and M are constant, and it makes no difference whether W or P is the first to rise.

If the quantity theory provides a reliable explanation of real world behaviour it may explain changes in prices, or inflation, and also in employment or unemployment. To use the quantity theory as a basis for policy it is necessary not only that V remains constant, or alters only in a predictable way, but also that M can be controlled; the effects of changes in productivity and the way these will be fed through into changes in prices or in output must also be known.

The Cambridge equation

Economists at Cambridge developed this reasoning to produce a formula to explain the demand for money before Keynes developed his concept of liquidity preference. They expressed the demand for money as $M_d = k(PY)$ where k is a constant and P and Y are as defined above. If k is a constant we have the same result as with the Fisher equation; changes in the demand for money or in the money stock will lead to changes in PY. However, we still do not know whether P *or* Y, the level of prices *or* the level of output and so employment, will be affected.

Prices or output or both?

We can conclude that changes in the money stock will have a direct proportional effect on the average level of prices only if we assume that the economy is always at the full employment level so that the level of output is constant. Everyday experience tells us that the economy does not produce an exactly constant amount of output. We will probably also doubt whether the economy is always at the level of full employment, but this might be because our notion of full employment is not necessarily the same as that used by those economists who claim that the economy operates, or has a tendency to operate, at its full employment level. There are two possible sources of difference: the definition of full employment, and just what is meant by 'having a tendency' to operate at its full employment level. How far away from full employment, however that is defined, can an economy be, and for how long, and still display a tendency to operate at full employment? This is an issue we will discuss in Chapter 16.

For the present we will concentrate on the question of whether changes in the money stock have a direct and proportional effect on prices. This is not a mere academic question. It lies at the heart of what is known as monetarism and forms the basis of economic policy of a number of governments.

The first important assumption, or assertion, depending on whether it is claimed as a matter of empirical evidence rather than merely assumed for expository purposes, is whether V, the velocity of circulation of money, is stable and constant. If it is not, if V varies, then changes in M may have no effect on either P or Y. An increase in the quantity of money stock from £10,000 to £20,000 could be cancelled out by a fall in V from 5 to 2·5. The total value of transactions in the period would remain at £50,000 so that the increase in M has had no effect on P or Y. Remember, since we cannot measure V directly, we cannot count how often each note, coin and £1 of bank account are used in a period. We have to relate what has happened to PY to M in order to decide whether V is constant or variable.

Some monetarists claim that V may change on occasion but remains stable for longish periods. Certain institutional changes such as the development and wide use of credit cards may affect V. Any form of extending credit or delaying payments means that fewer units of money are needed in a time period, or the same number of units will be used less often, to finance a given number and value of transactions.

The evidence seems to be that in the United Kingdom, V has been increasing slowly over a number of years, but not in an absolutely predictable way. While we may have a general idea of the size of V, therefore, we cannot be sure that it will not change in any given year. This means that we cannot be certain what will be the effect of a change in the money stock on the demand for goods and services, i.e. PY, in any time period.

If V is constant an increase in the money stock, M, must lead to an increase in aggregate money demand. Aggregate money demand is the amount of money stock multiplied by the number of times each unit of money is used in a period of time. If V is constant we can see why governments might consider it important to control the stock of money. If aggregate money demand rises and the volume of output remains constant, or even if it increases but at a slower rate than the increase in aggregate demand, there will be an increase in prices. This is the same sort of reasoning that we used to show that an increase in investment which generates multiplier effects will have only income-multiplier effects when the economy is at the full employment level. There cannot be an output-and employment-multiplier effect because there are no unused resources, so neither employment nor output can rise. All the effects take place on income. If aggregate money demand rises because M is increased and V remains constant, and Y does not or cannot increase, all the effects of the rise in M must be felt on P.

However, even if an increase in M leads to an increase in aggregate monetary demand for goods and services, whether this will lead to an increase in P, the general price level, or in Y, the level of output represented by the number of transactions at constant prices, depends *not* on what has happened to aggregate demand, but on what happens on the supply side. It is the response of producers to the increase in aggregate money demand which determines whether P or Y responds to the increase in M.

As we have seen, if it is assumed that the economy always operates at the full employment level so that the level of output is fixed and constant, then an increase in M will lead to an increase in P. However, even if we define full employment to mean that every person between the age of 16 and 65 is working a certain number of hours a week and there is nobody unemployed, it is still probable that output will increase. There will be an increase in productivity or output-per-worker or per-worker-hour as a result of technological improvements and the replacement of old capital equipment by newer, more efficient capital equipment which, by incorporating new technological advances, leads to higher output per hour worked. It is customary to refer to this as an increase in output-per-worker even when the increase is the result of a rise in the efficiency or productivity of capital equipment.

Thus there can be an increase in M without an increase in P as long as the increase in M leads only to an increase in aggregate money demand equal to the rate of productivity growth. If this happens output, and Y, rise by the same percentage as the rise in productivity, which is equal to the growth in M. Average prices can remain the same. This means that improvements in productivity are not passed on in the form of lower prices.

If the stock of money is reduced, V remains constant and Y remains at its former level, prices must fall. This supposes that when the total aggregate money demand (MV) falls, producers continue to produce the same level of goods and services but sell them at a lower price so that the new level of prices times the old (and current) level of output equals the lower stock of money times the constant V. Producers can be expected to do this only if their costs fall, or if they do so in the short run as a means of obtaining some contribution towards their fixed costs. In the long run they would cease production and the level of output, and Y, would fall. This would break the assumption that output and Y are constant.

For producers to continue producing the same level of output when faced by a reduction in aggregate demand it would be necessary for their wage costs to fall. If M and P fall, so must $(1 \cdot a)(EW)$. If Y is constant we can assume E is constant, although an increase in productivity could allow Y to be constant with a lower E. If E is constant, either W or $(1 \cdot a)$ must fall. If $(1 \cdot a)$ falls, producers are accepting lower profits. They might expect W to fall in the future. If this happened it is conceivable that a reduction in M could lead to the same Y at lower P.

However, it is very difficult to obtain a reduction in wage costs by reducing money wages. It is rare that money wages per hour worked are reduced. Workers and their trade unions generally resist fiercely attempts to cut money wages. Individual workers not in a trade union often believe that it is unfair to expect them to have a wage cut. Some may be willing to do so if the alternative is to lose their job, but many would not.

An actual reduction in the money stock, rather than merely a reduction in its rate of growth, requires money wages and prices to be flexible downward if the quantity theory, with a constant V, is to be operative as part of economic policy. As we have seen, if V is not constant we cannot forecast what will happen as a result of changing M.

However, even if M is not reduced but only its rate of increase affected, we still cannot be sure that an increase in M will lead to rising P rather than an increase in Y. Earlier we defined full employment in terms of all members of the population between certain ages being at work. In reality this never occurs. Even in wartime, when massive efforts to mobilise all resources are made, there are always some people who could provide additional labour input. In normal times the concept of full employment is extremely difficult to translate into measurable quantities of labour supply. In fact we often refer to full employment by reference to the level of *unemployment*. If unemployment is low we conclude that we are approaching or even passing the full employment level.

There are many difficulties about measuring unemployment, however, so that this too is an uncertain statistic in so far as it is used to indicate the amount of labour that might be available on certain terms and conditions to provide additional labour input into the productive process.

In practice we cannot be sure whether an increase in aggregate monetary demand will lead to an increase in P, in Y or in both. Some monetarists claim that there is, as a matter of empirical evidence, a direct connection between changes in the money stock and the average level of prices. However, these studies have been seriously challenged, and on both empirical and theoretical grounds it is now believed that even if there is some sort of relationship, the time-lag between changes in M and the resulting effects on P is both long and variable. If it is variable it is never really clear that the observed increase in P is the result of some previous change in M. It could be the result of some other factors.

However, there is one further serious criticism of the quantity theory and of modern monetarism. In order to test the theory and, more importantly, to use it as a basis for economic policy, it is necessary to provide a definition of money which forms M.

Definitions of money

As we have seen in the discussion of how banks can create money, there are different forms of money. Notes and coins are obviously money in their country of issue. Banks' deposits at the central bank are also money because they can be converted into notes and coins at will and because they also form part of the cash base of the other banks. These, plus banks' till money, are known as M_0 or high-powered money which provides the cash base. Current accounts (or as they are sometimes called, sight deposits, because they can be withdrawn at sight or on demand) provide immediate access to cash. Adding these together gives us a measure of money M_1. Some of the different definitions of money and liquidity are shown in Table 14.1.

The amount of M_1 that will emerge from a given level of total bank deposits can vary. The less of our deposits we hold in sight or current accounts and the more in deposit accounts – on which we are required to give notice of withdrawal – the lower will be the level of M_1. All that will have happened will be that we have transferred some of our deposits at the bank from one sort of account into another, but because sight deposits are included in M_1 and time deposits are not, there will be a reduction in M_1.

Obviously, if there is much switching between different sorts of accounts in this way which does not reflect or cause a change in the number or level

Table 14.1. Definitions of money in the United Kingdom

	Notes and coins in circulation with the public
plus	banks' till money
plus	banks' deposits with the Bank of England
Equals	M_0 (wide monetary base)
plus	private sector sight deposits
Equals	M_1
plus	private sector sterling time bank deposits
plus	private sector sterling bank certificates of deposits
Equals	sterling $M_3 - £M_3$
plus	private sector foreign currency bank deposits
Equals	Total M_3
£M3	*minus* private sector sterling time deposits original maturity over two years
plus	private sector holdings of bank bills, Treasury bills, local authority deposits and certificates of deposits
Equals	PSL_1
plus	private sector building society deposits and national savings (excluding SAYE and longer-term deposits and shares)
minus	building society holdings of bank and Treasury bills, LA deposits and bank deposits
Equals	PSL_2

Source: Bank of England Quarterly Bulletin, February 1984

of transactions, the money stock as measured by M_1 will be appearing to change without there being any effect on aggregate demand. It is possible that if interest rates rise many of us will switch some of our assets from current or sight accounts to time deposits in order to earn the higher interest. We might be prepared to put up with the inconvenience this causes if interest rates are higher.

M_1 might not be a very good definition and measurement of money, therefore, because its quantity can change without there being any change in the level of economic activity or transactions. This is the same as saying that V, the velocity of circulation, has changed. However, M_1 has the advantage that it is a measure of narrow money. It includes only cash and sight deposits. If it is thought that it is this definition of money which is the crucial determinant of aggregate demand, then this is the one the money authorities should seek to control.

Broader money

There are other assets which are almost as good as money or, in some cases, as good as money in that they can be used to finance expenditure today. Time deposits are an example. Some financial institutions permit immediate withdrawals from time deposits and deduct interest for a number of days equivalent to the usual period of notice of withdrawal. These deposits are as available as sight deposits. If we add private sector sterling time deposits and other public sector sterling bank deposits we obtain a measure of broad money sterling M_3 or £M3. If we then include UK residents' deposits in foreign currencies we obtain M_3. M_3 is not quite as accessible as £M3 since there will be additional delays and costs involved in converting the foreign currency deposits into sterling.

We can get even broader definitions of money by including other assets which have become as accessible or almost as accessible as those included in £M3. For example, Private Sector Liquidity 2 (PLS_2) includes M_3 and also other assets such as building society deposits and short-term bills which, because they are very liquid, can easily be converted into cash.

In the United Kingdom there is now a considerable number of definitions and measurements. If government, in pursuit of economic policies based on some version of the quantity theory, wishes to control the money stock it has to decide which particular definition of money it is to control. For economic policy purposes it should control that definition of money which most strongly influences the aggregate level of demand. Monetary policies are intended to influence the level of demand or, sometimes, the rate of interest in order to attract foreign lenders rather than to raise the rate of interest in order to reduce the level of demand for money. However, if banks and individuals do not wish to see the money stock reduced they will use some form of money which is not subject to the tighter controls of the monetary authorities.

Thus almost as soon as a particular definition of money becomes used for control purposes by the monetary authorities, it tends to lose the importance which led the authorities to select it as the appropriate money definition to control in the first place. If there is any predictive content to the quantity theory it must be derived from observed relationships between changes in the money stock and average prices. This means that a particular definition of money has to be used to establish the relationship. However, 'Any observed statistical regularity will tend to collapse once pressure is placed on it for control purposes.' This is referred to as Goodhart's law, and brings out the problems of using any particular definition of money stock to control the rate of change of prices.

If the money stock, M, canot be controlled by the monetary authorities, then even if the quantity theory expresses economic relationships and is not merely a tautology, it provides little basis on which economic policy can be built.

CHAPTER 15

Is there a general theory?

Keynes believed he had provided a general theory of employment, interest and money. By a general theory we mean two things. First, it can be applied generally and not merely to a particular economy faced with a particular set of economic conditions. Second, it is general in that it incorporates all the main economic variables and shows how they are interrelated, so that changes in one variable affect the others. We have set out the main features of Keynes's theory in Chapters 10–14. We will now fit them together to see how they seek to provide a coherent and comprehensive explanation of macro-economic activity.

We can do this by setting out a few simple equations or explanations of the determinants of certain economic variables. The basic statement is as follows:

1. $C + I = C + S = Y$.

The determinants of each of the components of (1) are explained by the following:

2. $C = MPC(Y), r$; and $S = MPS(Y), r$;
3. $I = mec, r$;
4. $Y = k(I)$ where k is the multiplier;
5. $k = 1/MPS$;
6. $r = LP, M$;
7. $LP = LP_1(Y), LP_2(r)$.

If we assume that the economy is initially in a state of equilibrium and then assume a change in one of the variables, we can follow through the effects. The numbers in parentheses refer to the equations above.

Shift in the propensity to save

If the MPS (and therefore the APS) increases and this is unanticipated by producers, there will be two effects. First, there will be an increase in I as a result of an unplanned increase in stocks since Y, in the short run, will be unaffected and $C + I = C + S$ (2). Second, we should expect I and output of C to fall as producers revise their forecasts of future sales (3 and 4). The reduction in the level of Y will lead to a fall in the rate of interest since LP_1 will fall as income falls and we assume the money stock remains unaltered (6). The fall in the rate of interest may have some effect in increasing the level of investment, but the reduction in the level of C will reduce the mec so that the effects of the lower interest rate may be swamped by the reduction in mec (3). The economy will contract until planned I = planned S and the planned level of C by households equals the planned level of output of C by firms. The initial increase in S will not lead to higher I except temporarily through enforced I in stocks. Because C has fallen employers will be less likely to invest in either replacement or net I.

Increase in the money stock

Unless the economy is in the liquidity trap, an increase in M will lead to a fall in the rate of interest (6). This will lead to an increase in I (3). Income will rise (4) even though there is a fall in the multiplier since MPC diminishes as income rises (5). The higher level of income will increase the demand for money (LP_1), so there will be a rise in the rate of interest from the lower level which followed the increase in money stock (6). This will lead to some reduction in the level of I from its new higher level (3), with consequential adjustments to the size of the multiplier (5) and the level of Y (4). This will again affect the demand for money and the rate of interest through LP_1 (6). The adjustment process will continue with oscillations in r, I, Y and k, until a new position of equilibrium is reached. The extent of the oscillations and the final equilibrium position will depend on the effect of changes in r on I (the interest elasticity of investment), the MPC and LP_1.

At the end of the process income should be higher since I is higher. This should occur even if the MPC falls and so the multiplier becomes smaller unless the MPC becomes negative. At the higher level of Y both C and S (and I) will be higher than in the initial equilibrium position. The multiplier might also change as a result of the fall in the rate of interest. If the reduction in r leads to a decline in S as the opportunity cost of current consumption is reduced, the multiplier will increase. The converse will occur if the reduction in r leads to an increase in savings if people are saving in order to acquire a specified sum in the future. The lower rate of interest might have a greater effect on C through the wealth effect. When the market value of shares rise consumption may rise as well. Thus the processes by which an increase in the money stock affects the level of output and income result in an increase in the level of I and C, so raising the level aggregate of aggregate demand.

We illustrate this in Fig. 15.1. We start with a position of equilibrium, where the level of investment at various income and aggregate demand levels is shown by I_1, and the level of consumption by C_1. If these are added together they provide aggregate demand AD_1. Because we are assuming a position of equilibrium so that planned output and spending equal actual

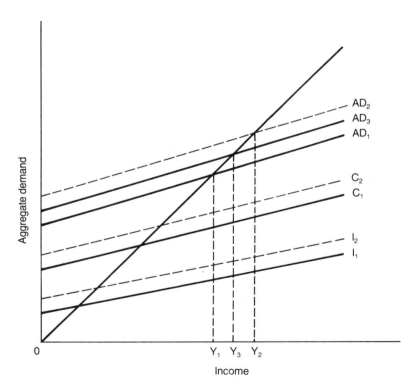

Fig. 15.1 Possibility of changing the level of aggregate income

income and output, the level of income and aggregate demand are equal. The level of income will be Y_1.

If the rate of interest falls as a result of an increase in the money stock there will be an increase in both I and C. I_1 will rise to I_2 and C_1 to C_2. The new level of aggregate demand will be AD_2 with a new, higher level of income Y_2. However, the higher level of income Y_2 will lead to a higher demand for money; LP_1 will rise, so there will be a subsequent rise in the rate of interest. This will cause I_2 and C_2, and therefore Y_2, to fall a little. The equilibrium position will be somewhere between Y_1 and Y_2. We have shown this as AD_3, with an equilibrium level of income at Y_3. For simplicity we have not shown I_3 and C_3 in the figure, but together these provide the total AD_3.

Effects of government spending

If government increases public spending this will have the same effect as an increase in I. There will be an increase in Y, and planned and actual S will rise to equal the new level of I (where I = investment in equipment, stocks, production of goods for export and government expenditure). If M remains fixed there will be an increase in r as Y rises (6). This will tend to reduce private investment (3). There will then be a fall in Y from its new higher level (4) and so a fall in the demand for money (7), leading in turn to a fall in the rate of interest (6). The ultimate equilibrium level of income, output and employment will be higher than before the government increased its expenditure but less than the higher levels which would have occurred if interest rates had not subsequently increased.

The effects are the same as illustrated in Fig. 15.1 although the causation is different. The increase in government expenditure increases aggregate demand from AD_1 to AD_2. The subsequent rise in interest rates affects I and C and leads to a decrease in aggregate demand from AD_2 to AD_3, with an equilibrium level of income at Y_3.

This consequential reduction in aggregate demand following an expansion of government investment is sometimes referred to as *crowding-out*. The argument is that some private sector activity is crowded-out as a result of the higher interest rates. This is really a form of pricing-out. Real crowding-out might be thought of as a reduction in private sector activity which results because increased government spending takes a larger share of the available physical resources and there are not enough of these available for the private sector to maintain its previous level of activity. If this happens there will be no increase in aggregate demand in real terms, merely a switching of activity from the private to the public sector. Real AD will remain at AD_1 and the real level of Y will remain at Y_1.

Some economists argue that most if not all of the increase in government expenditure will lead to the crowding-out of private sector activity. The extent of any crowding-out effects will depend essentially on two factors. First, there is the increase in aggregate demand that occurs as a result of increased government expenditure. This will be determined by the multiplier and the accelerator since the increase in income will induce additional investment which will itself have a multiplier effect. Second, there is the interest elasticity of private investment, which will depend on the mec and the extent of the rise in the rate of interest. The higher rate of interest makes some private investment unprofitable, while the higher level of income makes it more profitable.

IS–LM curve

It is possible to present the set of equations given at the beginning of this chapter in diagrammatic form. Basically, an equilibrium macro-economic position requires equilibrium in two different markets. There must be equilibrium in the product market. This is necessary to ensure that the planned output and planned expenditure on I and C are equal to the actual outputs and expenditures – requiring that planned and actual I equal planned and actual S. It is also necessary that the money market is in equilibrium so that the demand for money equals the money supply.

I–S or product market equilibrium

For each level of income there is one rate of interest at which planned I equals planned S; actual I will always equal actual S. We can connect these various combinations of interest rates and income levels at which planned I = planned S into an I–S schedule. The I–S schedule or curve will slope downward from left to right as in Fig. 15.2. This is because a higher rate of interest will provide equality between planned I and planned S only at a lower level of income. If the rate of interest rose and the level of income remained the same, so that aggregate demand was the same, planned I and planned S would no longer be equal. The higher rate of interest would lead to a reduction in planned I and to an increase in planned S. This cannot be an equilibrium position. A higher rate of interest can equate planned I and planned S therefore only if the level of income is lower. Both planned I and planned S will then be lower. Planned I will be lower because of the higher

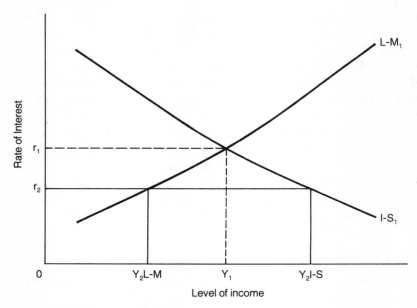

Fig. 15.2 IS–IM curve equilibrium

rate of interest and because the mec will have shifted to the left as a result of the lower level of income reducing firms' expectations of their future sales. Planned savings will be lower, even though the reward for saving and the opportunity cost of current consumption are higher, because the level of income is lower.

The I–S curve must slope downward from left to right therefore, but the steepness of the slope will depend on the interest elasticity of investment and savings (or consumption). If a change in interest rates has a large effect on aggregate demand, the I–S schedule or curve will be relatively flat so that a given change in r will lead to a relatively large change in Y. If changes in interest rates have only a slight effect on investment and consumption-saving decisions, the I–S curve will be relatively steep and changes in the rate of interest will not have much effect on Y or E.

L–M or money market equilibrium

We have also seen that for each level of income there is one rate of interest at which the demand for money will be equal to the money supply. As income rises the demand for money also rises for each rate of interest. This is the same as Keynes' LP_1 or the transactions demand for money. At each level of the rate of interest the demand for money will rise as income rises, and fall as income falls. If the quantity of money is given and unchanged, the demand for money as income rises can be brought into equality with the fixed supply of money only if interest rates are higher. Higher interest rates will reduce the higher demand for money that would occur at higher income levels with unchanged rates of interest. Thus to ensure that the aggregate demand for money does not rise, thereby getting out of line with the fixed money supply, it is necessary for interest rates to rise. This means that the L–M curve will slope upward from left to right, as shown in Fig. 15.2. If the rate of interest rose with a fixed money supply and income remained the same, demand for money would fall, thereby preventing equilibrium in the money market. If the money supply is fixed, a higher rate of interest can maintain equality between the demand for money and the fixed supply only if incomes are higher.

When the two curves, the I–S and L–M curves, are superimposed on each other we find the rate of interest and income level which provide equilibrium in both the product and money markets at the same time. This will be the equilibrium position for the economy.

Imagine that with the I–S and L–M curves shown in Fig. 15.2, the rate of interest were to fall from r_1 to r_2. The only levels of income at which an interest rate of r_2 could provide equilibrium in the money market is Y_2LM. However, the only level of income at which r_2 can provide equilibrium in the product market is Y_2IS, and this is a much higher level of income. Clearly, the level of income in an economy at any one time cannot be both Y_2LM and Y_2IS.

If the rate of interest were r_2 and income were Y_2LM, there would be an increase in investment. If income rose to provide the equilibrium income level Y_2IS there would be disequilibrium in the money markets. Demand for money would exceed the supply and interest rates would rise. This would reduce investment and lead to a reduction in income. Equilibrium would be restored at Y_1 with a rate of interest of r_1.

If the rate of interest were higher than r_1, the level of income would be too low, unless it was to the right of Y_1, to establish equality between the demand for and supply of money, and the I–S curve requires an income lower than Y_1 if interest rates are higher than r_1. There would be insufficient demand for money at an interest rate higher than r_1 to match the fixed supply. Interest rates would then fall to r_1.

The I–S and L–M curves therefore show us the only rate of interest consistent with a given income level which provides equilibrium in both the product and money markets.

The I–S curve can shift. Assume that firms become more optimistic about the future and revise upward their mec, or households may revise their consumption function upward or increase consumption because they believe there has been an increase in their permanent income. The I–S curve will then shift upward to the right. At each level of the rate of interest there would be an increase in aggregate demand so that equilibrium income would, for each rate of interest, increase.

With a given income level a change in the rate of interest would generate changes which caused the product market to move along the I–S curve for that level of income. A change in anything else, other than the rate of interest, which affects aggregate demand causes a shift in the I–S curve. It is the same principle as moving along a demand or supply curve and shifting the demand or supply curve. It is important not to confuse the movement along a curve with a shift in the curve.

The L–M curve can also shift. Each L–M curve represents the equilibrium positions for a given *real* money supply, i.e. the quantity of money in relation to the price of goods. The demand for money is assumed to be a real cash balances demand. This means that the amount of money we demand is influenced by the purchasing value of money, which is the same as its real value. This means that if money incomes and prices double, the demand for money will double as people choose to hold the same real cash balances. If the money supply rises by more than the increase in prices there will be an increase in real money supply. This will shift the L–M curve to the right.

Government fiscal and monetary policy

Let us assume that government increases its expenditure, say by an increase in public investment or expenditure on social security benefits. We will also assume that it finances this by issuing bonds which do not lead to any increase in the banking system's cash or liquidity bases and that there is no increase in the money supply. The higher government expenditure will increase aggregate demand and so shift the I–S schedule from IS_1 to IS_2 in Fig. 15.3. Because the quantity of money is unchanged the L–M curve remains at LM_1. The increase in aggregate demand leads to a higher level of income from Y_1 to Y_2 and a higher rate of interest from r_1 to r_2. The higher level of income will lead to increased employment if some of the multiplier effects are felt on output and employment. Any crowding-out effects are already incorporated in the new equilibrium level of income Y_2, since this is where the new IS_2 intersects with the LM_1 curve.

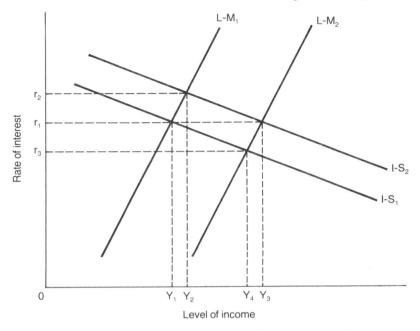

Fig. 15.3 Changes in I–S or I–M curves and adjustment to equilibrium

A similar effect can be obtained if the government increases the money supply. If, from an initial equilibrium position of r_1, Y_1, the government increases the money stock, the LM_1 curve will move to LM_2. With IS_1 unchanged this will lead to a reduction in the rate of interest to r_3, and an expansion of income to Y_4.

Government can therefore increase income from Y_1 to Y_2 either by fiscal policy – increasing government expenditure financed by issuing bonds, which does not affect the money supply – or by monetary policy through an increase in the supply of money. The latter requires that interest rates fall. This is the stimulus needed to increase aggregate demand.

With either approach there will be an increase in the equilibrium level of income. Whether there will also be a rise in the equilibrium level of employment will depend on whether the multiplier effects work only on income or whether the output and employment multiplier also operates. We shall consider this in more detail in the next two chapters.

By considering both the I–S and L–M curves together we can see that if the I–S curve is shifted as a result of increased government expenditure, there could be complete crowding-out only if the L–M curve were vertical.

As long as it slopes upward from left to right, no matter how steep the slope, there must be some expansion of income following an upward shift of the I–S curve. A vertical L–M curve requires that the demand for money is completely unaffected by the level of interest rates over the range of interest rates for which the L–M curve is vertical. For this to happen it would mean that an increase in income resulting from a rise in aggregate demand would lead to such an excess demand for money, given the fixed money supply, that no increase in interest rates could reduce the excess demand to bring it into equality with the fixed money supply. The rising interest rates would then reduce private investment and consumption by the total amount of the rise in government expenditure.

At the opposite extreme, the L–M curve may be horizontal. If there is a liquidity trap preventing the rate of interest from falling below some minimum level, the L–M curve will become horizontal at that level. If the rate of interest is already at this level, action by the government to increase income by increasing the money supply will have no effect on income. Shifting the I–S curve is then the only option open to a government which wishes to raise the level of income.

Whether we accept the complete general theory as put forward by Keynes, or whether we modify parts of it so that, for example, we give less importance to changes in the rate of interest leading to an increase in investment and more to their effects on consumption and savings, it remains the case that there are interconnections among the various economic variables so that some form of a general theory is required. The modifications may affect the slope of the I–S or L–M curves but not the general conclusions about the requirements for equilibrium.

Changes in any of the main economic variables will lead to a cycle of changes until a new equilibrium position is reached. Moreover, some changes which might not at first sight appear to be 'economic' can affect the economic variables. If there is a change in people's consumption and savings behaviour, the multiplier and aggregate demand will be affected. If the same aggregate level of income is received by a different composition of households we should expect changes in consumption and savings. Thus if there are more single-person households, both the propensity to consume and consumption patterns can be expected to change.

CHAPTER 16

Inflation and employment

We have seen that increases in income may lead to increases in output and employment, or merely to increases in money incomes and prices with output and employment remaining at the same level. It is obviously of great importance whether an increase in income has real or only monetary effects. If there are real effects, output and employment will rise.

We shall equate a rise in employment with a fall in unemployment so that $(E + U) = 1$. This, of course, may not be the case in the real world. Employment and unemployment may both rise, or both fall, in a given time period. If the population is growing, both E and U can rise together. Moreover, it is possible that an increase in employment actually induces more people to enter the labour force since they believe it is easier to find good jobs. This is referred to as the added-worker hypothesis. More jobs and higher employment encourage people who have not recently been employed or looking for work to enter or re-enter the labour force, and accept or look for a job. The converse is the discouraged-worker hypothesis. As jobs become more difficult to find, or wages fall and unemployment grows, some people stop looking for work. They come to the conclusion that it is not worth while looking because they are very unlikely to find a job, and the expense and effort of looking, or the sense of disappointment and failure they experience when rejected for a job, so discourage them that they withdraw from labour force participation.

The concept of unemployment is in fact quite a difficult one. We usually define someone as unemployed if they are not employed or self-employed, but are capable of work, willing to work and, perhaps, if they are also looking for work. We also generally limit our measurement of the unemployed to those people who satisfy these criteria and are between certain ages. Thus we would not regard children as unemployed even if they satisfy all the criteria. Also, we usually exclude people above a certain age, particularly if there are State-provided pensions.

These criteria, however, are sometimes very difficult to apply. We are not always sure who is capable of work. The only real test is whether an employer hires them, but then they are no longer unemployed. We may believe that someone is so untrained, weak, ill, or suffers from such physical or mental disabilities that he is incapable of work, and we cannot imagine any employer ever being willing to pay him wages. However, if product market conditions change so that even this person's marginal revenue product becomes equal to the wage which is offered and which he is willing to accept, he could become employed.

'Willing to work' is also an unclear criterion. Whether someone is willing to work may depend on the nature of the job offered and on the pay and conditions. I might be willing to work as a teacher for £100 a week but not willing to work as a coal-miner for £500 a week. Before we can say that someone is willing to work we have to specify the nature of the job, the type and amount of work-effort or effort-input required, the place of work, the times of work and the wages offered. Similarly, if we add the criterion of looking for work, we need to specify what sort of work, on what conditions, we will accept as reasonable before we can decide whether someone really is looking for work. If I say that I am looking for work as a professional football player at £1,000 a week, no one would take me seriously. I am too old and not a good enough football player.

It is necessary to exercise some element of judgement when deciding who is and who is not unemployed. This is because not everyone who is not employed or self-employed is regarded as unemployed. Some people are neither employed nor unemployed. They are not participants in the labour force. This may be because they have decided to spend their time raising their family or looking after the home, or because they have some means of support so that they do not wish or need to work.

Some people may be self-employed or engaged in cultivating family land. If jobs become plentiful and wages rise they may be capable of paid employment, willing to work and even looking for a job, but still regard themselves as self-employed rather than unemployed. If they found a job they would move from being self-employed to being employed but not appear as unemployed at all. If there is a State scheme for the payment of unemployment benefit, some people may claim to be unemployed in order to obtain the benefit and not really be looking for paid employment or, perhaps, not be willing to accept any of the offers of paid employment that are made to them.

In the real world, therefore, there are certainly three categories; employment, unemployment and non-participation in the labour force. We might sometimes also wish to add a fourth – self-employment. It is therefore a simplifying assumption to say that (E + U = 1). We make it so that we can refer to an increase in employment as being the same as a fall in unemployment and conversely, but we know that this is not necessarily the case. The assumption, therefore, not only ignores changes in labour force participation rates; it also ignores any demographic changes which mean that more or fewer young people are entering the labour market and more or fewer older people retiring from it.

Determinants of employment

As with most things in economics, it is helpful to start from the effects of demand and supply when considering the determination of the labour of employment. Demand will depend on the cost of labour to the employer and the MRP of labour. This follows the discussion in the early chapters and says that employers will hire labour when the cost of doing so, the MC of labour, is not more than the MRP of that labour. We can express this in terms of the *product real wage*. The product real wage is the relationship between wages – or really the total cost of labour including taxes, pension contributions and so on, as well as wages – and the price the employer expects to receive for the product of that labour. The concept therefore includes not only the cost of labour but also its MRP. It relates wages (taken henceforth as representing all the labour costs of employment) to the price of the products of that labour. Thus if there is a rise in the product real wage as a result of wages rising, the price of the products falling, or wages rising faster than the product prices are rising, we should expect to see a reduction in demand for labour.

The supply of labour, which can be expressed in terms of the trade-off between the utility obtained from receiving the wage-income and the disutility of undertaking the work-effort and giving up leisure, is usually regarded as being a function of the real wage. Thus if we want to know how much labour effort will be supplied at a wage of £50 a week we need to know the value of the £50 in terms of the goods and services it can buy. It is therefore the real wage level which attracts or fails to attract labour supply. For the worker, the appropriate price variable is not the price of the product he makes, as it is for the employer who hires him when he is assessing the product real wage, but the general level of prices of those goods and services which he buys or wishes to buy. Workers are therefore interested in the general level of prices in relation to their money wages, and their employers are interested in the price of their particular products in relation to their money wages.

If we assume that all prices rise together at the same rate, then changes in product real wages and changes in workers' real wages will be the same. We can illustrate the supply and demand conditions for labour as in Fig. 16.1. Each pair of demand and supply curves applies to one specific occupation or type of work in a given locality, and assumes that all other real wages are known and given. Thus, if Fig. 16.1 refers to bus drivers in a particular town, we conclude that at real wage W_1 demand and supply will be equal at a level of employment E_1.

If the employer wishes to recruit another bus driver he will have to raise real wages above W_1. This is because it is assumed that the labour market clears, so that at the existing level of real wages everyone who wants to work is employed at a wage at least equal to his labour supply price or his real reservation wage. The marginal worker represented by E_1 was not willing to work as a bus driver at a real wage lower than W_1. This is why the supply curve slopes upward; it indicates that in order to attract more bus

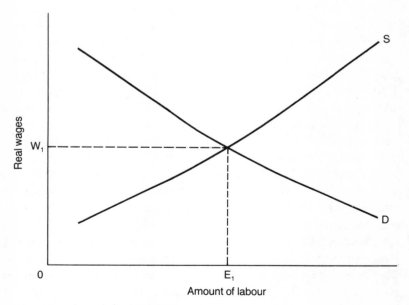

Fig. 16.1 Determinants of the level of employment

drivers it is necessary to increase the real wage. All the workers to the left of
E_1 would have been willing to work for a wage lower than W_1, as can be
seen from the supply curve. However, because all workers in the same
occupation, at least for the same employer, are assumed to receive the
same wage, they all receive W_1, the real wage necessary to induce worker
E_1 to accept employment. The intramarginal workers therefore receive
quasi-rent. If the employer's demand curve shifted to the right so that
additional workers were recruited and wages rose, worker E_1 would also
receive quasi-rent since he would no longer be the marginal worker.

The labour supply price or real reservation wage is the amount needed to
induce someone to offer his labour services to an employer; it is the lowest
real wage at which he is prepared to accept that job. It is called a reservation
wage because it acts in the same way as a reservation price at an auction. If
the price is not reached no sale or transaction takes place.

It is assumed therefore that at the prevailing level of real wages the
labour market clears, so that everyone who wishes to work at that wage is
employed and employers are able to obtain all the labour they demand at
that real wage. Those who are not employed are therefore either voluntarily unemployed because the prevailing real wages are below their real
reservation wages, or they are part of what is known as 'frictional'
unemployment in that they are in the process of moving from one job to
another. There will always be some frictional unemployment as people
change jobs. The analysis presented here however assumes that all the
others are voluntarily unemployed. They choose not to accept a job
because the level of real wages paid is lower than their real reservation
wage. To induce them to accept a job it is necessary for real wages to rise.

We might expect wages to rise more quickly when the level of employment increases or the level of unemployment falls. An increase in employment (equated to a decrease in unemployment) can be seen as an increase
in the demand for labour in relation to the supply; and wages, the price of
labour, ought to rise. In 1958 Professor Phillips produced an analysis which
appeared to show a close relationship between the rate of change of money
wages and the level of unemployment in the United Kingdom over many
years.

If product prices move with wages so that an increase in wages leads to a
rise in prices, any relationship between the level of unemployment and the
rate of change of wages will mean that there is also a relationship between
the level of unemployment and the rate of change of prices, or inflation.
Prices may not move by the same percentage as wages since improvements
in productivity or changes in the prices of imported materials and inputs

may lead to differing rates of change of wages and domestic prices. However, as long as the relationship between changes in wages and changes in prices remains the same, the Phillips curve, based on changes in money wages, can also be used to establish a relationship between the level of unemployment and inflation. Prices will rise more quickly as employment rises and unemployment falls, so that there will be a positive relationship between the level of employment and the rate of inflation, and an inverse relationship between inflation and the level of unemployment. This is illustrated in Fig. 16.2.

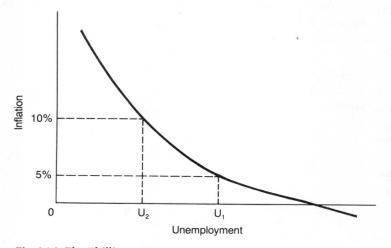

Fig. 16.2 The Phillips curve

In the 1960s it was believed that there was such a constant relationship in many countries, although the exact relationship, or the shape and slope of the curve, varied from country to country. This was important for policy-makers, for if there was a stable trade-off between unemployment and inflation, governments could have a relatively straightforward choice. They could choose less unemployment and more inflation, or less inflation and more unemployment. In Fig. 16.2 government could choose to have 5 per cent inflation and U_1 of unemployment, or reduce unemployment to U_2, but then accept an inflation rate of 10 per cent. However, the evidence turned against acceptance of the Phillips curve. If there had been steady relationships in the past they no longer appeared to hold.

However, this did not mean that economists concluded that there was no relationship between inflation and the level of employment or unemployment. The original Phillips curve was adapted into what is known as the expectations-augmented Phillips curve, which is an important part of the monetarist analysis and which is also accepted by some economists who are not monetarists.

It is called an 'expectations-augmented' Phillips curve because the expected rate of inflation is introduced and the analysis relates to real rather than money wages. There is a crucial difference from the original Phillips curve. The 'expectations-augmented' analysis is based, not on empirical observations as was Phillips' work, but on economic reasoning. It is assumed that wages rise more quickly the lower the level of unemployment, that workers base their decision to work or remain unemployed by looking at the level of real wages they expect to receive from work, and that the demand for labour is determined by the employers' expectations of future wage and price levels. From the supply side, or the workers' viewpoint, it is the expected real wages over the period of employment which is important; from the demand side, or employers' viewpoint, it is the expected product real wage level.

Figure 16.3 illustrates an expectations-augmented Phillips curve. The curve labelled 5 per cent shows the level of unemployment (or employment) which will result from any rate of inflation *when people expect the rate of inflation to be 5 per cent*. Thus if the rate of inflation is 5 per cent, and this is what employers and workers expect it to be in the future, the level of

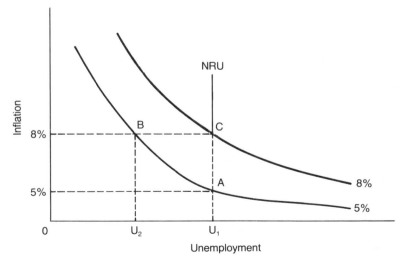

Fig. 16.3 Expectations-augmented Phillips curve and the natural rate of unemployment

unemployment will be U_1. We can also refer to this as the level of employment as we are assuming that $(E + U) = 1$. At employment level U_1 employers and workers expect prices to rise by 5 per cent per annum, and they rise at that rate. Employers are receiving the product real wage they expect and require, and workers are receiving the real wages they require to induce them to accept work.

It is now assumed that the government increases the quantity of money. Aggregate money demand rises and there is an increase in demand for goods. The level of demand facing employers will now be higher than they anticipated. Each employer now has to make a series of decisions. The first is whether the increased demand is an increase in real demand, or only an increase in money demand which will have no real effects. It is assumed that the employer believes that some of it at least is an increase in real demand. If he continues to expect the rate of inflation to be 5 per cent, presumably he should regard all of the extra demand as real demand, for if some of it were only an increase in nominal demand the rate of inflation could be expected to rise above 5 per cent – unless the increase in the money supply and its effects on prices had been taken into account when formulating the expectations of 5 per cent inflation.

Believing that there is an increase in real demand for his product, the employer now has to decide whether to meet that extra demand by increasing output or by raising prices with the same level of output. Because he believes it is an increase in real demand he will try to increase output to meet it. However, because it is an increase in real demand, he believes he can let his prices rise a little and still have an increase in the quantity demanded. Thus if inflation generally is 5 per cent, or he expects it to be 5 per cent, he may believe that he can increase his prices by 8 per cent and still increase the volume of his sales. He is therefore willing to let his prices increase by 8 per cent even though he still believes the general rate of inflation will be only 5 per cent.

If he wishes to increase his level of output it is assumed that he has to increase employment. To attract more workers he must increase real wages. He therefore raises wages and this has the effect of increasing the price of his products by 8 per cent. He will increase employment, and unemployment will fall to U_2 in Fig. 16.3. The equilibrium position moves from A to B in Fig. 16.3 with a lower level of unemployment (higher employment) and higher prices for the products of this firm.

It is important to emphasise the two stages in this process. The employer is able and willing to increase wages and see his prices rise because he believes that the general rate of inflation will continue to be 5 per cent, but that the demand for his product has risen so that even with an 8 per cent increase in his prices there will still be a higher level of real demand. The reason he actually increases his wages and therefore his prices is because he has to do this in order to attract more labour. If he could have recruited the extra workers at the existing wage levels he would presumably have done so to maximise his profits.

When he increases his wages by 8 per cent the unemployed, who are anticipating an inflation rate of only 5 per cent, believe that real wages have increased since money wages have risen by more than prices are expected to do. The 5 per cent curve in Fig. 16.3 is therefore essentially a short-run labour supply curve, for if extra workers had been willing to work for the prevailing wages – prevailing money and expected real wages – he would have been able to expand employment and reduce unemployment to U_2 without raising his money wages and increasing the price of his own products. The 5 per cent curve would therefore have been horizontal to the left.

Unemployment falls from U_1 to U_2 in the move from A to B, and prices rise by 8 per cent in this firm. However, it must also be assumed that many other firms are facing similar situations and making similar decisions. An increase in aggregate money demand will affect many of these firms. They too will be raising their wages and prices. In time, therefore, prices generally will rise not by 5 per cent but by 8 per cent. People will thus abandon the 5 per cent expected inflation curve and move to the 8 per cent expected inflation curve.

When this happens the employer will not need the extra workers since there will have been no increase in his real demand. Moreover, the extra workers will realise that the 8 per cent increase in money wages was not an increase in real wages because prices generally have also risen by 8 per cent. As real wages are now seen to be no higher than in the initial position, these additional workers will no longer be willing to work for the prevailing real wage and will choose to become voluntarily unemployed. The level of unemployment will therefore revert to U_1 with the rate of inflation at 8 per cent, as indicated by position C in Fig. 16.3.

Expectations will shift so that 8 per cent inflation is expected, and if the money supply continues at its present level a new equilibrium will be established with inflation of 8 per cent and unemployment back at U_1. Should the government again seek to reduce unemployment by increasing the money supply, the procedure will be the same as before. Firms will misinterpret the increase in aggregate demand and believe some of it is an increase in real demand. They will be prepared to increase money wages and prices because the increase in money wages will not lead to a rise in expected product real wages. Unemployed workers will misinterpret the increase in money wages as an increase in real wages and be prepared to accept the extra jobs. Unemployment will fall below U_1. However, as this will be happening to many firms prices will rise, there will be no long-term increase in real demand or real wages, and unemployment will revert to U_1.

In the long run, when employers and workers correctly interpret the signals and appreciate that prices generally will rise, the level of unemployment will be at U_1. This is the long-run level of unemployment and has come to be known as the Natural Rate of Unemployment (NRU). The long-run expectations-augmented Phillips curve is vertical at the level of the Natural Rate of Unemployment. It is not possible therefore for the government to increase the level of employment by increasing the money supply in the long run.

There may be an increase in employment in the short run but this will only lead to a higher rate of inflation and reversion to the Natural Rate of Unemployment. It is argued that the short-run gains occur only because employers and workers misunderstand the effects of an increase in the money supply. If they correctly appreciated that this would lead only to an increase in aggregate money demand and no increase in real demand, employers would not try to increase output and employment since they would realise that everyone else was doing the same, and workers would appreciate that the increase in the money supply would only increase money wages and prices with real wages remaining constant. The unemployed would not therefore be willing to accept the job offers because they would understand that real wages were not rising.

By this analysis monetarists conclude that the government can do nothing to lower unemployment by increasing the money supply. Such action will only increase the rate of inflation. This is the same conclusion that was reached by the quantity theory of money and the assumption that V was constant with output always at the full employment level – or, as we may now call it, the natural rate (or level) of output, employment or unemployment.

Criticisms of the expectations-augmented Phillips curve

The first criticism of this account of how the economy responds to an increase in the money supply is that it is not always necessary to increase employment in order to increase output. Firms may be able to expend output from existing•resources. This will lead to higher output but not necessarily to higher employment.

However, it does not follow that higher real wages are necessary in order to increase employment. This would be true only if the labour markets clear in real-wage terms, so that the unemployed are voluntarily unemployed, choosing not to work because the level of real wages offered is below their real reservation wages. Labour markets do not operate like markets for wheat or potatoes, where the forces of supply and demand may, in the absence of price support schemes or quotas, determine price in something approximating to the way in which perfect competition is supposed to work.

Labour markets are imperfect and there are various distortions from the perfect competition model. Trade unions may raise wages above their market level. This may mean that employment is lower than it would be, but it also means that wages are higher than market-clearing levels, and some unemployed people would be willing to work for the prevailing real wage levels. Increases in real wages might not therefore be necessary to induce unemployed workers to accept jobs. It might be enough merely to offer them jobs at existing real wages.

Indeed, it is possible that some of the unemployed would accept jobs at lower real wages. This is a situation explained by Keynes as demand-deficient unemployment.

Demand-deficient unemployment

Let us assume that at a given set of wage levels the product market is in equilibrium so that planned investment and savings are equal. If wages are set above market-clearing levels there will be some unemployed workers willing to accept jobs at prevailing wage levels, but insufficient demand in the economy for employers to offer them jobs. If product real wages were lower employers would offer more jobs. There are two basic ways in which product real wages can be reduced. Money wages can fall with product prices remaining constant or, if money wages remain constant, product prices can rise. Either method will also reduce real wages.

As we have said earlier, it is very difficult to cut money wages. Trade unions resist this fiercely, and individual workers often feel that their status is demeaned by a cut in money wages. If they are working as hard as they have in the past they do not see why they should receive less money. It is extremely difficult therefore to reduce real wages and product real wages by cutting money wages. However, the same result can be obtained by a rise in prices.

If an increase in the money supply leads to an increase in aggregate demand and output with some increase in prices, perhaps because employers are facing downward-sloping MPP curves, it might still be possible to recruit additional workers to produce extra output without an increase in money wages. Rather than having to increase real wages in order to recruit additional labour it could well be possible to recruit more workers even if real wages fell. If there is demand-deficient unemployment, therefore, it may be possible to reduce unemployment from U_1 to U_2 in Fig. 16.3 even though this will raise prices. Indeed, the rise in prices to reduce product real wages is a necessary condition for the increase in employment. An increase in employment might be associated with some lasting increase in prices rather than there being only a short-run trade-off. Action by the monetary authorities could therefore lower the level of unemployment and increase both employment and output.

This is the same sort of reasoning used in Chapter 15, which suggested that an increase in the money supply could raise aggregate demand, and this could lead to an increase in both prices and output. Or, put in terms of the quantity theory, an increase in M will lead to an increase in both P and Y. It will also lead to an increase in E. It need not lead to an increase in W, but this is because we have now abandoned the assumption that P and W move together, so that P is always a constant mark-up over W. This is the same as abandoning the assumption that if $MV = (EW) (1 \cdot a)$, a is a constant. We are in fact increasing a so that MV and PY can increase, as can E, but if W does not rise, EW will rise by less than MV or PY. This is merely a different way of saying that the product real wage has fallen, and we have seen that a reduction in the product real wage was necessary in order to induce employers to increase output and employment.

Far from government being unable to affect the level of employment/unemployment by monetary policy, it may be possible to increase employment by increasing the money supply in conditions of demand-deficient unemployment. Any other measures which governments can take to reduce the real wage and decrease the product real wage can have the same effect. Incomes policies, depending on their content, may be one way of doing this, although incomes policies do not necessarily have to lead to a reduction in real wages.

The Natural Rate of Unemployment (NRU)

Even if the account set out in the expectations-augmented Phillips curve is accepted, it does not follow that government cannot influence the level of unemployment. All that particular piece of theory says is that governments cannot influence the level of unemployment in the long run by increasing the money supply, and can reduce unemployment in the short run only at the price of increasing inflation. There may still be a range of measures open to governments to influence the Natural Rate of Unemployment and thus the level of employment and unemployment.

The NRU is the rate of employment or unemployment at which the economy will settle in the long run. At this level of employment, output and demand, the actual rate of inflation will be the same as the expected rate of inflation for, as we have seen in the examination of the expectations-augmented Phillips curve, if actual and expected inflation are different, producers or workers will revise their plans when they discover that their expectations of product real wages or real wages have not been met. It is only if the actual rate of inflation equals the expected rate of inflation that an equilibrium position will be maintained. The NRU is therefore the level of output, employment and unemployment at which expectations of future rates of inflation equal the actual rate of inflation which occurs. This is usually taken to be the same as a constant rate of inflation. *It does not mean zero inflation.* Unemployment level U_1 was an equilibrium position in Fig. 16.3 as long as everyone expected 5 per cent inflation.

It is important to emphasise that the term natural rate of unemployment does not mean that there is anything natural or 'proper' about it. It is merely a term to signify the level of employment consistent with a constant rate of inflation. Because the word 'natural' might have some association with laws, or rules of nature, and because the analysis which uses the NRU seems to rest heavily on the assumption that labour markets always clear, a new term and concept has been introduced to express a similar notion.

The non-accelerating inflation rate of unemployment (NAIRU) is the level of unemployment at which the rate of inflation remains constant. It neither accelerates nor decelerates. Provided that we remember that NAIRU, while very similar to the NRU, does not require the assumption that labour markets always, or ever, clear, so that there can be demand-deficient unemployment and some of the unemployed may be willing to work for existing wage levels or even less if jobs were offered, we can use the NRU to cover NAIRU as well.

Changing the NRU

The NRU or NAIRU is the level of employment consistent with the expectations of producers and workers regarding future wage and price levels being met. Emphasis is given to the expected and actual rates of inflation because it is assumed that the existing position is an equilibrium one, and that the factors which established the existing equilibrium will continue. For example, workers determine the supply of labour by their real reservation wages and employers establish the demand for labour by their product real wages. If workers were to reduce their real reservation wages so that they would work for lower real wages, employment and output could rise since employers would be able to expand employment when product real wages fell.

Monetarists argue that there are two main factors raising real reservation wages above their 'true' market level, or above the level they could be at. First, trade unions are able at certain times, if not always, to raise real wages of their members. Minimum wage laws or wages councils might have similar effects. Second, the existence of State-provided unemployment and social security benefits creates a floor of minimum income. It is necessary to pay wages higher than this floor in order to induce the unemployed to accept the disutility of work.

The combination of these two factors, it is argued, creates a situation where trade unions increase wages in the unionised sector of the economy. Some of the workers who would like to obtain jobs at these higher wages are unable to do so; the supply of labour at this higher level of wages exceeds demand and so they look for work in the non-unionised sector. If there were no unemployment benefits, wages in the non-unionised sector would be driven down by the excess supply of labour to that sector until everyone who wanted a job at the prevailing wages was able to get one. However, because of the floor of unemployment benefit, wages in the non-unionised sector do not fall sufficiently to absorb all the unemployed. The level of unemployment is therefore higher than it need be, and the NRU and NAIRU are higher than they need be, because wages, money wages and real wages are higher than they would be in a 'free' market due to the existence of trade unions and State unemployment benefits.

Two obvious measures to reduce the NRU which appear to follow from this analysis are the weakening of trade unions so that they are unable to raise wages above their 'market' level, or are able to do so to a lesser extent, and a reduction in the level of State unemployment benefits. Both of these might lead to a reduction in wage levels and an increase in employment. Reducing or abolishing statutory minimum wages might have the same effect.

Against this it can be argued that while there may be some unemployed workers who are voluntarily unemployed, choosing not to accept a job because the wage is insufficiently high in relation to unemployment and social security benefits, there are many others in employment who would be as well, or better off, unemployed. Many people work for wages which are not much higher than the amount they could receive if unemployed. The decision to work or be voluntarily unemployed does not seem to be as coldly calculating as the monetarist argument supposes. In economic terms, many people appear to obtain greater utility or satisfaction from income obtained from work than they do from the same amount of income received from the State for not working. There may be some for whom the position is reversed, but the view that it is right and proper that we should work seems to be widely accepted.

It may be that trade unions increase wages above the levels which would obtain in their absence. This is one of the purposes of trade unions. It is a political as well as an economic judgement whether the weakening of trade unions is desirable in a democratic society. However, measures to weaken trade unions can be regarded as attempts to lower the collective reservation wage in the same way that reducing unemployment benefits seeks to lower the individual's reservation wage.

Any measures or changes in people's views which lead to a reduction in their reservation wages and in the level of wages they are prepared to accept for working, will lead to an increased demand for labour, provided that the employers' estimates of the demand for their products are not adversely affected by the reduction in wages. If the reduction in wages, even though accompanied by an initial increase in employment, leads to a fall in aggregate demand, the end result may be a fall in total employment and a rise in the NRU to a higher level. As we saw earlier, wages are costs to employers but income to households, and if wages are reduced there will be a reduction in household income. More households may receive income as extra workers are employed, but it is the combined effect of the two contradictory pressures which will determine the net change in aggregate demand. Reducing real wages could merely increase demand-deficient unemployment.

However, if lower wage costs and lower product real wages lead to improved competitiveness in international markets, it may be that employment will rise as exports increase. In this case exports can replace, and exceed, any reduction in demand from the domestic market which may follow the reduction in wages.

If we accept some of the monetarist account of the development of employment and inflation following an increase in the money supply, as set out at the beginning of this chapter, it does not mean that we must necessarily accept its conclusions. Let us for example assume that the economy responds to an increase in the money supply as explained by Fig. 16.3, so that employment rises (unemployment falls from U_1 to U_2). The rate of inflation is now 8 per cent instead of the expected 5 per cent. It is then assumed that prices and wages will be increased to restore their previous real levels so that both prices and wages rise by 8 per cent. This is necessary, it is argued, in order to restore real wages and this must be done to maintain the original demand for and supply of labour.

However, it is possible that workers will accept a reduction in real wages (prices rise by a further 8 per cent and wages by less than this) in order to maintain their jobs. Even if their real reservation wages before they accepted the extra jobs were such that higher real wages had to be paid to induce them to accept the jobs, it does not follow that they will keep those higher real reservation wages once they are employed. They may prefer to keep their jobs and accept lower real wages. We do not know, but we should be careful before assuming that workers always maintain constant real reservation wages. They may well be willing to accept a reduction in real wages in order to keep their jobs. If they do this, employment can remain at U_2.

In addition to voluntary unemployment there will also be some frictional unemployment consisting of people in the process of changing jobs. Some of them will have left their previous job to look for a new one. During the time they are looking for another job they will be counted as unemployed and so included in the NRU. If it is possible to reduce the time needed to find another job, the NRU can be reduced. Any measures which lower frictional unemployment will lower the NRU. Measures to improve the working of the labour market by improving the flow and amount of information about jobs and vacancies, and provisions to help the unemployed find jobs more quickly through employment exchanges, will lower the NRU.

There will be vacancies for some sorts of jobs for which there may not be enough trained people. Measures to reduce the mismatch between the skills of the unemployed and the skills required by employers will reduce the NRU, and may also lead to lower wage increases since there will be a lower level of excess demand for these occupations. In the same way, geographical mismatch or imbalances between the unemployed and vacancies can lead to a higher level of unemployment. An active manpower policy and improved training facilities may lower the NRU and reduce the rate of wage increase.

While, in a strict monetarist analysis, it may not be possible for government to influence the level of unemployment by changing the money supply – and this has been challenged by Keynesian and other arguments such as that of demand-deficient unemployment – it may still be possible for government to influence the level of unemployment and inflation by other means. Some measures may reduce the NRU, and some may reduce the rate of wage increase which affects the rate of inflation. Even if the strict monetarist position is accepted, therefore, it does not mean that the government is unable to influence the level of unemployment or the rate of inflation.

CHAPTER 17

Government policies

In the previous chapter we discussed possible ways in which government can shift the NRU or NAIRU. This would allow it to influence the level of employment/unemployment. In Chapter 15 we looked at how government expenditure may increase aggregate demand and employment, and how monetary policy may lead to an expansion of output and employment. Both of these approaches may also increase the rate of inflation. Monetarists believe that an increase in the money supply will, in the long run, affect only the rate of inflation, but we have considered criticisms of this argument. In this chapter we will draw together the various possibilities for government intervention and consider different sorts of policy options. We will continue to concentrate on domestic economic developments. International trade and foreign activities will be considered in the following three chapters.

Demand management

Demand management is the use by government of fiscal and monetary policies to influence the level of income and economic activity. Fiscal policy is the combination of taxation and government expenditure decisions. Monetary policy is the collection of decisions affecting the money supply and the rate of interest.

Recalling the discussion in Chapter 15 we can see that fiscal policy affects the I–S curve and monetary policy the L–M curve. Fiscal policy determines the PSBR but the method by which the PSBR will be financed – by expanding the money supply by increasing the banks' cash base, or by selling bonds and borrowing from the private sector – is determined by the monetary policy adopted by government. Fiscal and monetary policies may be independent or interdependent.

Let us assume that the economy is at income level Y_1 in Fig. 17.1, with IS_1 and LM_1. Government believes this level is too low and seeks to increase it to Y_2. It may shift the I–S curve upward to IS_2 by increasing government expenditure. It can do this by introducing an expansionary fiscal policy which increases government expenditure, and/or reduces taxes to stimulate private spending. If monetary policy remains the same as before, with LM_1, there will be no increase in the money supply, and interest rates will rise from r_1 to r_2 as a result of the higher transactions demand for money as incomes rise. If government wishes income to be no higher than Y_2, the higher rate of interest r_2 is also necessary to restrict private sector spending to the appropriate level. If government has increased its expenditure there will be some crowding-out when interest rates rise, so the composition of aggregate demand will have changed as

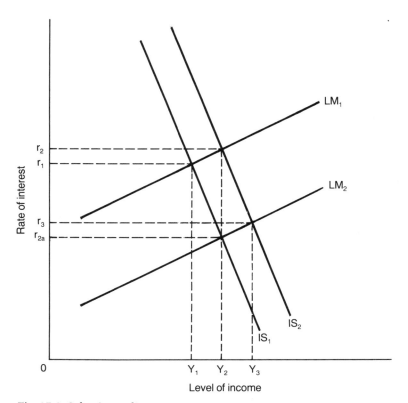

Fig. 17.1 Selecting policy measures

well as its absolute level. Expansionary fiscal policy with the same monetary policy leads to an increase in the government share of total economic activity.

Government could have induced an increase in income to Y_2 by maintaining its fiscal policy intact and adopting an expansionary monetary policy. If the quantity of money were increased to LM_2 and the I–S curve kept at IS_1, the new equilibrium level would be Y_2 with a lower rate of interest r_2a. The lower interest rate which was necessary to induce people to demand the larger amount of money would encourage investment and consumption expenditure by the private sector. There would be no crowding-out so the composition of total aggregate demand would move towards the private sector.

If government had adopted both expansionary fiscal and monetary policies by IS_2 and LM_2, income would increase to Y_3 with interest rate r_3. Income would then be even higher. However, it may be that government believed that the increase from Y_1 to Y_2 could take place without generating much inflationary pressure so that most of the increase in income was an increase in real income, output and employment; Y_2 may be the NRU or NAIRU. Any expansion of income beyond Y_2 may be regarded as leading only to an increase in money income with no additional real output or employment gains. Beyond Y_2 any increase in the money supply is seen as leading only to higher prices rather than to an increase in the real money supply.

In terms of the quantity theory, expansion from Y_1 to Y_2 is seen as affecting Y and E, with perhaps some slight effect on P and W. Expansion beyond Y_2 is seen as affecting only P and W. Government would therefore choose some combination of fiscal and monetary policies which expanded income from Y_1 but only to the level of Y_2. The range of combinations of fiscal and monetary policies which can achieve this growth of income is set by the movement of IS_1 to IS_2 and of LM_1 to LM_2. The first represents a policy based totally on fiscal measures, with the second totally based on monetary policy. It is open to government to choose any combination between these two extremes, so that fiscal policy could lead to a shift of the I–S curve but not as far as IS_2. It would then be necessary to shift the LM_1 curve until it intersected the new I–S curve at income level Y_2, but this would not require expansion as far as LM_2, once IS_1 has been shifted any distance to the right.

The mixture of fiscal and monetary policies adopted will depend on political as well as economic criteria. Governments may have different views about the desirability as well as the micro-level effects of increasing taxation. It may be thought that higher taxes will act as a disincentive.

Balanced budget multiplier

In our discussion of the multiplier in Chapter 12 we explained that government expenditure had the same effect as investment in generating a multiplier effect, and that taxation had the same effect as savings in reducing the size of the multiplier, by reducing the amount of income that is passed on through consumption as higher demand for the products of others. It might be thought therefore that an increase in government expenditure financed by an exactly equal increase in taxation would have no net effect on aggregate income. However, this may not be the case.

If government increases its expenditure by £1m and increases income tax by £1m, there will be two effects. The £1m of government expenditure will lead to an increase in aggregate demand of that amount. Higher taxes of £1m will reduce disposable income, i.e. income after tax and benefits. However, if the MPC out of disposable income is less than 1, total consumption will not fall by £1m but by (MPC)·£1m. The reduction in total consumption expenditure will therefore be less than £1m, so that even with a balanced budget where government expenditure is matched by higher taxes, an increase in government expenditure and taxation will still lead to an increase in aggregate income. The increase will not be as large as the rise in government expenditure because there will be some reduction in consumption following the tax increases, but there will be an increase.

Demand management policies, as we have seen, consist of a mixture of fiscal and monetary measures. For a number of years after 1945 British governments gave more importance to fiscal policy than to monetary policy. The more recent revival of monetarism has shifted the emphasis. We have noted that the policy mix may depend on other economic and political objectives of government. Fiscal policy works more quickly and directly. Monetary policy has its main effects through interest rates, and expansionary policies require that producers are optimistic about future sales. If they are not they will be disinclined to increase investment. Fiscal policy can generate an immediate increase in demand. This may still require producers to be optimistic that the demand will continue in the future before they decide to invest, but it may be more effective in generating confidence.

Inflation or real growth?

A crucial question is whether a higher level of income leads to a higher level of output and employment, so that it is a higher real income, or merely to an increase in prices. As we have also seen, we cannot be sure in advance whether an expansion of aggregate demand will affect only, or mainly, P and W, or Y and E. This uncertainty may affect not only government's choice of fiscal or monetary policy, if it believes that one is more likely to affect real growth than the other, but also, perhaps more importantly, its decision whether to try to generate an expansion of income at all.

In Fig. 17.1 we assumed that government believed it could expand income from Y_1 to Y_2 without generating much additional inflationary pressure, but that beyond Y_2 further expansion would be only in money terms with no increase in real output and employment. If government believed that any expansion beyond Y_1 would generate only inflationary pressures it would not embark on an expansion to Y_2. Its main concern would be to maintain income at Y_1. We have seen that the level of output and income where inflation begins to rise is the NRU or NAIRU.

Government may seek to introduce structural changes in the economy, or changes in attitudes and behaviour, which will lower the NRU (as we discussed in Chapter 16), but demand management policies will be aimed primarily at maintaining the level of income at the NRU. When assessing the possibilities for, and desirability of, expanding aggregate income, it becomes important to have a view about how wages and real wages, and therefore product real wages, are determined. If money wages rise faster than the rate of productivity growth there will be either a rise in product real wages if profits are squeezed, or inflation, so that the money wage increases do not lead to increases in real wages. If real wages rise faster than productivity, and product real wages rise, there will be a reduction in employment in the private sector as employers cut back production in response to the increase in product real wages.

Trade unions and wages

We should accept as a starting proposition that one of the purposes or objectives of trade unions is to increase the standard of living of their members. This means they seek to increase their members' real wages. Of course, they also wish to protect the jobs of their members so they do not push real wages up to the point where large numbers of their members are dismissed. This may mean that employment is lower than it would otherwise be, but the unemployed may not be union members, and so their interests are not served in the same way as are members' interests. At the same time there may be situations when trade unions and their members are much concerned to preserve employment so that the unemployed, who may be relatives, are able to get jobs. This will act as a restraint on their pressure to increase real wages.

Trade unions often place a great deal of importance on comparability. They believe that if other workers, particularly other workers with comparable skills and training, are receiving higher wages, their members should also receive higher wages. They also often seek to maintain, on their part, traditional pay differentials over less skilled workers. The less skilled on their part may seek to reduce pay differentials. Many individuals, whether in unions or not, also believe that comparability represents fairness. If others have received a pay increase they ought to receive one too. Fairness is very important in pay determination and in determining reservation wages. The amount we expect to receive for doing a particular job may be much influenced by what we think is fair. Economic analysis may try to explain that wages are determined by, or related to, the MRP of workers, but that does not stop people from having notions of fairness about their wage levels.

If other people doing the same sort of work as we do are getting higher pay we often believe we should get the same. Our employer may tell us that he cannot afford to pay but often we look not at the MRP of our labour, that is the value of the product or service that we produce, but at the effort-input required from us. We want to be paid for what we do; the employer determines how much he can pay us on the basis of what he can sell the product of our labour for. There may therefore be differences in the way the two sides of the labour market look at pay and fairness. Workers see fairness in relation to effort-input and employers see fairness in relation to MRP and product market conditions. Most of us do not know the value of our MRP, and many in the public sector do not have one; their product is not sold but provided free by the government.

While trade unions may seek to increase wages above their 'market' level, individual workers not in unions do not necessarily accept the outcome of 'market' forces. They too may seek to obtain higher wages on the basis of comparability or fairness.

However, as we discussed in Chapter 16, governments may seek to reduce the power of trade unions to increase real wages. They may try to do this by legislation which limits the ability of trade unions to take strike or other industrial action in support of their wage claims. They may also introduce incomes policy.

Often governments introduce both a prices and incomes policy, which is intended to impose restraints on the rate of change of prices and incomes.

We shall concentrate on the incomes side, not because price restraint is unimportant – indeed, without price restraint it may be impossible to persuade trade unions and their members to accept the incomes side of the policy – but because in the context of this discussion incomes are the more important.

Reducing inflation

Governments can seek to restrain the growth in incomes by demand management policies, as we have discussed. They may also seek to reduce inflationary pressure by improving the way in which the economy functions. All markets, but especially the labour markets, have distortions, which means that they do not work as smoothly and efficiently as economic theory sometimes suggests. For example, there may be mismatches in the occupational composition of labour supply and demand. The skills required by employers to fill their job vacancies may differ from those possessed by unemployed workers. Labour market forces can deal with this. Wages for those occupations in short supply can rise and this will induce some people to undertake the training necessary to acquire the skills. Supply will then increase. The higher wage level will also reduce some of the demand so that a smaller increase in supply will be needed. However, this can take a long time and the increase in wages of this occupation may lead to wage increases for others if comparability influences wages. This increases inflation. Government therefore may introduce and finance training schemes to help the market adjust and respond more quickly.

Similarly, while there are geographical mismatches, government may help the unemployed move from one part of the country to another where there is a labour shortage by providing removal grants or assistance with housing.

An alternative, which we shall consider later in this chapter, is for government to encourage firms to move to areas of high unemployment rather than expand in areas of labour shortage. Expansion in the labour shortage areas could increase wages if labour demand exceeds labour supply, and this could lead to higher wages elsewhere through pressure for comparability. Employment in areas of high unemployment could expand with less upward wage pressure.

On the product market side, measures to reduce monopoly and restrictive trade practices can lead to lower prices or lower rates of increase in prices.

These structural changes or improvements may make some contribution to reducing inflationary pressures and unemployment. They have the same effect as lowering the NRU.

Incomes policies

However, these policies may be insufficient to provide the level of output desired by government. Measures to contain inflation by a restrictive monetary policy may lead to a lower level of income than is desired. Government may therefore seek to persuade or induce those responsible for making pay and price decisions to make decisions which are different from those they would normally take in the prevailing economic conditions. They may seek to persuade pay bargainers to settle for lower pay increases than they would otherwise do, given the level of aggregate money demand. It might always be possible to get lower wage increases by reducing the level of aggregate demand, but government may believe this would also lower the level of employment and this they may not wish to do. They therefore seek to change economic behaviour.

They may do this by persuasion, seeking the co-operation of trade unions and employers, or they may use legislation which restricts pay increases to specified amounts.

Certain features of incomes policies should be noted from the outset. First, there is an assumption that those responsible for pay decisions are pay-makers and not pay-takers. If it is believed that pay levels are determined only by economic market forces, there is little point in trying to persuade people to settle for less than the market determines. This would merely mean that wages would rise, and those who paid less than the market rate would lose their workers to other employers. A government introducing an incomes policy must believe that at least some elements of wage increases result from institutional factors which are capable of, or amenable to, change.

Second, it must be believed that the effects of inducing the change in behaviour will lead to higher employment and output. If it is thought that it would lead only to a reduction in aggregate demand and lower investment with a fall in output and employment, the government should not advocate it. Other measures could achieve this result more easily and trade unions are unlikely to co-operate with a policy intended to reduce income and employment.

Third, it must be believed that the parties to pay determination are willing to co-operate, or that they can be induced or made to do so by legislation. It can be very difficult to enforce pay restraint on unwilling unions and employers in the private sector. In the public sector the employing authorities are under much more direct government control. In the private sector, if employers and unions or workers collude to evade the controls, it can be very difficult for government to do much about it. Pay increases can often be disguised as productivity or piece-work payments, or jobs can be regraded and 'phoney' promotions given to justify a pay rise. Some element of co-operation from at least one of the parties to pay determination is probably required for an incomes policy to be effectively imposed.

There is considerable disagreement among economists as to whether incomes policies have been or can be effective for long. There is more agreement that they can operate for a time, but some then argue that they inevitably lead to a wage explosion so that wages finish up as high as they would have been without the restraints. Others are less sure, and believe that if the policy content is right, it may be possible to operate an incomes policy for a long period. They also argue that even if incomes policy does no more than delay the increase in pay, this can be very advantageous. The slowing down, or deferring in time, of pay increases may reduce inflation-ary pressures for a while and this may be important.

Incomes policies may also seek to redistribute income by permitting higher wage increases to some groups, for example the low-paid. This will change pay differentials. They may also seek to change pay differentials as a result of productivity changes. Higher increases may be permitted to those who increase their productivity by changing their working practices or by increasing their effort-input. Without an incomes policy the pressures of comparability may mean that if one group of workers increase their effort-input and obtain higher wages, other groups will press for similar increases even though they have not changed their effort-input.

Incomes policy is seen by some as a necessary supplement to demand management policies if government is to maintain a higher level of employment. They believe that the pressures from trade unions for higher real wages will lead to too much inflationary pressure when employment is high. This is a different way of saying that the NAIRU is high in an economy with developed and strong trade unions, and an incomes policy can lower the NAIRU by reducing the upward pressure on wages. It does not mean that real wages will not rise, but that they will do so with lower rates of increase in money wages. This will reduce the general level of inflation.

Regional policies

All economies contain disparities in employment and income levels among different regions. They all have some areas which are relatively prosperous and some which are relatively poorer. The market system does not lead to equality of income and employment opportunities throughout an economy. This may be because some factors of production, possibly even all factors, are less mobile than may be assumed in economic theory. Labour is often reluctant to move to other areas, and when it does wages may not fall sufficiently to absorb all the unemployed. Capital may also be less than perfectly mobile.

Physical capital, represented by plant and equipment, is not spread evenly throughout the economy and we should not expect it to be. Plant and equipment will be located according to the relative costs of production, so that access to raw materials and product markets may influence the locational decision. In other cases location is influenced by the availability of a skilled labour force. Placing the plant in a different locality could lead to much higher production, distribution or labour costs.

However, there may also be some rigidities or distortions in the allocation of plant and equipment. Decisions in a multi-plant company may be influenced by the location of the head offices, so that research departments may be placed near to the head office even though costs are higher. Senior managers may be reluctant to move to certain areas of a country, and may have misconceptions about what it would be like to work and live there. Wives of senior or middle managers may not wish to live in certain areas and this may influence management decisions. Few decision-makers are completely cold total profit-maximisers. Even if they are, it could be argued that to locate in an unpopular area would affect morale and productivity and the ability to recruit and retain good people, and so would not be a profit-maximising decision. It is almost always possible in economics to argue that something is or is not profit-maximising if you make the right assumptions.

Regional imbalances in income and employment can be tackled in two main ways. Measures can be introduced to induce workers to move to the jobs, or jobs to move to the workers. Either approach involves intervening in the established market processes and practices but, as we have already discussed, the existing institutions, processes and practices do not represent 'pure' economic or market forces; even if they did, it is always open to government and society to decide that they do not wish the economy to be entirely dependent on the outcome of market forces.

Measures to induce workers to move to areas of higher economic activity can reduce labour shortages in the receiving areas, but they can also create additional shortages. An inflow of workers will lead to a higher demand for housing, schools, hospitals, transport facilities, shops, amusement and entertainment. There will be an increase in the demand for labour to supply these extra requirements. In the short run this could lead to an even greater shortage of labour than existed initially. There will also be pressure for increased government expenditure to provide the higher level of public services that will be needed.

At the same time there may be under-utilisation, or waste, of houses and services in the areas from which the labour came. Government may have spent considerable amounts on providing infrastructure which will now be wasted. Moreover, since it is likely that the migrants will be the younger and more active members of that region, there will be a shift in the composition of the population. It will have a higher proportion of older people. The area will be a less attractive location for future employers since it will have lost a part of its active workforce. There could be a downward cycle of economic activity.

Policies designed to change the location of investment and production might appear to avoid these problems. They do not lead to increased demand for housing and a wide range of additional services in the expanding areas. This moderates the inflationary pressure which would otherwise occur there. They allow the existing infrastructures and services in the areas of high unemployment to be more fully utilised. However, they require firms to make decisions which are not those they would otherwise have made.

This may be achieved by giving special allowances and grants to firms investing in specified areas. These may be investment allowances, tax rebates or exemptions, specially subsidised premises, or free training of labour. The intention is to alter the cost of investment in the special areas. This has the same effect as reducing the rate of interest or increasing the mec. It is hoped that by changing the relative costs of investing in one area in relation to another, firms will change the location of their investment. Sometimes this is reinforced by the imposition of controls on investment or expansion in certain areas. If the firm is prevented from expanding in some areas it may be more likely to invest in others.

The extent to which inducements will attract firms in the special areas depends on the size and type of inducement and on the reasons why the firms chose not to invest there in the first place. If a firm's investment and production decisions are strongly influenced by access to raw materials, it might require very large subsidies to induce it to locate elsewhere where it will face not only higher transport costs, but also greater distance from its supplies and therefore greater uncertainty about future deliveries. This will also apply if closeness to product markets is important. Much may depend on the relative importance of transport costs to total costs of production and distribution. The firm may be more influenced by the availability of a suitable workforce. For many products, transport costs are less important than they once might have been.

Some services have to be located very close to the customer. It would make little sense to centralise all hairdressers in one large shop in the middle of the country. However, some services can be relocated with few adverse effects. This is particularly true of government services where contact with the public is by post, such as the issuing of driving licences or passports. It also applies to some private sector activities such as the clearing office for credit or bankers' cards, where accounts are issued by post and payment made by post or at one of the many branches of the bank.

The general approach in the United Kingdom has been to encourage investment in special areas by influencing the location of new activity. At the same time there has been a considerable amount of interregional migration, and this has been in both directions. People move into, as well as out of, special areas. It is the net migration which leads to a reduction in population and possible under-utilisation of infrastructures.

In some countries there has been very large migration away from areas of low employment opportunities. Many people may have moved from rural areas into towns where there are insufficient jobs. Unemployment, or under-employment, on the land has been replaced by urban unemployment, or activity in the informal sector. The informal sector consists of economic activity of a self-employment type such as a street-trader or hawker, or provider of services, or employment for less than the minimum wage, or on a casual or part-time basis. In many developing countries the informal sector may be an important contributor to total economic activity, and may be one source of experience and training which leads to future employment in the formal sector.

Investment grants

We have seen that governments may offer inducements to firms to invest in certain areas. They may also offer general inducements for all investment in order to stimulate activity. Usually these take the form of a grant, subsidy or tax concession, based on the amount of investment in new plant and equipment. The larger the amount of investment, the larger the amount of grant or subsidy.

If effective, this leads to an increase in investment over the level that would have taken place without the subsidy. Any grant or subsidy paid in respect of investment that would have taken place in any event is dead weight. It has had no effect in leading to more investment, but has become a dead-weight burden round the neck of the government, which has to pay for something which would have happened without the grant. Governments seek to minimise the dead-weight effect but it is not easy to ascertain which investment would have occurred, and which took place only because there was the grant.

If the government is seeking to increase output and employment, a subsidy to investment may have contradictory results. There may be more investment and output but less employment. The key factor is whether the investment is labour-adding or labour-substituting. Labour-adding investment leads to an increase in the amount of labour employed. Labour-substituting investment leads to the replacement of labour by capital and therefore to a lower level of employment, although possibly a higher level of output.

Investment grants and subsidies may encourage labour-substituting investment because it alters the ratio of prices or costs of capital and labour. A firm decides on its factor mix between capital and labour by varying the quantities of each factor employed until the ratios of MRP/MC are equal. If there is a subsidy to investment in capital this must lead to a shift towards capital instead of labour. The increase in investment should therefore be seen in two parts. The first is that resulting from a change in relative factor costs, and will take place until the ratio of the MRP/costs of the factors are again equal. That will reduce the level of employment. Second, there will be an expansion in investment if the total marginal costs of production after the first increase in investment are still lower than the MRP or MR obtained from increasing output. Any further investment on this account will lead to more employment, but only to an increase in total employment after the reduction in employment from the first stage has been made good.

The increased investment may also lead to a change in the type of labour needed. If new technology is used different skills may be required. The firms may retrain their existing workers or may dismiss them and recruit new workers, who either have the skills required, or are considered more suitable for training to acquire the new skills.

There will be a further increase in employment to provide the plant and equipment forming the new investment. This may lead to higher temporary employment in the area where the investment takes place. It may, however, lead to higher temporary employment elsewhere, even overseas, depending on where the equipment is manufactured. Any investment in new buildings, roads or other infrastructure will lead to some temporary rise in employment in the special area. The important point is whether the employment multiplier effects are experienced in the special area or elsewhere.

Tax concessions are sometimes used instead of investment grants. These have the disadvantage that they do not provide a cash flow until taxable income has been received. An investment grant, if paid in cash, can make an earlier contribution towards the cost of investment and, as we saw earlier, the sooner a cash sum is received the higher is its current discounted value. Tax concessions may nevertheless be effective if they apply to profits earned on activities in special areas. By lowering taxes they increase the mec.

Because investment grants and subsidies tend to encourage the substitution of capital for labour, it is sometimes proposed that regional policy should subsidise new jobs rather than new investment. There are two main problems with this kind of proposal. The first is the dead-weight effect, as with investment grants. The second is a different form of dead weight. To be effective in creating new jobs, employment subsidies should be paid only on *additional* jobs created, just as investment grants apply only to additional investment. It is difficult to find a way of accurately measuring new or additional jobs, particularly when firms merge. Proposals to subsidise all jobs in certain areas, as with the old Regional Employment Premium in the United Kingdom, mean that for a given amount of government expenditure the subsidy per job is small since it has to be spread over all the existing jobs, as well as any new ones created. However, this is sometimes advocated as a means of protecting existing jobs rather than encouraging the creation of new ones.

Some form of subsidy on new jobs created, if suitably devised to overcome the problems of differentiating additions to employment from the effects of mergers, would have a more direct effect on stimulating employment in special areas. However, it would also work against investment in new capital equipment, and this could be undesirable. If there are significant technological changes taking place in an industry's production methods, measures which discourage their adoption in one country could leave it less able to compete in international markets.

The problem is complicated by the fact that we wish both to encourage improved efficiency in production and to increase the level of employment of labour. These might be contradictory objectives given the relative costs and efficiencies of labour and capital. Of course, if wages were to fall it would be easier to invest in new technology and increase employment, but the government also wishes to maintain and improve real wages and living standards. The difficulty is that we do not yet know how to achieve all the various objectives simultaneously.

Foreign investment

By foreign investment we mean investment in our own country by foreigners. Investment in foreign countries by residents of the United Kingdom is referred to as overseas investment.

Foreign investment is an emotive political issue as well as an economic one. It is often seen as exploitation of the nationals of the country in which the investment takes place, and as a modern version of past colonialism. The greater part of the profits may be expatriated, the senior positions may be filled by foreign nationals, and there may be a feeling that the crucial decisions are made overseas by people who do not pay much attention to the interests of the domestic country. Multinational corporations (MNCs) which invest in a variety of countries are subject to considerable criticism.

At the same time many governments, of developed as well as developing countries, spend considerable time and offer various inducements to attract foreign investment to their countries. They see MNCs or foreign investment as a source of new jobs and additional economic activity, and as contributors to output and income.

Part of the apparent contradiction may stem from the different sorts of foreign investments. Some consist of old investment from colonial times. These may be plantations, or producers of primary products, competing in unstable international markets where prices are subject to considerable fluctuations, and where labour costs traditionally form a high proportion of total costs. In addition, these activities may have been the major source of employment. These companies may be seeking to reduce employment by substituting capital for labour, as with the mechanisation of sugar-cane harvesting. They may be facing shrinking international markets, increases in international supply as more countries start producing, say, tea or coffee, and be trying to reduce their total labour costs. There may be genuine conflict between the employers' views of the economic situation, and the social and economic aspirations of the workforce, which wants job security and higher wages. The extension of political independence has been accompanied by demands for improved social and economic conditions, and these demands are not necessarily constrained by the economic factors which may determine the producers' actions.

There are also new foreign-owned enterprises producing consumer goods, or working on relatively new primary products, where working conditions and wages overseas may be more attractive to MNCs. Foreign investors may have been attracted by the lower labour costs in relation to those in their own country, the appropriate comparison of labour costs being total labour costs – wages plus statutory or other fringe benefits and contributions – and labour productivity. While labour costs in relation to productivity may be lower than in the home country, wages may be relatively high for the country in which the investment has taken place.

It is noteworthy that workers in many developed countries object to their company investing abroad where wages are lower. They believe that they are denied employment opportunities because of worse conditions of employment overseas. If wages, labour costs and labour productivities were identical in all countries, investment would be determined by transportation costs plus any non-economic factors.

Countries have to decide whether they want to obtain the benefits of higher output and employment which accrue from foreign investment, and accept that foreign firms will wish to repatriate at least a part of their profits, or whether they so object to this that they prefer to forgo the additional investment and employment. This choice is the more difficult because the investment-receiving countries, particularly if they are developing countries, are aware that domestic sources are insufficient to provide the required amount and type of alternative investment. The foreign investment raises the I–S curves and so the level of income and employment. There will be relatively little crowding-out of domestic investment since this is usually too low to attain full employment. These countries then face the hard choice of accepting the terms on which foreign countries will invest, including the repatriation of profits, or tolerating lower levels of output, income and employment.

In some cases – and for some countries it is a marked feature of their economies – domestic resources are insufficient to generate a level of aggregate demand which provides full or high employment. To increase investment it is necessary to attract foreign investment. This may lead to political and social problems, but so does the high level of unemployment and low incomes. It is a choice of political economy whether to encourage foreign investment.

Measures may be introduced to ensure that local nationals are employed and trained for higher managerial posts. This will lead to higher incomes and also provide a source of trained manpower which can move to other industries and employment. Legislation can also provide for minimum wage levels and certain working conditions. However, if these lead to an increase in costs or a reduction in expected MPP and MRP, it could mean that the company about to invest might decide that the project is no longer worth while.

Foreign investment may be regarded by some as bringing undesirable features as well as benefits to the host country. Political as well as economic choices may be involved in the formulation of policy regarding foreign investment.

It is extraordinarily difficult to ensure that the various policies support and re-enforce each other. Different policies are designed to deal with different problems, and governments have a number of different economic, social and political goals. The selection of economic policies therefore inevitably involves value judgements and the making of political choices. Within the framework of its own value judgements and policy objectives, a government should try to create as much consistency between its various policy measures as it can.

CHAPTER 18

International trade

Although we have occasionally referred to international competition, and imports and exports, the previous chapters have been concerned primarily with a domestic, or closed, economy – one not open to international trade. This is, of course, a simplification adopted for expository purposes. It is now time to introduce international trade. In this chapter we will consider the basic theory of international trade and consider why trade takes place across national boundaries. The basic explanation refers to two countries, each capable of producing only two goods, but the concepts can be applied to many countries capable of producing many different goods.

Comparative advantage

At the heart of all explanations of international trade is the notion of comparative advantage. Some countries are comparatively better at producing certain goods than others. They may be absolutely better at producing all goods, but that will not lead to international trade unless there are comparative advantages in specialisation.

As noted, to present the basic concept we will assume that there are only two countries, that each of them is capable of producing only the same two goods, that labour is the only factor of production, and that there are constant returns to scale. Assume that each worker in country A can produce either two units of tea or one unit of wheat. The two commodities can be measured in different units so that a worker can produce two chests of tea or one ton of wheat. In country B each worker can produce one unit of tea or two units of wheat. The differences may be the result of climatic conditions, the nature of the soil, and possibly the skills and training of the workers in the two different countries. While skill and training may not seem very different for tea and wheat production, the importance of the capabilities and skills of the workers in the two different countries would be obvious were the two commodities assumed to be cut and polished diamonds, and moon rockets.

We will assume that each country has 200 workers and that before specialisation and international trade, each country uses half its workforce to produce tea and half to produce wheat. The production of each commodity will be as set out in Section I of Table 18.1. The combined output of the two countries before international trade will be 300 units of tea and 300 units of wheat.

Table 18.1. Gains from international trade: each country with advantage in one product

	Tea		Wheat	
Country	Workers	Output	Workers	Output
I Before trade				
A	100	200	100	100
B	100	100	100	200
Total	200	300	200	300
II After specialisation				
A	200	400	–	–
B	–	–	200	400
Total	200	400	200	400
III				
A	200	250	–	150
B	–	150	200	250
Total	200	400	200	400

Note that the assumption that there are constant returns to scale means that a worker can transfer from the production of one commodity to the production of the other and be as efficient as every other worker in his country already employed in that sector. Each worker in country A who moves from the production of wheat to tea will add two units of tea, and the production of wheat will fall by one unit.

The opportunity cost of one unit of wheat in country A is two units of tea, and the opportunity cost of one unit of tea is a half unit of wheat. In country B the opportunity cost of a unit of tea is two units of wheat, and the opportunity cost of a unit of wheat is one half a unit of tea. There is a difference in the *relative* efficiency of the two countries in producing wheat and tea, where relative efficiency means the production of one good in one country relative to the production of the other good in that country, compared with the other country.

Country A is relatively more efficient at producing tea than wheat, so tea has a lower relative cost in terms of wheat than it does in country B. A unit of tea costs only one half a unit of wheat in country A, but costs two units of wheat in country B. Similarly, country B is relatively more efficient at producing wheat.

If the two countries specialise in the production of the good in which they are relatively more efficient, so that country A employs all its 200 workers to produce tea and country B employs its 200 workers to produce wheat, as shown in Section II of Table 18.1, the combined output will rise to 400 units of tea and 400 units of wheat. In this example, therefore, specialisation leads to an increase of 100 units of tea and 100 units of wheat. International trade can take place and allow each country to have more of each commodity than it had before specialisation and trade.

If international trade takes place each country can consume more of each commodity than it did before specialisation. Exactly how much more of each commodity each country will have will depend on the terms of exchange, i.e. the rate at which the two commodities are exchanged or traded between the two countries. If we assume that the rate of exchange of the two commodities is one unit of tea for one unit of wheat, each country can gain 50 units of each commodity, as illustrated in Section III of Table 18.1.

We cannot say exactly what the terms of trade, or rate of exchange between the two commodities, will be, but we can determine the range within which it must fall if specialisation and international trade is to take place. If the rate of exchange was three units of tea for one unit of wheat, country A would not be willing to specialise and trade. It can obtain wheat from its own production by giving up only two units of tea (the opportunity cost of wheat in A). Clearly, it would not trade with country B if it had to give more units of tea in exchange for a unit of wheat than are needed by transferring its own resources to wheat production. In the same way, country B would not specialise and take part in international trade if the rate of exchange was three units of wheat for one unit of tea, for it could grow tea itself at an opportunity cost of only two units of wheat.

For specialisation and international trade to take place, therefore, the rate of exchange of the commodities must be more favourable to each country than its own opportunity costs for the commodities. This is because the opportunity cost of producing one commodity rather than another in the same country is, in effect, the internal rate of exchange of one commodity for another, and no country will take part in international trade on worse terms than it can get from internal trade. The rate of exchange of the commodities between the countries will therefore be somewhere between the internal rates of exchange or opportunity cost ratios of the two countries.

It need not be exactly half-way between them. This was assumed in Section III of Table 18.1 as an illustration. For example, if the rate of exchange, or terms of trade, were one and a half units of tea for one unit of wheat, and each country specialised, country A could exchange 150 units of tea for 100 units of wheat. It would then have 250 units of tea, which is more than we assumed it had before specialisation and trade in Section I of Table 18.1, and would have 100 units of wheat, which is the same as it had before. It could then trade more tea for wheat and still have more of each than it had before trade, although not as much as it had when the terms of trade were assumed to be one-for-one.

Gains even if one country has absolute advantage in both commodities

In the example we have just looked at we assumed that each country had a relative, or comparative, advantage in the production of one commodity, and also that one country had an absolute advantage over the other in the production of one commodity. Country A was better at producing tea than was country B, as each worker could produce two units, while each worker in B produced only one unit. The position was reversed for the production of wheat. However, there can be benefits in specialisation and trade even if one country is better than the other in producing both commodities, and so has an absolute advantage in the production of both goods.

In Table 18.2 we assume that country C is more efficient than country D at producing both coffee and cars. We again assume that each country has 200 workers and that there are constant returns to scale. Before specialisation, if each country devotes half of its labour to producing each of the goods, the combined output will be 116 units of coffee and 54 cars. Country D has an opportunity cost of four units of coffee for each car, and country C has an opportunity cost of two units of coffee. If country D stopped producing its four cars it could produce 16 units of coffee. If country C produced an extra four cars it would forgo eight units of coffee. Total production would increase if country D concentrated its total workforce on the production of coffee. If it produced only coffee, country D would employ its 200 workers in that sector, and produce 32 units. Country C

Table 18.2. Gains from international trade: one country with advantage in both products

Country	Coffee		Cars	
	Workers	Output	Workers	Output
I Before trade				
C	100	100	100	50
D	100	16	100	4
Total	200	116	200	54
II After specialisation				
C	84*	84	108*	54
D	200	32	–	–
Total	284	116	108	54

* Country C has 8 workers available to produce either cars or coffee

could then employ 84 workers to produce 84 units of coffee so that the combined production of coffee remained at 116 units. Country C could also employ 108 workers to produce 54 cars so that the combined output of cars remained at 54, as shown in Section II of Table 18.2. The combined output of both cars and coffee would then be exactly the same as before specialisation, but country C would be employing only 192 of its workforce of 200. It could then use the additional eight workers to produce an extra eight units of coffee, or four cars, or any combination of cars and coffee. This extra output represents the gains from specialisation and trade, and the extent to which each country would gain would depend on the terms of exchange.

It must be noted that for the output of *both* commodities to rise, or for the total output of one good to remain the same and the output of the other to increase after specialisation and trade, where one country has an absolute advantage in the production of both goods, *it is essential* that the country with absolute advantage transfers some of its workforce to the production of one good made in the less efficient country, and uses some of its workforce on the production of the other good. Only the less efficient country specialises in the production of one good – that in which it has the relative advantage. The other country must produce both goods. If each country had specialised, country D would have produced 32 units of coffee, and country C 100 cars. This would have led to less coffee. Specialisation the other way would have produced 200 units of coffee and eight cars. In either situation there would have been more of one good than before specialisation, but a smaller output of the other commodity. We cannot conclude that this would be preferable.

We cannot add together the total output of coffee and cars before and after specialisation. The units for coffee are not the same as the units for cars and cannot be aggregated. To demonstrate that both countries can benefit from specialisation and trade it is necessary to show that the output of *both* commodities can rise. In the example shown in Table 18.2 the eight workers in country C could, for instance, produce an extra four units of coffee and an additional two cars.

Causes of gains from international trade

The gains from specialisation and international trade are possible because of differences in the relative advantages, or opportunity costs of production of different goods, in different countries. If the two countries had the same opportunity cost ratios there would be no advantages from specialisation since the internal and external opportunity cost ratios would be the same. Relative advantages arise from various causes.

Factor endowment Countries have different combinations of factors of production. Some have much land while others, such as Singapore or Hong Kong, may have relatively little land but a relatively large population, and a larger relative supply of labour. They can be expected to produce labour-intensive goods, while the countries with more land will be better suited to the production of goods which are land-intensive, such as agricultural products. Some countries have a plentiful supply of raw materials and other natural resources.

Factors of production are not homogeneous. Land is not the same in all countries. Some is desert with no natural resources and has little economic use. Land in other countries is extremely fertile. Some land is better suited to the production of some products than of others.

Labour too is not homogeneous. A country may have a large population and an abundant supply of labour, but it may be relatively unskilled and have low productivity. Often countries with a relatively plentiful supply of capital produce goods for international trade which contain a high proportion of labour, i.e. labour costs are a high proportion of total costs. The theory of comparative advantage might lead us to expect that they would concentrate on the production of goods with a high capital content, and import labour-intensive commodities from countries with an abundant labour supply. This is not always the case, and the reason is that the developed countries have a different sort of labour supply which is more highly skilled.

Some factor endowments cannot be changed. We cannot make tropical countries into ones with temperate climates. We cannot alter the natural resources to provide oil if none exists. However, technology may allow adverse climatic conditions and unfavourable natural conditions to be changed, albeit at a cost. Discoveries and inventions may allow us to develop and exploit natural resources which previously were physically impossible or too expensive to develop.

Labour is especially amenable to change. It is possible to increase the skill of a workforce by education and training. While, therefore, a workforce may be currently relatively unskilled, training and experience may lead to a different qualitative factor endowment.

Obviously, the amount and type of capital can be changed. Investment can alter the relative amount of capital both in relation to the other factors in a country, and in relation to the factor mix compared with other countries.

If there are changes in the relative efficiency of factors in a country, say as a result of new discoveries, new inventions, additional investment or improvements in the training and skill of the workforce, there will be changes in the type of goods in which countries specialise. The examples in Tables 18.1 and 18.2 were based on an assumption of constant opportunity costs or comparative advantages. If these change, so too will the specialisation and the relative contribution each country makes to total output.

Economies of scale We assumed constant returns to scale. All the differences between the relative efficiency of the two countries might therefore be assumed to result from differences in endowments. However, it is possible that some of the differences assumed to exist were the result of economies of scale. For example, in Section I of Table 18.2, country D may have had a relatively high opportunity cost of cars in terms of coffee because its car industry was operating on a small scale. If production expanded it could conceivably have a relative advantage in car production provided there were large economies of scale available to it.

In the real world specialisation among different countries may be the result of economies of scale since the assumption of constant returns, *over all levels of production*, is unrealistic. We adopted it merely to simplify the explanation and make the numerical examples easier to follow. The theory of comparative advantage can easily accommodate economies and diseconomies of scale. All that is needed is to adjust the output figures as production expands or decreases. However, such adjustments should be based on estimates of the actual returns to scale. Merely selecting numbers which lead to the desired answer is misleading.

Product homogeneity We assumed that the products of the two countries were homogeneous. Thus in Table 18.1 there was no difference in the quality of tea and wheat produced in countries A and B, and in the example in Table 18.2 people were indifferent as to whether the coffee and cars were produced in country C or D. If the products of the two countries are not homogeneous so that, for example, people prefer cars from country D to those from country C, and prefer coffee from country C, then we have four goods and not two. We can no longer substitute the output of one country for that of another and show that total output can rise.

In the real world people often have preference for the product of one country. All coffee is not the same and tea varies not only from country to country, but also from each estate, and parts of estates, in one country.

Important assumptions

We specified certain assumptions at the beginning of this explanation, and it is important that their relevance be fully understood. If the assumptions are not met, the expected gains may not occur.

Returns to scale We assumed that there were constant returns to scale. This is important, for if there are diseconomies of scale, the addition to output following specialisation will be less than would occur with constant returns to scale. In practice it is unlikely that workers can be transferred from the production of one good to the production of another and be just as efficient as people already employed in the new industry. Different skills, abilities and training would be required. Labour is not homogeneous and some workers are better at doing some types of work. However, it is possible that after training, which involves costs, the new labour may become as efficient as those already employed.

Capital equipment The illustrations we used assumed that no capital equipment was necessary, so that extra output could be obtained merely by transferring labour. In reality, additional capital equipment would be necessary, particularly if we expect to have constant returns to scale. Costs of other factors need to be included.

Land Some land in some countries cannot be used to produce some agricultural products, or could be used to do so only if extremely expensive production methods were used. It might be possible to grow pineapples in northern countries with cold climates if heavy costs were incurred in providing artificial heating and glasshouses. This would raise the costs of production considerably.

Transport costs The increases in output resulting from specialisation may well be reduced by the need to transport the traded goods from one country to another. In the example in Table 18.2 we saw that the same total output produced by 400 men in countries C and D could be obtained from the employment of 392 men after specialisation. This meant that total output could then rise by the employment of the eight workers in country C and could consist of various combinations of cars and coffee. However, after specialisation, it would be necessary to transport some coffee from D to C and cars from C to D. This would involve costs or, in our example, the employment of some of the 400 workers to provide the transport facilities.

If the transport of the commodities traded between the two countries required more than eight men, it would be necessary to take some workers away from the production of cars or coffee in one of the countries and this would mean that the combined output of the two countries would be less than before specialisation and trade. In this case there would be no gains from specialisation and trade, but a loss. However, if transport required the employment of only two workers, total output of cars and coffee would rise by the employment of six workers.

If workers in both countries were equally efficient at providing transport services, it would be beneficial to use workers from country D to provide these services. This would reduce the output of coffee by 0.32 units. If two workers from country C were employed in providing transport, the loss of coffee would be two units or one car.

For specialisation and international trade to result in an increase in the total output of both commodities, it is necessary that the costs of transport, whether expressed in terms of costs of production or, as we have done, in terms of the number of workers needed, are less than the gains resulting from specialisation. International transport costs reduce the increases in output that would otherwise occur.

International free trade

The theory of comparative advantage is often used to conclude that specialisation of production and international free trade, uninhibited by tariffs or restrictions of imports and exports, will lead to the highest level of total output, and therefore to the highest standards of living. For example, the gains from trade in Tables 18.1 and 18.2 could not take place if there were restrictions which prevented imports entering both countries, or if quotas limited the amount of imports which were allowed.

When we look at the real world we find that there are many restrictions on free trade, and a plethora of measures to protect domestic production, which apparently prevent output from being maximised in the way we would expect by following the theory of comparative advantage.

Protection, or restriction of free trade

There are a number of ways in which domestic producers may be protected from foreign competition. These restrict free trade.

Tariffs Tariffs are a tax on imports. They therefore operate in the same way as an indirect tax except they are applied only on foreign-made imported goods. Because the tariff is not applied to domestically produced goods, they raise the price of imports in relation to the same category of goods produced by home suppliers. They therefore reduce the price attractiveness of foreign goods. If there are no domestic producers of the goods, tariffs should be seen as an additional indirect tax. In this case the intention is not to protect the home industry, because there is no home industry, but to raise government revenue or to discourage the consumption of those goods and so reduce imports.

Quotas A government may impose quotas limiting the amount of certain goods which can be imported. Sometimes this is done to protect home producers, and sometimes, often in the case of developing countries, to limit the amount of foreign exchange needed to pay for imports.

Tariffs and quotas have different internal effects. Many developing countries limit the importation of cars. Many countries which do so have no domestic car producers. Assume that the demand for imported cars is represented by D–D in Fig. 18.1 and the supply by S–S. If there were no government intervention, demand would be for Q_1 cars and the price would be P_1. Total demand for foreign exchange would be $(Q_1 \cdot P_1)$. The government does not wish to see this level of demand for foreign exchange. (We will consider why this might be so in Chapters 19 and 20.) It is prepared to allow Q_2 number of cars to be imported and this would require $(Q_2 \cdot P_1)$ foreign exchange.

At the price of P_1, however, there are more people wanting a car than the quota allows. Some way of allocating the quota of Q_2 cars has to be devised. One way would be to allocate them randomly among the applicants, say by

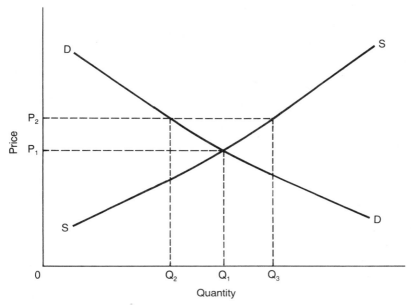

Fig. 18.1 Effect of a tariff on demand and price

drawing names out of a hat. If this happened the number of people applying for one of the cars would rise. Since there are only Q_2 cars available, the internal or domestic price will rise to P_2 because at that price there are Q_2 people willing to pay price P_2. Anyone obtaining one of the quota cars could immediately sell it for P_2 and make (P_2-P_1) gain. The demand would therefore increase above Q_1 as the demand curve shifted to the right.

Moreover, because there are Q_2 people willing to pay price P_2, they might offer a gift or bribe to those allocating the quota. They could give any amount between P_1 and P_2 and still be satisfied. Indeed, if they were to give, say, one-half of the difference between P_1 and P_2 they would benefit by obtaining the car below the price (P_2) they were willing to pay. The person allocating the quota would benefit by half the difference between P_1 and P_2. Quotas often lead to corruption and other unlawful methods to obtain one of the scarce permits to purchase.

The government could impose a tariff equal to (P_2-P_1). This would have the effect of raising the market price of cars to P_2, at which level the market demand would be equal to the administratively determined quota supply of Q_2. This would not be a market equilibrium, since at price P_2 the market would supply Q_3 cars, but is not allowed to do so by administrative action.

With quotas, individuals fortunate enough to obtain one of the scarce commodities are in a position to benefit from the imbalance between supply and demand. With a tariff, the government can benefit by receiving additional revenue.

Other restrictions Governments may restrict the amount of foreign currency available to their nationals. This limits the demand for foreign goods and services in a general way. Discrimination may be applied, so that importers of essential equipment or raw materials from overseas are treated more generously than those wishing to buy imported consumer goods or travel abroad on holiday. To some extent this can be seen as a generalised quota system, since only a certain total amount of foreign goods can be purchased. As with specific quotas, this approach tends to encourage dishonesty. The demand for foreign currency exceeds the available supply at the prevailing price, or exchange rate, and some people are willing to pay more than the market price.

Many governments give preference to domestic suppliers when making government purchases of goods. In some cases this may be for political and defence reasons. A government may not wish to be dependent on foreign suppliers who might withhold supplies in times of war. Governments may also make it difficult for foreign exports to enter the country by instituting various administrative difficulties. There may be special safety requirements which foreign firms find difficult to meet and which are essentially protective measures for domestic producers.

Granting subsidies or allowances to domestic producers is a disguised form of tariffs. If home suppliers are given special terms on plant or equipment, cheap loans or tax concessions, it is equivalent to a tax on foreign imports.

The case for protection

Economic analysis seems to suggest that protection is undesirable because it prevents full specialisation and international trade and thereby leads to a lower level of total output than would occur if free specialisation and free trade were to operate. However, there may be arguments in favour of protection.

Infant industry This is analytically the most powerful economic argument in favour of protection, and also the most abused in practice. Put simply, the infant industry argument is that some industries may potentially have comparative advantage even if they do not currently do so. A period of protection to allow the infant industry to develop would lead to a change in comparative advantage. This argument can be derived from the earlier comments which indicated that the analysis on which comparative advantage is based often relies on assumptions that the opportunity costs in the two countries and the relative efficiencies remain constant or static. If, for example, there were a large inflow of capital equipment into country D in Table 18.2, and a period of training and acquisition of skills by the workforce, country D might be able to produce cars more efficiently than country C.

There can be no doubt that the relative and absolute advantages of countries change through time. In the early nineteenth century, England was more efficient at producing many manufactured goods than was the United States. This is not true today. If relative advantages had remained constant, the United States would still be primarily a producer of agricultural products.

The infant industry argument emphasises the importance of change – change in skills and abilities, factor endowments, and relative efficiencies. There is much evidence from actual developments that considerable gains can be obtained from encouraging new industries. If these are not protected in some way they may be unable to survive, since foreign producers who are already established may be more efficient and so undercut the new firms from the beginning – thereby preventing them from gaining the experience and skills which would ultimately lead to their becoming more efficient.

However, there is a considerable danger that the infant industries will prefer to remain protected rather than make strenuous efforts to become more efficient. Political and economic pressures will develop to maintain the protection. Those employed in the industries will not wish to lose their jobs to foreign competition, and the government may have given financial assistance, as well as protection through tariffs or quotas, and so may not wish to see those investments destroyed by foreign competition. If this happens, the infant industries may continue to be relatively inefficient.

Government may continue to provide protection even though efficiency is low because the infant industries are producing goods which would otherwise have to be imported and there may be a shortage of foreign exchange. Many governments in developing countries have adopted protection policies and encouraged infant industries. In some cases there was no realistic possibility that the enterprises could become sufficiently efficient to be able to compete with foreign suppliers.

The basis of the infant industry argument is that the protection is a temporary measure necessary to provide time in which experience and skill can be acquired. The danger is that the temporary support becomes part of the permanent features of an economy.

Cheap labour Protection is sometimes advocated on the grounds that foreign goods are undercutting domestic products because of low wages and living conditions abroad. It is argued that this is 'unfair' competition and that domestic producers ought to be protected by tariffs or quotas. However, as we have seen, the basis of specialisation and international trade is that each country should concentrate on the production of goods in which it has comparative advantage, and even if one country has an absolute advantage in all products, trade can still benefit both countries as we saw in Table 18.2. This rests on the assumption that there is free trade in all the products in every country. If some countries impose tariffs or quotas which distort free trade, the gains which are possible may not be achieved. Often, however, the cheap labour argument is used to limit competition, so that unpleasant or undesired adjustments in the pattern of employment and production do not have to be made in the home country.

Specialisation and free trade may provide benefits to all countries, but may nevertheless impose undesirable changes and reductions in living standards on some sectors in some countries as other countries become more efficient and replace them in international markets.

With complete specialisation and free trade, given the absence of monopolistic or monopsonistic distortions from the perfect competition model, there will be a tendency for factor and product prices to be equal. Any differences should reflect only transport costs, and in the case of labour, the costs of movement from one country to another. Otherwise, the international market should operate in the same way as the domestic market, and wages and prices for the same or homogeneous factors and products tend to equality.

This does not mean that wages in every country will be the same. It does mean that wages for the same type and quality of labour in all countries should tend to be the same, if by labour of the same type and quality we mean labour which has the same marginal physical productivity. If the MPP of labour in different countries is the same, and competition in the product market means that the MRP of the workers is the same, we should expect their wages to be the same.

There may be some differences between the MPP and MRP of workers in one country compared with another if it costs more to transport raw materials or finished products in one country. Thus if the MPP of shirt manufacturers is the same in Sri Lanka and Hong Kong, but if there are greater transport costs in Sri Lanka, perhaps because the product markets are further away, and if the products of both countries are homogeneous and sold in the same market, the net MRP of labour in Sri Lanka will be less. They will be producing the same physical quantity of output but it will have a lower value on the international market. Buyers of the shirts in the United States will pay the same price in the United States for the homogeneous products, and the producer will have to bear the transport costs. The higher transport costs will have to come from profits or wages, and we might expect the returns to both factors of production in Sri Lanka to be lower.

The argument against cheap labour is unwarranted if labour is paid the value of its marginal product. If, however, there are distortions preventing wages in one country from rising to their free market level, the criticism of cheap labour undercutting home producers may have more justification if wages of the home producers are themselves determined by market forces.

Unemployment A consequence of the cheap labour and unfair competition argument is that unemployment may rise in the importing country if domestic producers are displaced by imported goods. An increase in imports has the same effect as an increase in savings in generating a downward multiplier effect. However, the government can respond to this by appropriate demand management measures to stimulate the economy. As we have already discussed, this may involve structural adjustments in employment and output, and this may be unpleasant or undesirable to those affected. There may be a conflict of interest between the gains of the national economy, and all economies in general, and the losses of those engaged in particular sectors.

Anti-dumping Protection is sometimes justified if foreign countries are 'dumping' their products on the international market by selling them below their costs of production. We have seen that firms will remain in production in the short run if they are able to cover their variable costs and make some contribution to their fixed costs, even if they are not covering their total average costs. There may be occasions therefore when firms sell below their normal or long-run price in either the home or the foreign market. It can be very difficult to know whether a firm is 'dumping' or taking the sort of action we would expect any firm to take to minimise its losses in the short run.

Some firms will also sell at a special low price when introducing a new product on to the market in order to attract new customers away from existing suppliers. This would be a natural occurrence in some forms of imperfect competition. The firm might later increase its price, regarding the lower introductory price as a marketing expense similar to advertising costs. Firms may do this in the international market, hoping to kill off the domestic producers by their low price competition. This may then allow them to establish a monopoly position which they will later exploit by raising prices considerably. It can be very difficult to ascertain the motives and intentions of firms in competition.

On occasion governments may provide subsidies to firms to allow them to compete in international markets in order to avoid a rise in unemployment at home. The subsidy may allow the firm to sell below the cost of production and can be seen as a different form of dumping.

Most countries oppose the dumping of foreign goods in their markets. It is regarded as unethical and as a source of potential monopolistic exploitation. However, it is often very difficult to establish whether dumping is taking place, and to separate the short-term pricing and production decisions which we would expect a firm in conditions of perfect competition to make from those actions which are attempts to establish a monopoly.

Strategic and defence As we have already indicated, governments may protect some home producers on grounds of national security. They may wish to ensure that supplies will not be cut off in the event of hostilities. This consideration could apply to food supplies as well as armaments. If a government does wish to maintain domestic production for strategic reasons, it would be better to do so by granting subsidies rather than imposing tariffs. This would keep prices lower.

Trading arrangements

If we look around the world we see very few examples of international free trade. Countries impose tariffs and many impose other restrictions. Sometimes this may be done for good economic reasons, as with infant industries, and at other times it may be the result of political pressure and an attempt to avoid the painful structural adjustment that might be involved in adapting to changing comparative advantages. In addition to measures to provide protection, which are determined individually by each country, some countries have entered into various forms of agreement with other countries to establish some uniformity.

Free trade areas Countries may agree to impose no tariffs or restrictions on trade among themselves. In this case goods produced in one of the member countries may be exported to other members without tariffs or duties, and subject to no quotas. This will encourage specialisation among the member countries. Obviously, the greater the differences in comparative advantages among the members, the greater the gains to be expected. Free trade areas are therefore more likely to produce greater benefits when they contain countries with different sorts of economic specialisations, factor endowments and natural resources.

Common market A free trade area removes tariffs and controls on the movement of goods produced and sold by member countries among themselves. It allows each member to decide on its own tariff and protection policy in regard to imports from countries outside the free trade area. A common market goes further than this. It includes free movement of goods among member countries, and should also include the free movement of all factors of production among them. The intention is to allow factors of production, production decisions and the movement of goods to take place among the member countries in the same way that they do among different regions of a single member country. However, because each member country may be free to pursue its own demand management policies, it does not follow that the outcome of a common market in terms of the allocation of resources and the equalisation of factor prices will be the same as within a single country. Moreover, we saw in our discussion of regional policy in Chapter 17 that substantial regional differences can exist within a single country.

A common market also seeks to establish a uniform policy in all member states regarding tariffs and other forms of protection against imports from non-members. Unlike a free trade area, which allows each member to determine its own policy on tariffs against non-members, a common market seeks to establish a common tariff policy. We should expect to see more specialisation and trade among members of a common market than would be the case were they pursuing independent policies, but this will be influenced by the extent to which they have similar comparative advantages and whether the common tariffs and economic rules are equally suited to all members.

Commodity agreements Producers of a single commodity may band together to try to control the total supply of their product. This is often found among producers of agricultural or primary products. High prices may lead to a large increase in supply (as was discussed in Chapter 5). Countries which depend on a single commodity for a large part of their employment and earnings of foreign currency may be particularly hard hit if there is a sharp decrease in price following a large increase in supply. They may therefore seek to regulate the price of the product by controlling aggregate supply.

This can be done by allocating each producing country a quota so that the aggregate supply is the total of the individual country quotas. However, if prices rise, it can be extremely difficult to ensure that every member abides by the quota allocation since there will be great temptation to increase supply in order to take advantage of the higher price. This is especially the case where the product is a natural resource such as oil, whose supply can be increased relatively quickly. It is more difficult to increase the output of some agricultural products very quickly, but if the high prices are expected to continue countries may increase their output the following year.

It can prove difficult to reach agreement on the size of each country's quota. Sometimes this is done on the basis of percentage shares in previous output. However, this may prevent new and cheaper sources of supply from developing, and some countries may wish to increase their output in order to obtain higher foreign exchange earnings.

In some cases buffer stocks may be established. Member countries provide funds, perhaps raised by a small percentage levy on all sales of the product, which are used to buy surplus stocks when supply exceeds demand at the desired market price. These stocks are then sold when demand exceeds supply at the prevailing price. In this way some of the extreme fluctuations in price may be avoided. Buffer stocks are appropriate only where the commodity is non-perishable. There can be problems if the agency intervenes to maintain the price by buying the excess supply for too long or on too large a scale.

By preventing or limiting the fall in price, a buffer stock scheme may perpetuate the excess supply and encourage more producers than are necessary to continue producing. If the fall in demand is the result of a change in tastes, perhaps resulting from the appearance of a substitute, so that the demand curve has shifted, measures to try to stabilise the price will lead to a permanent excess supply. Buffer stocks work best when there are random fluctuations in demand and supply around stable levels. In practice it is often difficult to know whether an imbalance in supply and demand is a random fluctuation or the beginning of a new equilibrium position with a lower level of demand and a lower price. Thus buffer stocks may delay the adjustments in supply that would otherwise emerge from the market forces.

Comparative advantage and costs

We have considered comparative advantage in terms of physical productivity – the number of units of output that can be produced by a worker in each industry in each country. Obviously, we could have expressed this in terms of the number of workers, or worker-hours, needed to produce one unit of each commodity in each country. It would have altered the figures but not the basic explanation. We would still have been considering MPP and APP, and, because we assumed constant returns to scale, these would have been the same.

We can present the analysis in terms of costs of production and relative prices. Let us assume two countries, X which is an industrialised developed country, and Y which is an agricultural developing economy. To illustrate the more complicated example we will also assume that for the two goods considered, X has an absolute advantage because it can produce both goods more efficiently than country Y.

In Section I of Table 18.3 we show the domestic costs of producing the two goods, television sets and shoes. We assume that labour is the only factor of production so that the unit cost of producing each good in each country is the number of hours of labour necessary to make one unit of the good, multiplied by the hourly wage. In country X costs are expressed in dollars, in country Y in rupees. The labour requirement for a unit of each commodity is lower in X than in Y, so X has an absolute advantage in the production of both TVs and shoes.

Table 18.3. Exchange rate limitations of benefits from trade

	TVs			Shoes		
	Hours of labour	Wages per hour	Cost	Hours of labour	Wages per hour	Cost
I Labour costs of production						
		Dollars	Dollars		Dollars	Dollars
Country X	40	10	400	6	10	60
		Rupees	Rupees		Rupees	Rupees
Country Y	80	4	320	10	4	40
II Costs from X at different exchange rates						
			Rupees			Rupees
$1 = Rs1.25			320			48
$1 = Rs1.375			290.9			43.6
$1 = Rs1.50			266.7			40

To compare the relative prices of the two goods it is necessary to have a rate of exchange between dollars and rupees. In Section II of Table 18.3 we show the prices of both goods in terms of rupees at three different rates of exchange. If the rate of exchange is $1 = Rs1.25, TVs from country X will cost Rs320, the same as those produced in country Y, and shoes will cost Rs 48 compared with Rs40 in country Y. At this rate of exchange, and assuming no transport costs, some people might be willing to buy TVs from country X since they are the same price as those from country Y, but no one would buy shoes from X. If the exchange fell by just 1 cent so that $1 = Rs1.24, the price of TVs from X would rise to Rs322.58 and shoes would rise to Rs48.4. In these circumstances no one would buy any goods from country X. For trade to take place the exchange rate of the dollar must not be less than Rs1.25.

In the same way, if the exchange rate were $1 = Rs1.50, the price of TVs from X would be Rs266.7 and shoes would be Rs40. TVs would be cheaper and shoes would cost the same as from country Y. If the exchange rate then rose to Rs1.51 = $1, both shoes and TVs from X would be cheaper than from Y and no one would buy any of Y's goods.

The exchange rate must therefore lie between $1 = Rs1.25–1.50. If the exchange rate is exactly midway between these two limits, at $1 = Rs1.375, TVs from X would be Rs290.9 and shoes Rs43.6. It would be cheaper to buy TVs from X and shoes from Y. International trade could take place, both countries could benefit, and following the analysis of Table 18.2, output of both commodities would be higher than if no trade took place.

CHAPTER 19

Exchange rates

In the previous chapter we considered comparative advantage and the benefits of international trade in terms of physical productivity – the number of units of output that can be produced by a worker in each industry, in each country. We could have expressed this in terms of the number of man-hours or the number of workers needed to produce one unit of output of each commodity in each country. This would have altered the figures but not the basic explanation. We would still have been considering the MPP and APP and, because we assumed constant returns to scale, these would have been the same.

The benefits of specialisation and international trade were illustrated by the number of extra units of goods that were available, and we showed that each country could benefit if the rate at which the goods were exchanged lay between certain limits determined by the opportunity cost ratios in the two countries. The illustration pretended that goods were physically exchanged or bartered. In the real world there may be a few examples of barter at the international level, but the overwhelmingly greater part of international trade takes place for money payments, as it does in a national economy.

There is a major difference between international and domestic trade. Trade within a single country takes place through the medium of a single currency. There is one unit of currency in which costs and prices are expressed. With international trade there is a great variety of currencies. Each country has its own currency. Exporters, or sellers of goods to purchasers in other countries, will wish to be paid either in the currency of their own country, or in some currency which they wish to own.

Freely floating or market-determined exchange rates

We will assume initially that exporters – those who sell goods to residents in another country – require payment in their own domestic currency, so that British producers and exporters require payment in sterling, Sri Lankan exporters in rupees, Americans in dollars, and so on. We will also assume for the present that no one holds foreign currency as a form of wealth assets or for speculative motives, and that the only purpose of wishing to obtain foreign currency is to pay for imports (i.e. the foreign country's exports). If an importer wishes to obtain a foreign currency he will do so by buying it in the foreign exchange market. This is where the currency of one country can be bought, or exchanged, for the currency of another.

For international trade to take place on these assumptions, it is necessary that each importer be able to pay the exporters in the exporters' own currencies. In one respect, foreign currency is like any other commodity. It has to be bought by importers. We will assume that the price of foreign currency is determined in a free and competitive market by the forces of supply and demand.

The price of one currency expressed in terms of another is the rate of exchange between those two currencies. If £1 costs 10 rupees, the rate of exchange is Rs10 = £1, or 1 rupee = 10p (£0.1).

Because we have assumed that the demand for a foreign currency is only in order to pay for imports, it follows that the amount of foreign currency demanded by the importers or residents in any one country will depend on the total quantity of imports from a particular country multiplied by the price of the imports. If the British demand for Sri Lankan rupees is determined solely by the need to pay for imports of Sri Lankan tea into the United Kingdom, the total demand for rupees will be determined by the quantity of tea imported multiplied by the cost per unit of tea.

However, the quantity of tea demanded will depend on its price in sterling and this will not be known until the exchange rate between the two countries is known.

In Fig. 19.1 we show the demand for and supply of sterling at different exchange rates, with the quantity of sterling on the horizontal axis. The important point to remember is that the demand for rupees *is* the supply of sterling, for we are assuming that the only reason people wish to obtain rupees is to purchase goods from Sri Lanka, and therefore the only sterling which is available for Sri Lankans to buy is the amount of sterling that British importers are prepared to pay for rupees.

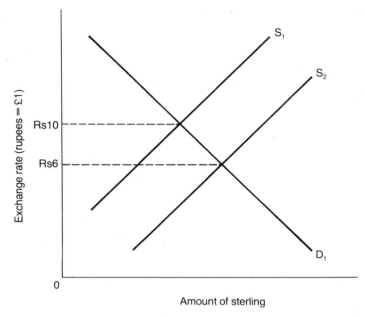

Fig. 19.1 Effects of changes in the exchange rate

The supply of sterling rises with its price in rupees. If tea costs Rs500 a chest in Sri Lanka and the rate of exchange is Rs10 = £1, the price in sterling to the UK importer is £50. If the exchange rate for the rupee falls to Rs15 = £1, the UK sterling price of tea falls to £33.3 a chest, and given a normal price elasticity of demand, we would expect more chests of tea to be demanded. If the price elasticity of demand for tea is greater than 1, there will be an increase in the total amount of sterling supplied. We will assume that the demand for tea is price-elastic so that it increases relative to the fall in the exchange rate; in this case the amount of sterling entering the foreign exchange market to buy rupees will also increase. If the demand for tea was price-inelastic, so that a fall in the exchange rate led to a less than proportionate increase in the demand for tea, the amount of sterling entering the foreign exchange market would decline, and the supply curve would slope downward. The supply of sterling is determined by the *total value* of demand for imports at different rates of exchange and not by the physical quantities demanded or supplied. The demand and supply curves for a currency in the determination of rates of exchange are not therefore the same as supply and demand curves for products, which do refer to physical quantities.

The demand for sterling from Sri Lankan importers will slope downward from left to right. If UK cars cost £5,000, the Sri Lankan price in rupees will be Rs25,000 if the exchange rate is Rs5 = £1, and Rs75,000 if the exchange rate is Rs15 = £1. Again, as a result of the price elasticity of demand, we would expect the demand for UK cars to be higher when the Sri Lankan price is Rs25,000 than when it is Rs75,000. The demand for UK sterling by Sri Lankans will therefore be higher when the exchange rate of rupees into sterling is lower. If the demand for Sri Lankan tea is such that the amount of UK sterling seeking rupees is represented by S_1 in Fig. 19.1, and the Sri Lankan demand for UK cars which provides the demand for UK sterling is represented by D_1, the exchange rate will be Rs10 = £1.

If there is a change in tastes, or a rise in the price of coffee, so that British demand for Sri Lankan tea increases, the supply of sterling will increase so that S_1 is replaced by S_2. Because more UK importers are demanding rupees in the foreign exchange market, there will be an increase in the supply of sterling; and given the demand for sterling, D_1, the new equilibrium exchange rate will be Rs6 = £1.

If this happens there will be a *depreciation* in the exchange rate of UK sterling and an *appreciation* in the exchange rate of the rupee. The pound has depreciated because it can now buy only 6 rupees, and the rupee has appreciated because 1 rupee can now buy 16.6p instead of 10p. Every appreciation of a currency's rate of exchange must be accompanied by a depreciation of the other country's currency.

Capital movements and speculation

In presenting this simple explanation we assumed that the only demand for a foreign currency was to pay for imports. This is an unreal and restrictive assumption. People may demand foreign currency for other purposes. They may wish to buy assets or invest abroad and to do this they must buy that country's currency. If foreigners wish to invest in UK Treasury bills, they purchase them in London with sterling. If a multinational corporation wishes to buy or build a factory abroad it needs foreign currency. There will therefore be a demand for foreign currency for capital transaction purposes.

Some people may hold foreign currency for speculative purposes. If, when the exchange rate was Rs10 = £1, I believed that it was going to change to Rs6 = £1, I might have bought rupees. I could have obtained Rs50,000 for £5,000. After the depreciation of UK sterling to Rs6 = £1, I could sell my Rs50,000 for £8,333, making a profit of £3,333. If the exchange rate is free to move, and people expect movement to take place, there will be some speculative demand for some foreign currencies. This is similar to the speculative demand for money rather than bonds considered in Chapter 14.

The exchange rate and prices

Changes in the exchange rate lead to changes in the domestic prices of imported goods. When the rupee appreciated from Rs10 = £1 to Rs6 = £1, the price of tea in the United Kingdom rose from £50 a chest to £83·3, and the price of UK cars in Sri Lanka fell from Rs50,000 to Rs30,000. A depreciation of a country's currency causes the prices of its imports, expressed in its own, or the domestic currency, to rise, and the prices of its exports, expressed in terms of the foreign currency, to fall. Conversely, an appreciation of a country's currency causes the prices of its imports, expressed in its own currency, to fall, and the prices of its exports, expressed in terms of foreign currencies, to rise.

In both cases – tea and cars – we assumed that the price in the country of origin remained the same. The fall or rise in price in the foreign, or importing, country was therefore the result of changes in the rate of exchange and not of changes in the domestic costs of production.

The alteration in the exchange rate, and so the cost of imports in terms of domestic currencies, will have effects on the demand for imports. When the rupee appreciates and the rupee price of British cars in Sri Lanka falls, we would expect there to be a rise in demand for British cars. At the same time, the increase in the UK price of tea will lead to a reduction in the demand for imported Sri Lankan tea.

Exchange rates are important therefore because they affect the level of demand for imports, and since every country's imports are someone else's exports, they affect the level of activity, output and employment in the exporting country through the multiplier effect of exports.

Exchange rate policies

We assumed that the supply of a currency on the foreign exchange market was determined by the demand of the residents of that country for imports, and that this would be determined in free market conditions; thus the total supply of a currency depended on the domestic demand for imports resulting from the price and income elasticities of demand of its residents. We then recognised that there could be additional demand for foreign currency for capital or investment purposes and as a result of speculation. However, in many countries, and particularly in developing countries, exchange rates are not determined by free market forces. The government may impose a fixed exchange rate.

Under a regime of fixed exchange rates, governments, through the central bank or other institutions, undertake to maintain the exchange rate at a predetermined level. This may be an exact rate of exchange such as £1 = \$2.25, or may be a fairly narrow range such as £1 = \$2.15–2.30. It is possible to maintain a fixed exchange rate only if the supply of and/or demand for the currency can be controlled.

As we have seen, the demand for a currency and its supply are unlikely to remain constant through time. They will change as the demand for imports and exports alter, and technological change – the development of new or more competitive products from other countries – will affect the demand for imports and exports. Even if it is possible to control the demand for imports by imposing import controls, tariffs or quotas, it is not possible to control the foreign demand for the exports of the domestic country. Sri Lanka may control the import of cars from the United Kingdom, and from all other countries, but the British demand for tea is not within the control of the Sri Lankan government. Thus the demand for rupees may fall because Britain buys tea elsewhere, or because there is a change in tastes away from tea.

Some of the movements in the supply and demand curves for a currency may be the result of short-term or seasonal factors. For example, tea is cropped and sold at different times of the year, so the demand for rupees will not be constant each day or week. There may be fluctuations round a more or less stable rate of exchange, but there is always the danger that a movement in the exchange rate will stimulate speculative activities which will exaggerate the fluctuations and lead to undesirable effects on the foreign demand for the country's exports, as a result of price elasticities of demand.

Assume, for example, that the government is committed to maintaining a fixed exchange rate of £1 = \$2.25. If supply and demand for sterling are represented by S_1 and D_1 in Fig. 19.2, this will coincide with the free market rate. However, if demand for sterling falls to D_1, the market rate of exchange would be £1 = \$1·50. There would be an excess supply of (Q_2–Q_1) sterling at a rate of £1 = \$2.5. In order to keep the exchange rate at £1 = \$2.25, the government must either shift the supply curve to S_2, which means cutting the demand for imports, or it must generate an artificial demand for sterling equal to (Q_2–Q_1).

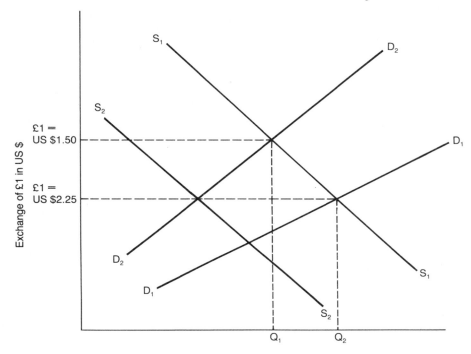

Fig. 19.2 Effect of a shift in demand for a currency with a fixed exchange rate

As we have seen, import controls and tariffs may shift the supply curve of sterling, i.e. the demand for foreign currency. In addition, the demand curve can be shifted by generating artificial or non-market demand for sterling. This is done by the government, or its agency, buying sterling and paying in foreign currency. This is the same as selling foreign currency for sterling, since the demand for sterling is the same as the supply of foreign currency seeking to buy sterling. To do this the government or its agency needs a supply of foreign currency.

Thus, with a fixed exchange rate the government must have a stock of both foreign currency and its own currency, which it can use to remove any differences between supply and demand for its own currency. When demand for its currency falls below the level necessary to maintain the fixed rate of exchange, given the supply of its own currency in the foreign exchange market, i.e. the demand for imports, the government must intervene by providing foreign currency from its stocks or reserves. If it does not do this the exchange rate cannot remain at the fixed level. Similarly, if demand for its currency exceeds the supply at the fixed rate of exchange, the government will supply its own currency from its reserves and exchange or sell this for foreign currency. The foreign currency it obtains in this way can be used when demand for its own currency is less than supply.

Two important points should be noted. First, even though a government imposes a series of controls on imports and the domestic demand for foreign currencies, it may still be unable to ensure that supply and demand for its own currency balance at the fixed exchange rate. It cannot control foreign demand for its currency even though, through its controls, it can determine the supply of its own currency to the foreign exchange market. Second, it will be able to maintain the fixed rate of exchange in the face of excess supply of its own currency, or deficit foreign demand for its currency, only to the extent that it has stocks or reserves of foreign currency.

Once the UK stocks of foreign currency, in this case dollars, are exhausted, it cannot maintain the fixed exchange rate of £1 = $2.25 if demand for sterling is less than the supply. When the demand for dollars (the supply of sterling) exceeds the supply of dollars (the demand for sterling), the price of dollars will rise and the price of sterling will fall, so that the exchange rate will fall below £1 = $2.25.

If, with a fixed exchange rate regime, foreigners believe that a country's reserves of foreign currency are running low, that it is unlikely to be able to obtain replacements by borrowing from other countries or from an international agency, and that an imbalance between supply and demand is likely to continue, they will anticipate a devaluation. A devaluation is the same as a depreciation in the exchange rate, but it is the result of the decision of the government or government agency rather than the outcome of the current supply and demand for the currency in a free market. Because it is an administrative decision, devaluation is by a specified amount. For example, the exchange rate is altered from £1 = $2.25 to £1 = $1.75. Both before and after the devaluation the rate of exchange is known and the new exchange rate of £1 = $1.75 will continue until there is another devaluation. The amount of depreciation depends on market forces, so the exchange rate may continually change.

As already noted, a depreciation means that the currency is worth less in terms of other currencies. If an American investor bought £10,000 worth of sterling at £1 = $2.25, he would have paid $22,500 for his British stocks and shares. If there is a devaluation of sterling so that £1 = $1.75m when he sells his British securities for £10,000 and converts the sterling back into dollars, he will receive only $17,500. Even though he will have received interest on the British securities he will suffer a capital loss when he repatriates his dollars.

If foreigners believe that a country will be unable to maintain its fixed exchange rate and will devalue, they will sell their assets in that currency and convert the proceeds back into their own or another currency. When they convert their holdings of that currency into their own (in this example when Americans convert their sterling back into dollars), there will be an increase in the demand for foreign currency which will reduce the government's dwindling reserves.

This reduction in reserves will make devaluation even more likely and so more Americans will sell their sterling assets and convert the proceeds into dollars. The pressure can become so strong that the British government could be unable to maintain the exchange rate and devaluation would take place. If, under a fixed exchange rate regime, there is a strong belief that devaluation is a possibility, the self-interested actions of foreign holders of that currency can lead to pressures on the foreign exchange markets which greatly increase the probability of devaluation. In some cases, if foreigners hold enough assets in the country and are able to convert them into other currencies at will, they can almost ensure that devaluation takes place.

Residents of the country may wish to convert their assets into a foreign currency, but it is easier for the government to impose restrictions on them. In many countries, nationals are limited in the amount of currency they can convert into foreign currency. If there are no restrictions on the sale of a currency for other currencies, we say that the currency is freely and fully convertible. Some currencies are freely convertible by foreigners but not by its own nationals. In some cases foreigners can convert certain amounts for specific purposes. The ability to repatriate profits and convert them into foreign currency can be an important factor influencing the decision of overseas companies to invest in a country.

Fixed exchange rates prevent the working of supply and demand as the determiners of the rate of exchange. They operate to create stability in the rate of exchange and this is important, since it affects the domestic price of imports. As we have seen, a depreciation or devaluation leads to an increase in the domestic price of imports. This may have two important repercussions.

First, it increases the cost of living. Domestic prices rise and this is generally followed by pressure to increase money wages in order to maintain real living standards. This can lead to an inflationary spiral as wages rise to compensate for higher import prices, and domestic prices then rise to reflect the higher labour costs so that there is further pressure for higher wages to compensate for the increased prices, and so on. Second, if the country imports raw materials which it processes or turns into manufactured goods for export, the higher import prices will lead to a rise in the prices it charges for exports to reflect the higher import input prices. The initial decreases in the foreign currency price of its exports following the depreciation or devaluation will therefore be offset to some extent by the subsequent rise in its domestic prices.

The terms of trade

The terms of trade compare the prices of a country's exports with the prices of its imports. In the illustration of the principle of comparative advantage, where we used only two commodities, we could express the terms of trade as the ratio in which the two commodities were exchanged or traded. In the real world, where countries exchange and trade thousands of different commodities and services, we cannot use physical units to quantify the exchange ratio. We therefore use indices of the prices of the goods exchanged. To do this we calculate an index of export prices. This is an index number showing how the prices of goods exported, expressed in the domestic currency, have changed over a time period. Thus if the index is based on 1976 = 100, and currently stands at 250, we know that export prices are on average two and a half times higher than they were in 1976.

We can also construct an index of import prices which shows how the average prices of imports, measured in the domestic currency, have changed. It is crucial to remember that both indices measure the change of prices through time. They do not measure the absolute level of export and import prices at a particular time. Thus if the export price index is 250 and the index of import prices, based on the same year, is 300, we can say that the average price of imports has risen since 1976 by more than the average price of exports. We cannot say that imports cost more than exports for we do not know from the indices of prices what the average price of a unit of exports or imports is. Nor do we know what the average units of exports and imports are. For example, if all imports are chests of tea and all exports are cars, we would expect the average price of exports to be higher than the average price of imports – if we are measuring in units of a car and a chest of tea. A car is more expensive than a chest of tea. If the unit of tea was expressed in tons, the tea may be more valuable. Comparison of the two price indices allows us, therefore, to say that the price of imports has risen by more than the price of exports, but not that imports are more expensive than exports. We can say that the average price of imports has risen more quickly, or that imports are *relatively* more expensive than exports compared with 1976, but that is not the same as saying that they are more expensive.

We compare the index of export prices with the index of import prices to obtain an index of the terms of trade:

$$\text{Index of terms of trade} = \frac{\text{Index of export prices}}{\text{Index of import prices}} \times 100$$

Using the example above we would calculate the index of terms of trade as $250/300 \times 100 = 83.3$. Currently, in relation to 1976, the base of the two price indices, the terms of trade have fallen from 100 to 83. This means that the prices of exports have fallen relative to the prices of imports. Both sets of prices have risen, but those for imports have risen by more than those for exports.

It is conventional to refer to a reduction in the index of the terms of trade as a worsening of the terms of trade. Thus, in the above example, the terms of trade are worse than they were in 1976. They may be better than they were last year because last year's index of the terms of trade might have been 80, and have risen to 83 this year.

Depreciation or devaluation always worsens a country's terms of trade. It does this by raising the cost of imports in the domestic currency.

When a country devalues it deliberately turns the terms of trade against itself. It makes imports dearer in terms of its own currency, and it makes exports cheaper in terms of the foreign currency if the domestic price of its exports remains unaltered. However, as we have seen, if imported raw materials are used in the production of its exports there will be some increases in the domestic price following devaluation; but since raw materials do not account for the total costs of production, the increase in the domestic price after devaluation will still be less than the fall in price in the foreign currency resulting from the devaluation.

After devaluation, and as a result of price elasticities of demand, there will be a change in the demand for imports in both countries. The devaluing country will demand fewer imports since their prices will have risen. Foreign countries will demand more imports from the devaluing country because their prices in foreign currencies have fallen. The devaluation leads to an alteration of the price of the same product in the two currencies, so that the devaluing country can charge the same price for its exports in its own currency and foreigners will be able to buy them at a lower price in their currency. Similarly, the foreigners' exports will be priced at the same amount in their currency but will cost more in the devaluing country's currency.

The effect on the aggregate demand for and supply of the devaluing country's currency in the foreign exchange market will depend on the price elasticities of demand of the products being sold in the different countries. If both countries have price-inelastic demands for imports, the higher prices in the devaluing country will not lead to much decline in the quantity demanded, and because each unit bought requires more domestic currency to buy the same amount of foreign currency to pay the constant foreign price, there will be a large increase in the demand for foreign currency. Because foreign demand is price-inelastic it will not rise by much, even though the foreign price of exports and the devaluing country's currency have fallen, so there will be a reduction in the supply of foreign currency in the foreign exchange market. In this situation there will still be an imbalance between supply and demand in the foreign exchange market and the new exchange rate will not be an equilibrium one.

If the demand for imports in both countries is price-elastic, there will be a reduction in the total amount of demand for foreign currency in the devaluing country and an increase in the total demand for its currency by foreigners wishing to buy a proportionately larger amount of imports from it. The aggregate demand for the currency will increase and the aggregate supply of it will fall in the foreign exchange market, thereby leading to an imbalance, but an imbalance which results in foreign currency flowing into the country's reserves.

A devaluation will lead to an improvement in the country's aggregate demand and supply position according to the relationship of its price elasticity of demand for imports and the foreign price elasticity of demand for its exports. If the sum of the two price elasticities for imports is greater than 1, the result of devaluation or depreciation will be to increase aggregate demand for the currency in relation to aggregate supply and thereby improve the currency's position in the foreign exchange market.

This simple rule becomes more complicated, however, once we allow for the effect of imported raw material prices in the costs of the country's exports, for this means that some of the expected gains from the price elasticity of demand will be lost as a result of the higher prices. Also, the rise in the price of imports in the devaluating country will raise prices and, as we have seen, may lead to pressure for higher money wages. In addition, there will be changes in output and employment following devaluation since the alterations in relative prices will affect demand for products. This will lead to changes in income so that the income elasticity of demand for imports becomes relevant. The simple rule of price elasticities may be overridden by other factors.

There may be even more complications. The sum of the price elasticities of demand rule operates on the assumption that the higher demand for exports from the devaluing country can be met by increased output at a constant price. It may not be possible to increase output, or be possible to do so only at a higher price if producers are faced with upward-sloping cost curves. For example, if Sri Lanka devalued, it might not be possible to increase the supply of tea even if foreign demand was price-elastic.

Similarly, when import prices rise in the devaluing country and demand for foreign exports falls, foreign producers may reduce their prices in order to maintain their markets. For example, producers of primary or agricultural products may be faced with an inelastic supply which forces them to keep the prices of their exports at the same or even at a reduced level after devaluation.

Price elasticities of supply therefore should also be taken into account when a country is considering whether to devalue its currency.

There is one further complication. Producers in the devaluing country may know that they are faced with a price-inelastic demand for their products in foreign countries. If they charge the same price in their own currency for their exports, so that the price in the foreign currency falls, there may be relatively little expansion in demand. They may therefore decide to increase the price of their products in their own currency so that the price remains the same in the foreign currency. For example, if British producers were selling whisky to the United States at £5 a bottle, or $11.25 when £1 = $2.25, they may decide to increase their sterling price to £6.40 when sterling is devalued to £1 = $1.75. This will keep the dollar price of whisky at $11.20. They could take the higher sterling price as extra profits, or finance improved advertising campaigns or retail outlets to try to increase demand through non-price competition.

Producers of exports in a devaluing country will maintain their home currency price for exports at the pre-devaluation level only when the price elasticities of demand and supply for their products are favourable.

Alternatives to devaluation

We have seen that if there is imbalance between aggregate demand and supply of a currency in the foreign exchange market, the exchange rate will change if there is a floating exchange rate system, or there will be changes in the reserves of foreign currencies if there is a fixed exchange rate regime. Where demand for a currency on a fixed exchange rate is less than the supply, there will be a running down of the reserves of foreign currencies which might lead to a devaluation. This can improve the position if the various elasticities of demand and supply are appropriate.

There are other options open to a government seeking to protect or maintain its exchange rate.

As we have seen, some of the demand for a currency is for the purchase of its exports, but some is also to enable capital movements and investments to take place. If a government increases the rates of interest available to foreigners, it may attract foreign capital and thus increase the aggregate demand for its currency. Some capital is internationally mobile, willing to move from country to country in response to relative interest rates: it will go where the interest rate is highest on assets of the same risk. Thus in order to attract overseas capital, it is necessary to raise interest rates in a country not in relation to their past levels in that country, but in relation to prevailing rates of interest in other countries. Moreover, the comparison is of interest rates for loans of comparable risk. If it is thought that a country is likely to devalue by 20 per cent, then interest rates that are 5 per cent higher than in other countries where there is no risk of devaluation will not attract foreign capital.

Relatively higher interest rates may, however, be used to increase the demand for a currency by attracting foreign investors as long as the extra rewards are not swamped by perceived higher probabilities of devaluation and capital loss, or as long as there is no fear that the government will subsequently introduce legislation preventing the repatriation or convertibility of the funds invested. However, it should be recognised that this inflow of capital may be reversed if other countries increase their rates of interest.

A government may also seek to persuade foreign companies to undertake long-term fixed investment in plant and equipment. The funds transferred to do this will increase the aggregate demand for the currency and so stem the outflow of foreign currency from its reserves. However, in some cases relatively little of the total investment costs may be in the local country's currency. The foreign company may purchase the capital equipment elsewhere or produce it at home, so that while there is a large amount of capital invested in the country, not much of it requires local currency.

A government may encourage its nationals working abroad to repatriate some of their earnings, or require national companies with overseas earnings to remit part of their earnings or profits home. This will increase the demand for the local currency.

Where foreign exchange controls are imposed, the government is attempting to limit the demand for foreign currency. It may do this by limiting the amount of foreign exchange that its nationals can demand for buying imports or for travelling abroad on holiday. It is seeking to reduce demand by some non-price means. It could presumably always have a rate of exchange at which the demand for foreign currency would equal the supply, but this exchange rate might impose great burdens on the economy. A country may feel that it has to import certain commodities such as oil, some foods, some machinery or defence weapons. It may believe that both economic and political stability would be seriously threatened were the exchange rate set at the level which equated supply and demand for its currency, for that could lead to a very large devaluation so that the price of imports would increase a great deal. It therefore seeks to maintain an exchange rate at which the demand for foreign currency is higher than the supply, and to do this it has to impose controls to limit the demand through licences, quotas or by rationing foreign exchange and insisting that all its nationals hand over all their earnings of foreign exchange to the central authorities.

Because the exchange rate is an artificial one there will be an unofficial or black-market exchange rate, since some nationals will be willing to pay more than the official price for foreign currency. Some nationals with earnings of foreign currency from exports will retain some of it rather than hand it over to the authorities. Others will seek to purchase foreign currency from tourists at a higher rate of exchange. This will happen because demand exceeds supply at the prevailing fixed price and some people are willing to pay more, and risk suffering penalties, in order to obtain foreign currency.

CHAPTER 20

The balance of payments

We saw in the previous chapter that imports incur a liability to payment in a foreign currency and exports lead foreigners to demand the domestic currency in order to pay for them. If the exchange rate is free and floating, the rate of exchange of a country's currency with those of other countries will be determined by the aggregate supply of and demand for its currency. If there is a fixed exchange rate regime, imbalances between aggregate demand and supply can be adjusted through the reserves of foreign currencies held by the government's agency or exchange equalisation account, although a persistent excess of supply over demand will lead to the exhaustion of reserves and devaluation.

Countries produce an annual balance of payments account, which is a record of all transactions between its residents and the rest of the world. This is essentially a record of the inflow of domestic currency into the country and the outflow to purchase foreign currencies. The practice is easier to understand if we take one country as an example.

The UK balance of payments account records all credits from all transactions with people overseas which lead to an inflow of sterling to the United Kingdom, and all outflows of sterling are shown as debits. As with all double-entry bookkeeping the two sides of the accounts, the credits and debits, must balance. The overall balance of payments account is made up of subdivisions which differentiate the various types of activity which create credits or debits.

Details of the UK balance of payments account for 1984 are given in Table 20.1.

We separate the account into three main sub-accounts: the current

Table 20.1. UK balance of payments account 1984

		£ million	
(1)	Visible exports	+70,409	
(2)	Visible imports	−74,510	
(3)	Balance of visible trade (1–2)		−4,101
(4)	Invisible trade (services) exports	+21,327	
(5)	Invisible trade (services) imports	−17,342	
(6)	Balance of invisible trade (4−5)		+3,985
(7)	Balance of trade (3+6)		− 116
(8)	Interest, profits and dividends received	+50,744	
(9)	Interest, profits and dividends paid	−47,440	
(10)	Net transfers	− 2,253	
(11)	Current account (7+8−9+10)		+ 935
(12)	Balancing item	+ 1,040	
(13)	Foreign investment in UK	+ 3,619	
(14)	UK private investment overseas	−14,585	
(15)	Investment in banking sector (net)	+ 9,312	
(16)	Other	− 1,637	
(17)	Official financing	+ 1,316	

Notes: 1. These figures will be revised by the government as more accurate information becomes available.
2. The overall balance of payments is (11+12+13−14+15−16+17), which must always sum to zero.

account, the capital account, and official financing. The current account shows the balance between inflows and outflows in respect of current activities, and the capital account shows the inflows and outflows of capital. Official financing reflects the intervention of the government or its agency to maintain the exchange rate by buying or selling sterling.

The current account

This records the value of inflows and outflows of goods and services, and other income. We distinguish 'other income' from capital movements so that receipts of interest or dividends by UK residents from their investments overseas are counted as income in the current account, and payments of interest and dividends, etc., to people overseas by UK firms or the UK government are counted as a debit in the current account. The transfers of the money used to purchase the stocks or investments which earn the dividends or interest are classed as capital movements and so included in the capital account. Put simply, therefore, if a UK resident sends £5m abroad to invest in shares in a foreign country, that would appear as a debit of £5m in the capital account of the UK balance of payments. When dividends or interest were received they would appear as a credit payment in the current account of the UK balance of payments. At the same time, the country in which the investment, or purchase of stocks, took place would record the inflow of the £5m (in units of its own currency) as a credit in its capital account, and the subsequent payment of dividends or interest would appear (again in units of its own currency) as debits or outflows in the current account.

The current account includes all trade and income payments and receipts.

The balance of trade The most obvious forms of trade are the imports and exports of goods resulting from specialisation and trade. These are referred to as *visibles*: we can actually see the goods entering or leaving a country as imports and exports. We refer to the difference between the value of visible imports and exports as the balance of visible trade. In 1984 the United Kingdom had a deficit of £4,101m on its balance of visible trade because it imported that amount of goods more than it exported. It is usual for the United Kingdom to have a balance of visible trade deficit.

Countries also import and export services such as banking, insurance, shipping and tourism. These are called *invisibles* although we can actually see tourists spending money in a country, and the banking services are no less real than the work of the accounts clerk in the factory producing cars which are exported and counted in the visible trade balance. The balance of invisible trade is the difference between the credits and debits of these invisible items.

Interest, profits and dividends As we have seen, residents in the United Kingdom receive interest and other income from assets abroad and foreigners receive income from their assets in the United Kingdom. These have exactly the same effect as payments from or for the export or import of physical trade. Receipts from abroad increase the demand for sterling and the supply of foreign currency, and payments to foreign nationals have the opposite effect.

There may also be transfer payments like contributions to international organisations such as the UN or EEC, and the receipt of foreign aid. These are included in the current account since they are seen as payments for activity taking place in the year.

If we add together the visible and invisible trade (which gives the balance of trade), interest, profits and dividends, and transfers, we obtain the current account balance.

In 1984 the United Kingdom had a surplus of £935m. The UK current account has been in surplus since 1980. Previously it was often in deficit, but the development of North Sea oil reduced imports of oil.

The current account balance is an important economic indicator. It tells us whether the country is currenty earning more from its international activities than it is paying out. Details of the balance of trade can indicate whether the country is becoming more or less competitive in international trade. If a country has a net surplus on interest, profits and dividends, a deficit on the balance of trade is less serious, since this surplus can offset it. A deficit on the current account has to be offset or 'paid for' by a surplus elsewhere in the balance of payments.

The capital account

The capital account shows the international sales and purchases of assets. These are often financial assets such as government securities, stocks or equity shares in private companies. They may also include investment in new plant and equipment in factories already owned by nationals of one country in another. In the UK balance of payments accounts, capital movements are usually separated into short-term (those in assets with a life of less than one year) and long-term.

Sometimes the long-term balance and the current account are added together to provide the *basic balance*. This is taken as an indicator of the underlying position of the country; short-term capital movements and official financing are sometimes seen as accommodating transactions, since they are undertaken or induced in order to accommodate a desired movement in funds in order to obtain a smaller deficit or larger surplus. As we saw in the previous chapter, a government may increase interest rates in order to attract internationally mobile capital. This would generally come to purchase short-term securities or make short-term loans, and would be seen as accommodating a balance of payments deficit by increasing the inflow of foreign funds, albeit on a temporary basis.

There has been a large outflow of long-term capital funds from the United Kingdom since 1980–82, when controls which restricted investment overseas were removed.

The capital account can provide a surplus to offset a deficit on the current account.

Official financing

If we add up the debits and credits of the current and capital accounts we find that they do not balance. In 1984 the UK balance of payments showed that after adding together the current and capital accounts there was a deficit of £1,316m. This deficit had to be covered from somewhere, since the total amount of inflow of foreign funds converted into sterling has to equal the total outflow of sterling converted into foreign currencies.

If the exchange were completely free and floating there need be no official financing, since the rate of exchange would be determined each day, or each minute that the foreign exchanges were working, by the aggregate supply of and demand for sterling and foreign currencies. The total of the current and capital accounts would always be exactly equal. However, no country has a perfectly or completely free and floating exchange rate. As we have seen, governments intervene to smooth out day-to-day fluctuations or to maintain an exchange rate within some predetermined limits. Even if governments are committed to allowing market forces to determine the general level of and movements in the exchange rate, they may wish to influence the precise movements.

Because governments seek to exert some influence on the exchange rate, they intervene in the foreign exchange market. They will buy their own currency by providing foreign currencies from their reserves when the market forces would push the exchange rate below the desired level, and they will sell their own currency for foreign currency when the aggregate supply and demand pressures would lead to an unwelcome rise in the rate of exchange. These interventions are the official transactions, or official financing. They therefore indicate the extent to which government has intervened in the foreign exchange market.

The amount of official intervention or financing is always equal to the difference between the sum of the current and capital accounts and has the opposite sign. This can be confusing. A plus in official financing means that government or the exchange equalisation account has intervened to provide foreign currency. It has removed the excess supply of sterling in the foreign exchange market by providing more foreign currency than appeared from foreign demand for UK exports or as a result of foreigners wishing to invest or lend funds to the United Kingdom.

The balancing item

If we add together the current and capital accounts we find the net balance of the country's international trade and capital movement. In practice there is another entry called the 'Balancing item'. The balancing item is *not* the amount necessary to make the credit and debit entries of the current and capital accounts balance or sum to zero. This function is performed by official financing. The balancing item represents the fact that we cannot measure the total values of all international transactions precisely and accurately. There are always some errors in the figures. Some of the entries may be estimates based on samples. The balancing item is the correction made to the recorded figures to bring them into line with the known outcome of international activity. In 1984 the balancing item in the UK balance of payments was +£1,040m. When all the estimated figures for the various components of the balance of payments were added together, there was an imbalance of −£1,040. Since both sides of any double-entry bookkeeping system must balance, it was necessary to add in £1,040m. It is possible that the debits are actually overstated by £1,040m or that the credits are understated. The figures for 1984 will be revised at a later date when the government statisticians have more accurate information. The balancing item might change, but it will always be whatever is necessary to make the debits and credits equal. The best way to look at the balancing item is to regard it as a measure of the inaccuracies of the balance of payments statistics.

Surpluses and deficits

In one sense no country can ever have a surplus or deficit on its balance of payments. The balance must balance and come to zero. However, as we have seen, there can be surpluses or deficits on each of the component parts of the balance of payments, and the overall balance may be obtained by official financing which reflects government intervention to influence the exchange rate. If there were an overall deficit it would mean that some people who wished to exchange their sterling for a foreign currency could not do so, with the result that some foreigners would not be paid for their exports to the United Kingdom, or some foreign investors would not be able to convert their dividends and interest into their own currency. If this happened there would be a major threat to international trade with the country because foreigners would be unwilling to export to or invest in the United Kingdom. Governments can restrict the access to foreign exchange of their nationals, but problems arise if they do this with foreigners.

If the total value of imports, plus payment of interest, etc., to foreigners, exceeds the value of exports plus interest received, a country must attract foreign capital or use its reserves of foreign currency. As we have seen, it can seek to attract foreign capital by raising interest rates, but this is hazardous since the foreign funds may leave if interest rates rise elsewhere. It can try to attract long-term capital and it can borrow from other governments or international organisations.

These debts will increase future outflows of interest and dividends but will provide inflows in the short run. Some countries have borrowed such large amounts of foreign funds that a substantial part of their future earnings of foreign currency from exports is already committed to debt servicing or repayment.

An overall deficit offset by official financing cannot continue indefinitely. A deficit in the basic balance, which is offset by increased foreign borrowing to restore the overall balance, postpones the need to reduce the outflow or increase the inflow of foreign funds. Many developing countries are faced with immense difficulties. There is a high demand for imports; some of these are essential, such as oil. Others may be necessary if the country is to undertake a programme of development, since plant and equipment may have to be imported. Some of the demand for imports may reflect the desire to have a higher standard of living than can be provided from domestic resources. There may be little opportunity to expand exports because the country may be uncompetitive in new products and there may be declining markets for traditional products.

It is important to recognise that each component of the balance of payments does not have to balance exactly. A deficit on visible trade can be offset by a surplus on invisible trade or on interest and dividends. Temporary deficits can be covered by official financing. However, in the longer run, continuing deficits in the basic balance will create considerable problems. At some stage it will prove increasingly difficult or impossible to obtain further foreign loans. Drastic reductions in imports will then be necessary.

Policies for imbalances

There are three types of policies to deal with persistent deficits in the balance of payments.

Deflation If a country has a persistent imbalance in the balance of trade it may deflate the economy. It can introduce restrictive demand management policies so that the level of economic activity is reduced. This might lead to a reduction in wages and prices or a slower rate of growth of wages and prices. In turn, this may increase the competitiveness of exports in the international market and so lead to an increase in demand. However, if that restores the level of economic activity to its former position, the previous rate of inflation may reappear so that there would be no lasting improvement.

Deflation may also improve the balance of trade if lower incomes lead to a reduction in the demand for imports. Thus both exports and imports could benefit, but both could then revert to their previous positions if the policy is effective. In some situations deflation could worsen the balance of trade. Lower incomes might lead to an increase in the propensity to import rather than to a reduction. This would depend on the type of goods consumed at different income levels.

Devaluation As we have seen, devaluation may stimulate exports and reduce imports by raising the price of imports in the devaluing country's currency, and lowering the price of exports in other countries' currencies. Much will depend on the price elasticities of demand in the various countries. It is also important that the elasticities of supply be appropriate.

When a country devalues there will be an increase in the price of imports. One of the objectives of devaluation is to reduce the demand for imports and so the aggregate demand for foreign currency. If there is a high price elasticity of demand for imports, demand for them will fall in the devaluing country. However, this will mean that if incomes and consumption remain the same, there will be an increase in demand for home-produced goods which are now more price-attractive than imports. Domestic demand for domestic products will rise. This could lead to producers reducing their exports. It may be easier to sell on the home market, there are fewer difficulties than in dealing with foreign buyers, and payment may be received more quickly.

There will also very likely be an increase in foreign demand for exports since their price may be lower. This will depend on whether the domestic producers in the devaluing country have maintained their prices after devaluation or raised them to take advantage of devaluation. It is possible that there could be a significant increase in demand for products from the devaluing country as both internal and foreign demand increase. This could lead to an increase in costs and prices if firms are faced with upward-sloping cost curves, and also because wages may rise as a result of the increase in the cost of imports following devaluation. There is a strong possibility therefore that devaluation might be followed by rising prices which would negate some if not all of the effects of devaluation.

Often deflationary policies are introduced with devaluation to try to reduce home demand and thus avoid this additional inflationary pressure. Devaluation will be more successful if there is excess domestic capacity or if producers are faced with constant cost curves.

Devaluation worsens a country's terms of trade. A country does this because it hopes thereby to improve the balance of trade. As we have seen, whether the balance of trade will improve after a change in the terms of trade depends on the price elasticities of demand. It is possible that either an improvement or a worsening in the terms of trade could lead to an improvement or a worsening in the balance of trade. The greatest effect is likely to be on the balance of visible trade, since these are the items included in the calculation of the terms of trade, but devaluation could improve the invisible trade balance.

The difference between the terms of trade and the balance of trade is important. The terms of trade refer to differences in the rate of change of import and export prices expressed in the domestic country's currency. The balance of trade refers to the difference in the aggregate value of imports and exports expressed in the country's currency. Paradoxically, a worsening of the terms of trade could lead to an improvement in the balance of trade, either visible trade or visible plus invisible, and an improvement in the terms of trade resulting from a greater increase in the price of exports than of imports could lead to a worsening of the balance of trade if the demand for both imports and exports is price-elastic.

Controls and restraints The third way to try to reduce a balance of payments deficit on current account is to impose controls and restraints on the free importation of goods. Quotas and tariffs will lead to a reduction in the quantity of goods imported and in the demand for foreign currencies. Foreign exchange controls can be introduced which limit the amount of foreign currency nationals may acquire. The controls may be general or discriminate between different types of users of foreign currency. Those importing essential commodities may be given large allowances, and those wishing to purchase imported luxury goods, or obtain foreign currency for a holiday abroad, may be severely limited in the amount they can have.

As we have already discussed in Chapter 18, quotas will lead to demand exceeding supply at the prevailing price, and some increase in price, or the opportunity to make gains by selling the limited amount of imported goods for their higher market price, will arise. Tariffs raise prices so that demand at the higher price can be equated to supply. Controls create distortions in the market allocation of goods and expenditure by preventing either supply or demand from being effective at its market level.

A current account deficit can be improved by encouraging more exports. Subsidies to exporters can be seen as a negative restraint. They are positive encouragements to exporters and may have the same effect on the foreign price of a country's exports as devaluation: by subsidising production costs they allow the export price to be lower than it was previously. Unlike devaluation, export subsidies do not lead to a rise in the domestic price of imports. However, many international agreements discourage or ban export subsidies. In practice, such prohibition may be difficult to enforce.

Non-trade items

A country may seek to reduce a current account deficit by reducing the outflow of dividends, profits and rent to foreigners. This might be achieved by imposing a tax. However, if the rate of return on foreigners' investment in the country is reduced, foreigners may withdraw their investment, thus creating a large outflow on the capital account.

A country may impose controls on overseas investment by its nationals. This will reduce the outflow of funds on the capital account.

Surpluses

Countries seek to avoid a deficit on the combined current and capital accounts. They may try to obtain a surplus in order to build up their reserves of foreign exchange. A surplus in one country means that there must be a deficit elsewhere. Countries which consistently have a surplus on their combined current and capital accounts are ensuring that some other countries have deficits. A surplus may appear to be good for a country. If it is exporting more than it imports it is obtaining the benefits of the multiplier effects of exports, and may be maintaining a higher level of employment than would be possible were its imports and exports to balance.

However, if other countries are running deficits on their balance of trade, they may be compelled to take action which leads to a reduction of imports. This may lead to a reduced demand for exports from the surplus countries, but could also lead to a reduction in the exports of other deficit countries. It need not follow therefore that the long-term reduction in international trade which may follow the corrective action of deficit countries will lead to a reduction in the exports of surplus countries.

Countries which have a continuing surplus create problems for others. Persistent surpluses are therefore undesirable from the general viewpoint, although they may bring benefits to the individual surplus countries. It can be difficult to take effective action against persistent surplus countries. The best solution is for their surpluses to be reduced or eliminated by an increase in their imports, as other countries sell them more exports. However, the surplus countries may resist a growth of imports. Other countries could reduce their imports from surplus countries, but this might require them to introduce discriminatory restrictions against specific countries, and this could deny people the opportunity to import and purchase goods at prices which they prefer.

International agreements may seek to condemn the maintaining of persistent surpluses and permit discrimination against exports from countries which run them, but it may prove difficult in practice to prevent a country from having a surplus on its basic balance.

CHAPTER 21

National income accounts

We have seen from our discussion in Chapter 12 that there is a circular flow of income from firms to households and back to firms, with government intervening through taxation and government expenditure, and with imports and exports deducting from or adding to income through multiplier effects. We have also seen that the value of net output or value added by a firm is equal to the incomes of all those employed by the firm, and of its shareholders or entrepreneurs. We can use these relationships to measure the income or output of a country.

Gross domestic product

Initially we shall take gross domestic product (GDP) to measure the income or output of a country in a period of time. Usually we measure GDP for a year, although it is possible to measure it for a month or a quarter. Gross domestic product is the total output produced by the factors of production in an economy.

We know that the total value of output must equal the total incomes received from the production of that output, so that $Y = O$. Because all income must be consumed or saved, and savings must equal investment, it follows that income must equal expenditure on consumption and investment goods (X), so that $Y = O = X = C + S = C + I$.

If we were to add together all incomes from production, the total, Y, would equal the total amount spent on consumption and investment, which would also equal the total value of output produced by those factors of production. There are therefore three different ways in which we can measure GDP – by measuring income, by measuring expenditure, or by measuring the value of output – and they will each give us the same total of GDP.

As we saw in Chapter 12, it is important to avoid double counting, so that when we measure the output of each plant or industry we include only the *addition* to output. We do this by subtracting the value of bought-in materials, components and semi-manufactured items from the value of sales. We can take a short cut by counting only final output sold to consumers or to other producers as investment goods. Similarly, when we measure expenditure we include only final sales to consumers or purchasers of investment goods. The intermediate transactions are excluded or there would be double counting of expenditure.

The two most frequently used measures of GDP are the income method and the expenditure method.

Income Method

While there are some differences in the way in which different countries compile their national income statistics, they all follow the same general rules. No great distortion will be caused by using the UK figures to illustrate general practice, but readers in other countries should examine their own national accounts so that they are familiar with their national statistics.

As is shown in Table 21.1, there are six major categories of income. The most important is income from employment, which accounts for approximately two thirds of total domestic income in the United Kingdom. This proportion will vary from country to country according to the relative importance of employment and self-employment and the relative gross profit ratios.

All the figures are gross in that they are the amounts shown before the deduction of income tax or other direct taxes, and also include workers' and employers' contributions to pension schemes, whether these are private pension schemes or statutory pension contributions to a government or national pension or provident fund. We also include any payment in kind such as free meals provided by the employer or free quantities of products such as coal or agricultural products.

Income from employment is differentiated from income from self-employment because the former is what is usually meant by employment – payment received for working for someone else – while self-employment can be seen as a mixture of income from employment and gross profits. A self-employed person may be a small farmer working his own or rented

Table 21.1. UK national income accounts 1984

	£ million
A. *Factor incomes*	
Income from employment	180,342
Income from self-employment	26,885
Gross trading profits of companies	47,900
Gross trading surplus of public corporations	8,732
Gross trading surplus of general government enterprises	− 250
Rent	18,937
Imputed charge for consumption of non-trading capital[1]	2,526
Gross domestic income	285,072
less stock appreciation	− 5,163
Gross domestic product	279,909
Residual error	− 5,336
Gross domestic product at factor cost	274,573
Net property income from abroad	3,304
Gross national product at factor cost	277,877
Capital consumption	−38,371
National income	239,506
B. *Expenditure*	
Consumers' expenditure	194,673
Government final consumption	69,655
Gross domestic fixed capital formation	55,319
Value of physical increase in stocks and work in progress	− 177
Total domestic expenditure	319,470
Exports of goods and services	91,736
less imports of goods and services	−91,852
Gross domestic product at market prices	319,354
Plus subsidies less taxes on expenditure	−44,781
Gross domestic product at factor cost	274,573

[1] This represents imputed income of government and private non-profit-making bodies from owner non-trading fixed capital assets.

land, using members of his family as helpers. Or he may be a small shopkeeper. Some of his income is the equivalent of a wage and some is the profit he has made. It is often difficult to obtain precise or accurate information about the exact income from self-employment. For example, a small farmer may consume a large part of his output, and the actual income he receives for selling his surplus may be quite small in relation to his total level of consumption, so that the expenditure figures will also understate the actual level of consumption. There will be a difference between actual consumption and the level of consumption and income financed by the payment of money. Total output and total actual consumption of goods will be higher than the figures of income received from working or profits received from selling surplus products would suggest. The total quantity of goods and services produced and consumed will therefore be higher than calculations based on market transactions suggest.

In many developed countries this might not make very much difference since most transactions take place through market activity of buying and selling products. However, if production for one's own or family consumption is important, and provides a large part of some people's activity, attempts may be made to estimate the value of this production and consumption. The goods produced and consumed are as much part of total output or GDP as if they had been produced and sold for cash, and the money income received then used to buy back those, or alternative, goods.

Measuring income from self-employment can be difficult, and some countries may not try to do this. They may include the cash income from self-employment with gross profits. This can be misleading, however.

The third major category or source of income is gross trading profits of companies. Again, the profits are gross of direct taxes. Fourth, in the United Kingdom there is also the gross trading surplus of public corporations owned by the State. They can be seen as the equivalent of gross trading profits of companies except that they are State-owned rather than privately owned.

The fifth category is the gross trading surplus of general government enterprises. These enterprises are not incorporated as are the public corporations, but include central and local government trading activity. It is a relatively unimportant source of GDP.

Rent is the final category of income. This includes the gross receipts from the ownership of buildings and land minus the actual expenditure by owners on repair and maintenance. In addition, an amount is included for imputed rent to provide the equivalent of rent for owner-occupied dwellings. The amount of rent is not therefore the actual amount of rent paid since it includes imputed rent for owner-occupiers. It is assumed that owners of their own houses receive an equivalent income from rent as they do not actually pay rent to anyone. If this adjustment were not made GDP would appear to fall if more people bought their homes, since the amount of rent actually paid would decline. When imputed rent is included as income in the national accounts, we must also include an imputed item of expenditure of an equal amount on rent. We thus assume that owner-occupiers receive and pay rent to themselves.

When the various sources of income are added together we obtain total or gross domestic income. However, some of the gross profits of companies will include an element of stock appreciation if the prices of a constant amount of stocks held at the beginning and end of the year have risen. For example, if a company holds 1,000 cubic feet of timber at the beginning of the year, and also 1,000 cubic feet at the end of the year, but the value, or price, of timber has risen from £4 to £5 a cubic foot, the firm's assets will appear to be £1,000 higher at the end of the year than at the beginning, and this will be included in its gross profits. This £1,000 is in no way a contribution to output or income during the year and should therefore be deducted from the gross profits for national accounts purposes. Deduction of stock appreciation leads to the reduction of gross trading profits by an amount equal to the rise in value of a fixed quantity of stocks over the year. It is the increase in value of a constant amount of stocks that is deducted. If the firm has actually increased the amount of timber held in stocks and this value is included in the gross profit, it should remain included, for that represents additions to output and real economic activity.

When stock appreciation is deducted from gross domestic income we obtain GDP at factor cost. It is referred to as GDP at factor cost because the items are the cost of each factor of production. This is why income and profits are shown gross of tax and contributions to pension schemes, etc. These items are part of the cost of the factor and should therefore be included. Moreover, if they were excluded the total of income would not equal the total of output. If a firm bought £5,000 of raw materials and paid its workers £10,000 in wages plus £1,000 pension contributions, and made £3,000 gross profit, it would sell its final output for £19,000 and its total value added would be £14,000. The output of the firm supplying the raw materials would be £5,000. Total income, expenditure and output would thus be £19,000.

There is actually one slight complication. Although in principle the three methods should all give the same total of GDP, in practice the numbers may differ because of the difficulty of collecting absolutely accurate information. This is the same point we made in the previous chapter when discussing the measurement of the balance of payments account. It is customary to regard the expenditure figures as the most accurate. The figure for GDP at factor cost, therefore, includes an item 'Residual error', which is the figure needed to ensure that the same total GDP is obtained by both the income and expenditure methods. Residual error is the same as the balancing item in the balance of payments accounts.

Expenditure method

We measure GDP by the expenditure method by following the same approach of totalling the main items of expenditure. The first and largest component is consumers' expenditure. This is the total amount of expenditure by consumers on goods and services. Second, we include government final consumption. This is the expenditure by government on goods and services and on payment to civil servants. Government expenditure includes central and local government. Remember, income from employment and profits was shown gross of tax. Not all of the gross amounts shown were paid to employees or shareholders. The difference, that which was taken in direct taxes, is used to finance government final consumption. If it were not shown, the total consumption by workers and companies could not equal their income because some of their income was taken in taxation.

In effect we regard the provision of government services, such as education, justice, the provision of defence through the armed forces, and the work of civil servants and local government employees, as goods and services which are consumed by individuals and purchased through taxation or other forms of government financing, even though no price, or only a part payment, may be charged. When we estimate the total output of goods and services in a country over a period of time, we wish to include these services as part of the well-being and output of the economy. Because most of these are not bought and therefore do not appear in expenditure, we value them by adding together the cost to the government of providing the services. This cost is their wages plus any materials or bought-in services used, minus any direct charges made by government for the services.

The third item is gross domestic fixed capital formation, which is broadly equivalent to investment in plant and equipment. Since investment equals savings, this can be regarded as equivalent to savings so that we have now included consumption and savings, and this amount should equal income.

We also have to make an adjustment for the value of the physical increase in stocks and work in progress. Some of the output will not have been sold as consumption goods or be part of investment in plant and equipment. It will be an addition to stocks. This forms part of output during the year and income has been received from its production. The same is true for work in progress. A company may have begun building a ship in October. It will not have been finished by the end of the year, but workers will have received income for three months and there has actually been an increase in output – a part of a ship has been built. We therefore add the value of the physical increase in stocks and work in progress. If stocks have been run down during the year we would subtract the value of the reduction.

It is important to note the difference in the treatment of stocks in the two approaches to the measurement of GDP. In the income method we measure the change in value of a *constant* physical amount of stocks, as this increase in value of a constant physical amount is not part of output during the year. With the expenditure method we include only the value of the *change* in the physical amount of stocks; increases in value of the constant amount of stocks are ignored.

If we total these items we obtain total domestic expenditure, which is the amount spent domestically or within the country.

However, there will have been some output produced and income earned from exports. The value of exports should therefore be included so that the total output will equal total income. By the same token, imports should be deducted since they are not part of the output of the country, nor have they provided incomes for residents of the country. If exports are added, and imports deducted, we obtain gross domestic product at market prices.

GDP at market prices will not be the same as GDP at factor cost. This is not because of mistakes in the collection of statistics – we have already allowed for that by the residual error. The difference arises because of indirect taxes and government price subsidies.

If, in the example above, the output of a firm was £14,000 and that of the firm supplying the raw materials £5,000, total output and income would be £19,000. However, if we assume that the government imposed a 10 per cent indirect tax, the charge to consumers would be £20,900. Clearly, this is higher than output and income, and government expenditure of the £1,900, or the expenditure of those receiving government grants or transfer payments, will already be included in consumers' expenditure. We should therefore deduct indirect taxes from consumers' expenditure. In the same way, we should add government price subsidies to the value of expenditure; with price subsidies the amount paid by consumers is less than the value of output and the incomes received by those producing the consumer goods.

We then obtain GDP at factor cost, which is the same as that obtained from the factor income method.

International recommendations on the compilation of national accounts, and statistics published by international organisations, use GDP at market prices. One reason for preferring the market price method is that market prices reflect the prices actually paid for the goods and services. If consumers equate the ratios of prices and marginal utilities or satisfaction, an increase in GDP, with all market prices constant, might be thought to show that there has been an increase in total satisfaction of the community. We will consider the interpretation to be placed on an increase in GDP or other measures of national income below.

The United Kingdom prefers to use the factor cost method, although figures at market prices are also published. One advantage of this is that it allows comparisons to be made of the share of GDP going as income from employment, or as gross trading profits, and thus gives some indication of how resources have been allocated among factors of production. However, if GDP rises because employers' contributions to pensions have risen, thereby increasing income from employment and the share of income from employment in GDP, this will not mean that workers have a greater share of current output and income. They may be building up an entitlement to a larger share in the future when they get higher pensions, but not currently. The proportion of GDP received by different factors is not therefore always a reliable indicator of how resources are distributed, especially when factor incomes are gross of taxes. Changes in the incidence of taxation can change what appears to be a rising share of gross income into a falling share of net disposable income.

Gross national product

GDP is a measure of the output, income and expenditure from domestic resources. However, the residents of a country may have additional income, which they can consume or save, as a result of receiving income from assets abroad. Or, some income may be sent abroad as property income so that not all of the gross trading profits of companies are available to residents. Some will go to foreigners as dividend payments, as may some of the rent.

In order to obtain a figure for the gross national product (GNP), it is necessary to convert the domestic product, or GDP, into the national product, or GNP. We do this by adding the net property income from abroad. This is the difference between property income received from abroad, and property income paid abroad. It may be either positive or negative according to whether residents in the country have received more or less income from their assets overseas than has been paid to foreign owners of assets in the home country.

GNP is the measure of the total amount of resources available to the residents of a country during a year.

National income

GNP is a gross figure in that it measures the total amount produced or received in a year by the residents of a country. However, some of the capital assets will have been used in the process of producing that income or output. There will have been some physical depreciation of the capital equipment.

We may want to know the net output or income of a country in a year. This is the amount of output which has been produced and is therefore available for consumption or to add to investment, after allowing for the physical depreciation of the capital used to produce that output. If we deduct this from GNP, we arrive at a figure for the value of goods and services which have been added during the year: it is the net output, or net income, after allowing for the depreciation of capital.

We therefore deduct an item for capital consumption from GNP to arrive at national income. This is the value of output which is available for consumption or adding to investment and which will leave the value of capital stock at the end of the year equivalent to its value at the start of the year. It does not follow that the capital equipment used up in the course of production has actually been replaced. Replacement investment may be greater or less than capital consumption. The figure for capital consumption is the estimated amount that is necessary to replace that proportion of the existing capital stock at the start of the year which was used up in producing the year's output.

In national accounts terminology we use 'capital consumption' rather than depreciation in order to distinguish the amount estimated to have been used up in production from the depreciation which companies may make in their own balance sheets or which the tax authorities may allow as a pre-tax deductible item. We cannot actually measure how much capital consumption there has been in a year so we have to estimate it. There are two basic decisions in estimating capital consumption:
1. The value of the stock of capital at the beginning of the year.
2. The amount that has been used up during the year.

The first can be estimated from company balance sheets adjusted to take account of changes in the price or value of capital equipment, and by sample surveys. The second can be dealt with in two main ways. The 'straight-line' method assumes that assets depreciate or are consumed by a constant amount each year. If the asset is assumed to last for ten years, one-tenth of its value will be used up each year, and if it is expected to last for 40 years, one-fortieth will be consumed each year. With the 'reducing-balance' method, the depreciation each year is a constant *proportion* of the written-down or depreciated value at the beginning of each year. Accountants may favour this. International practice, followed by the United Kingdom, is to use the 'straight-line' method.

The annual amount of capital consumption is valued at current replacement cost rather than at the historical or original actual cost of the capital equipment. This is because this year's output and income are valued in current prices, and if we wish to know how much of the gross output, or GNP, has been used up in the process of producing that GNP, we should value the used-up capital in the same prices as this year's output. We can calculate capital consumption at replacement cost from details of historical cost of the capital equipment in one of two ways. We can take the actual cost of the capital equipment currently in use, calculate the capital consumption for this year on the basis of the original cost of the assets, and then revalue this year's capital consumption to take account of the increase in prices since the capital equipment was first bought. Thus if we have consumed one-tenth of capital equipment which originally cost £100,000, we can estimate capital consumption this year as £10,000. If the price of this type of capital equipment has doubled since its date of purchase, we can then revalue this year's capital consumption to £20,000.

Alternatively, we can start by revaluing the item into current prices, so that the capital equipment this year would be valued at £200,000 because prices have doubled since it was installed. A physical depreciation rate of one-tenth will then give us a figure for capital consumption of £20,000.

Whichever set of conventions is adopted to estimate capital consumption, the resulting figure is deducted from GNP to provide an estimate of national income, or net national product (NNP). Net national product (net of capital consumption) and national income mean the same thing.

Comparisons of national income

Figures for national income in different years are often used to assess whether a country is becoming better off. If national income rises, and there have been no increases in prices, it means that there are more goods and services in real terms available for consumption or investment. If national income doubles over a period, but all prices double, then there will have been no increase in real national income. To distinguish between increases in nominal national income and real national income, we often measure national income at *constant prices*.

The first calculation of national income for a year is made in current prices. These are the prices prevailing during the year for which national income is being measured. As we have seen, an increase in national income at current prices may be merely the result of inflation, or may be the result of an increase in real national income. If we select a base year and convert all prices in later years into the prices which prevailed in the base year, we obtain a series of national income figures at constant prices. They are expressed in the prices of the base year. This is usually done for GNP or NNP using the expenditure method, since the figures collected by that method are more readily converted into a price index series.

An increase in GNP at constant prices means that the total output of goods and services in real terms has risen. This does not necessarily mean that people are consuming more. The increase may have been in investment goods. This could lead to higher consumption in the future but not currently.

Even if real consumption has increased it does not necessarily mean that everyone is consuming more. This will depend on what has happened to the distribution of income. It does mean that total consumption has risen, but if the population has risen by more than real consumption, average consumption per head will have fallen. If we wish to ascertain whether the change in real national income was sufficient to permit an increase in average consumption, we therefore often use the concept of per capita national income, or national income-per-head. We divide the national income at constant prices by the population.

It is difficult to compare movements in real national income over long time periods. The longer the time period covered, the greater the probability that there will have been changes in products, so that it can be very difficult to estimate the current price of goods which were consumed 20 years ago but which are not consumed, or consumed only in small quantities, today. Changes in the quantities of goods consumed may have affected the level of costs and prices by leading to changes in returns to scale in production. It is even more difficult to estimate a price in the past for new products. For example, if we were comparing the real national incomes of today and 30 years ago, there would be many products included in current consumption which were not available 30 years ago. Videos, Walkman tape recorders, and the latest car models with new advanced technology were not available then.

Price indices have two major disadvantages. The items which are included in the basket of goods and which provide the basis for the index change through time. Either some goods disappear and new ones are developed, or what might appear to be the same good (or is called the same) changes as a result of technological innovation. Some of the price increases in this latter category may not be the result of higher prices for the same product but a different (higher) price for a different product. What appears to be a price rise will therefore include some improvement in quality which is not actually a price increase. Attempts are made to adjust the price index for changes in quality and periodically new products are introduced into the basket of goods, but these are both subjective elements.

In addition, changes in consumption patterns mean that some goods and services become more important items in people's expenditure and others become less important. The basket of goods which forms the basis of the price index should therefore seek to reflect the actual current patterns of expenditure. If too many changes are made in the basket of goods, however, it becomes unclear whether changes in the price index are the result of changes in prices of the same collection of goods, or the result of changes in the composition of the items making up the components of the index.

Comparisons of national income between countries

If it is difficult to compare national income at constant prices in one country through time, it is even more difficult to compare national income in different countries at the same period of time. Each country may estimate its national income in the same way but there may be considerable differences in the importance of some items.

Different countries have different baskets of consumption items. This reflects differences in tastes, in goods available and in climatic conditions. Fuel is a much less important item of consumption in tropical countries than it is in northern countries. Some foods which are cheap and plentiful in some countries are expensive in others. If we selected a single basket of consumption goods to measure prices in both countries we would have to include some items which were important in one but not the other; or, if we confined ourselves to those items which were significant items of consumption in both countries, we would finish up with a basket which was unrepresentative of consumption in both countries.

Moreover, to compare the absolute average GNP or NNP in different countries we must convert each country's figures into a common unit of measurement. We cannot compare an average NNP of Rs1,000 with one of $5,000. It is usual to convert each country's national income into US dollars. However, this provides a common basis for comparison only if the exchange rate used to convert from one currency into another accurately reflects the differences in the purchasing power of the various currencies. We know from everyday experience that this is not the case. Some countries are 'cheap' countries in that US$1 will buy a disproportionately larger amount of many goods in that country than it will in others. The official rate of exchange may be an artificial one managed by the government or exchange rate authorities and maintained by many controls on the convertibility of the currency.

Comparisons of the published NNP per capita figures can be extremely difficult. Moreover, it does not follow that the official NNP statistics provide a constant measurement of 'economic well-being' in all countries. Any one country's national accounts may provide a consistent measure of economic change and well-being in that country over a period of years, but may not be comparable with the national accounts of other countries even though they all follow similar international conventions.

We have seen that with the major exception of imputed rent for owner-occupiers, the UK national accounts include only 'market transactions'. Unpaid services are not included. Thus the services and the economic well-being derived from the services of housewives are not included in national income. If a housekeeper were employed her wage would be included, as would the value of her output. This gives rise to the old story that if enough men marry their housekeepers, national income will fall, although the housekeeping services provided might remain exactly the same.

In some countries non-market activities are an important part of economic well-being in that they provide a larger proportion of the total goods and services consumed and produced. The greater the proportion of non-market activities such as family help, the growing of one's own food, or the collection of firewood for fuel, the smaller will be the market-activity-based national accounts in relation to total consumption and output. The statistics of GNP or NNP will provide a lesser indication of the level of consumption and output, and comparisons of NNP per head with countries which have relatively little non-market activity will therefore be confusing. The economy with a greater degree of non-market activity will appear relatively poorer than, in another sense, it is.

However, comparison of GNP, NNP or some other measure of national income per head is the best means we have for trying to compare standards of living and economic well-being in different countries. The important point is to remember the various qualifications that need to be attached to such comparisons.

Glossary

Absolute advantage. One country is more efficient than another at producing all goods.

Accelerator. The effect of changes in national income or consumer demand on investment. The accelerator principle shows that under certain conditions (e.g. existing capital equipment is fully utilised), an increase in aggregate consumer demand will lead to a proportionately larger increase in net investment.

Aggregate consumer demand. The total demand for consumption goods in an economy in a specified time period, expressed in money terms. A change may be the result of changes in prices, in quantities demanded, or some combination of these.

Aggregate real consumer demand. The total demand for consumption goods in an economy in a specified time period expressed in terms of constant prices, so that a change indicates a change in the physical quantity of consumer goods demanded.

Appreciation. A rise in value. An increase in the exchange rate or value of the currency of one country in terms of the currencies of other countries.

Balance of payments. An account, normally covering a period of a year, of the transactions of residents of one country and residents of all other countries, expressed in the currency of the country concerned. All entries indicate either currency flows into the country, i.e. demand by foreigners or residents of other countries for the currency of the country, or outward flows of the country's currency representing demand by residents of the country for the currency of another country.

Balance of trade. A section of the balance of payments showing the net trading position – a currency inflow if there is a surplus, or outflow if there is a deficit – as a result of international trade in goods between the residents of one country and residents of all other countries. It therefore indicates whether the country is spending more on the import of goods than it is receiving from the export of goods.

Balancing item. An entry appearing in balance of payments accounts which is necessary to ensure that the two sides of the accounts (the inflows and outflows of currency) balance. It indicates the extent of the deficiencies or inaccuracies in the official statistics which make up the balance of payments account.

Capital. A factor of production with land and labour. It is the physical stock of goods not used for current consumption. Capital may also refer to the money value of goods used to produce other goods.

Capital consumption. A term used in national income accounts to estimate the amount or value of capital goods used up in the process of producing the output of goods and services included in gross domestic product. The deduction of capital consumption from GNP provides figures of national income in a period.

Capital–output ratio. The relationship showing the amount of capital needed to produce a given level of output.

Cash ratio. The proportion of a bank's assets which are held in cash. Cash may include notes and coins or till money, and deposits at the central bank.

Ceteris paribus. A term used to specify that all other things are equal or remain unchanged except for the specific change assumed to be taking place.

Comparative advantage. The ability of a country to produce a good or goods relatively more efficiently than it can produce another good or goods.

Consumption. The purchase and use of a good or service for the satisfaction to be obtained from so doing. This excludes the purchase and use of a good or service to produce other goods or services.

Consumption goods. Goods which are produced for sale to consumers rather than for stock.

Deflation. A fall in the general or average level of prices.

Deflationary gap. The amount by which aggregate demand is less than the level of aggregate demand associated with the full employment level of output and national income.

Demand. The quantity of a product, good or service which a consumer is prepared to buy at a specified price at a given time, given the price of all other goods, his income level, etc., i.e. *ceteris paribus.*

Demand curve. A graphical expression of the demand for a product at different prices, *ceteris paribus.* A demand curve may indicate the various amounts an individual consumer will buy at different prices, or may be an aggregate demand curve indicating the total or aggregate demand of all consumers at different prices.

Demand schedule. The quantities of a product that will be bought at different prices, *ceteris paribus.* This may refer to an individual or aggregate demand.

Demand–deficient unemployment. A Keynesian concept which ascribes some unemployment in some circumstances to a deficiency of aggregate demand. If aggregate demand were increased and prices rose a little with constant money wages, employers would demand more labour and unemployment would be reduced. It is a form of involuntary unemployment.

Depreciation. When referring to a currency, depreciation is the fall in its value under a system of floating exchange rates. When referring to investment or capital, depreciation is the amount of the capital equipment used up during a time period.

Devaluation. The reduction in value of a currency expressed in terms of the currency of another country, under a system of fixed exchange rates.

Diminishing returns. The combination of additional units of homogeneous variable factors of production with a fixed amount of another factor of production will, after a point, lead to diminishing quantities of output from each additional unit of input of the variable factors.

Direct tax. A tax levied on the income or wealth of individuals or companies.

Diseconomies of scale. An increase in unit production costs or marginal costs as output increases. Diseconomies of scale may be short-run where there is some fixed factor of production or long-run when all factors are variable.

Economic agent. An individual or organisation whose decisions or actions influence economic activity.

Economic model. A set of assumptions or relationships which provides an explanation or hypothesis of economic behaviour, or the effects of some economic variables on others.

Elasticity of demand and supply. The responsiveness of demand or supply to a change in some other variable, usually either price or income. Because the change in demand or supply examined is always a function of a change in some other variable, reference should be made to either price or income elasticity of demand or supply.

Equilibrium. A situation in which there is no pressure or tendency for change, *ceteris paribus.*

Exchange rate. The price or value of one country's currency expressed in terms of the currency of another country.

Fiscal policy. Government measures to alter the rates and levels of taxation and/or government expenditure.

Fixed costs. The costs of those factors of production which cannot be altered in the short run. Average fixed costs are total fixed costs divided by the number of units of output produced. Since the total amount of fixed costs is given, average fixed costs displayed graphically are a rectangular hyperbola. Short-run marginal fixed costs will always decline but at a diminishing rate.

Floating exchange rate. The exchange rate of a currency whose price is determined by supply and demand and which therefore may vary. This is sometimes referred to as a freely floating exchange rate.

Frictional unemployment. Those unemployed who are in the process of moving from one job to another. Sometimes a distinction is made between ex ante-frictional unemployment – those who have left one job and experience a spell of unemployment before taking up another job they have already arranged; and ex post-frictional unemployment – those who have left one job to look for another which they may or may not find within some short period of time.

Giffen good. A good which has an unusual or perverse demand schedule – since the demand for it increases when the price rises and decreases when the price falls, *ceteris paribus*. It is a special kind of inferior good since the negative income effect outweighs or swamps the positive substitution effect.

Gross domestic product (GDP). The total output of goods and services produced within an economy in a time period, usually a year, by the domestic factors of production of that country. It is also equal to the total income received from the production of goods and services within an economy.

Gross national product (GNP). The total income received by residents of a country from domestic production (GDP) plus income received by them as a result of their ownership of assets overseas minus income paid to non-domestic residents as a result of their ownership of assets in the domestic economy.

Income consumption curve. The relationship between demand for a commodity and income changes.

Income effect. A part of the explanation of the effect of a change in the price of a good on its demand with all other prices and a consumer's income remaining constant. Following the change in the price of a good there will be an income effect since the consumer's real income will have been affected if he previously purchased the good. There will also be a substitution effect because the relative prices of goods will have altered. The price elasticity of demand for the good will depend on the combined income and substitution effects.

Income elasticity of demand. The effect of a change in income on the quantity of a good demanded, with all prices remaining constant. A product with negative price elasticity of demand, where less is demanded as income rises, is referred to as an inferior good. Products with a positive income elasticity of demand are referred to as normal goods or sometimes as luxuries.

Income elasticity of supply. The effect of a change in incomes on supply. This concept is more commonly used in relation to labour. An increase in income may lead to a reduction in the amount of labour supplied if people decide that the decreasing marginal utility of income is insufficient to offset the disutility of providing marginal units of work or effort.

Indirect tax. A tax on expenditure such as purchase tax or value added tax (VAT). Tariffs and customs duty are forms of indirect taxes.

Inflation. A rise in the general or average level of prices.

Inflationary gap. The amount by which aggregate demand exceeds the full employment level of output or income.

Investment. The expenditure of income on plant and equipment or goods intended to produce goods or services. Investment is undertaken by entrepreneurs or companies in anticipation of sales, or by government. Increases in stocks or inventories are regarded as investment. The purchase of securities on the stock exchange is not investment.

Invisible trade. The import or export of services or payments of rent, interest and dividends, etc. Invisibles are contrasted with visible items of trade such as imports of goods which can be seen moving from one country to another. Invisibles include tourists' spending and earnings from or payments for insurance and banking services by foreigners.

Involuntary unemployment. This concerns unemployed persons who are able and willing to work for the prevailing wage level but who are unable to find employment.

Isocost. A curve showing the various amounts of factors of production which can be employed or bought for the same cost.

Isoquant. A curve showing the various combinations of two factors of production needed to produce a given amount of output.

Liquidity. The closeness of an asset to money. This refers to the ease and certainty with which an asset can be converted into or exchanged for money.

Liquidity preference. The decision to hold assets in cash or money rather than in other assets such as bonds, shares, land or physical assets.

Liquidity ratio. The proportion of a bank's assets which is held in liquid assets. The definition of 'liquid assets' may vary from time to time and from country to country.

Long run. The period of time in which a firm can vary all factors of production, as opposed to a period during which it is unable to change some of these factors (the fixed factors).

Macro-economics. The part of economics which is concerned with the behaviour of the economy as a whole rather than with individual consumers and producers.

Marginal. The effect of a small change.

Marginal cost (MC). The cost of producing one extra unit of output. Marginal cost is obtained by subtracting from the total cost of producing the total output (including the additional unit) the total cost of producing that output *less* one unit.

Marginal efficiency of capital (mec). The expected receipts from an act of investment expressed as a percentage rate of return on the cost of the investment.

Marginal propensity to consume (mpc). The proportion of an additional unit of income spent on consumption goods rather than saved. All income must be either consumed (i.e. spent on consumption goods) or saved.

Marginal propensity to save (mps). The proportion of an additional unit of income that is saved rather than spent on consumption goods. On some occasions this definition of 'savings' will include taxation and expenditure on imports (mpc + mps = 1).

Marginal revenue (MR). The change in total revenue as a result of selling one additional unit of output.

Marginal revenue product (MRP). The change in total revenue obtained from selling the extra output produced by the employment of an additional unit of a variable factor of production.

Micro-economics. The part of economics concerned with the behaviour of individuals rather than that of the economy as a whole.

Monetary authorities. Those responsible for taking decisions and actions on monetary policy in an economy. In the United Kingdom the monetary authorities are the Treasury and the Bank of England.

Monetary policy. Measures taken by the monetary authorities to influence the stock of money and/or the rate of interest.

Money. That which is usually accepted in an economy in settlement of debts. This includes notes and coins as legal tender and some bank accounts. Different definitions of money include different types of bank accounts so that some include only 'sight' deposits which can be withdrawn immediately and on which no interest is payable, while other definitions include a broader range of accounts. Some definitions may also include deposits in other forms of financial institution.

Money supply. The total amount of money stock in an economy at a given time.

Monopolistic competition. A market structure with a large number of small firms each producing very similar products which are differentiated in some way, either by small differences in the product or as a result of advertising or marketing campaigns by the individual producer.

Monopoly. A single producer of a commodity or product.

Multiplier. The ratio by which an increase in investment (including exports and government expenditure) leads to an increase in aggregate income. In numerical terms the multiplier is 1/mps, where mps is the marginal propensity to save, or the reciprocal of (1−mpc) where mpc is the marginal propensity to consume.

National income. The total amount of incomes accruing to the residents of a country in a time period as a result of their involvement in the production of goods and services domestically and overseas, after allowing for the depreciation of capital goods used in the process of production. It is GNP minus capital consumption. The total national income is equal to total net national output.

Natural rate of unemployment (NRU). The level of unemployment associated with a constant rate of inflation. This does not mean a zero inflation rate but one that remains the same.

Non-accelerating inflation rate of unemployment (NAIRU). A different term for the natural rate of unemployment used by some economists who do not accept all the implications or assumptions of some of the analysis and explanation underlying the NRU.

Normal good. A good with a positive income effect.

Normal profit. The level of profit which is sufficient to ensure that existing producers stay in the industry and maintain their level of output but not high enough to attract new entrants. It is therefore the level of profit associated with the maintenance of the existing level of production.

Oligopoly. A market structure with only a few producers of a product.

Opportunity cost. The cost of a good or service expressed in terms of the next-preferred good or service which has to be forgone in order to make this purchase. The opportunity cost of producing a good is the commodity which was not produced because resources were employed in producing this good.

Optimum output. The level of output at which the firm's average costs are lowest. Short-run optimum output is the level of output with lowest average costs given the firm's existing fixed factors of production. Long-run optimum output is the level of output with the lowest average costs which the firm can achieve by changing the quantity of fixed factors.

Price discrimination. The situation where a firm sells the same product at different prices in different markets or to different consumers for reasons not arising from differences in costs of production or distribution.

Price effect. The effect on demand of a change in price, *ceteris paribus*. The price effect is the result of the combination of the income effect and the substitution effect.

Product real wage. The relationship between the cost of labour and the price the employer receives or expects to receive from the sale of the product of that labour.

Profits. The return to the entrepreneur or firm bearing the risk of production.

Public Sector Borrowing Requirement (PSBR). The amount of borrowing by the government to cover the combined deficits of central and local government and public corporations. Roughly speaking, it is the difference between the amount of public spending in a time period, usually a year, and the amount of public receipts from taxes and public corporation revenues.

Residual error. An entry in the national accounts necessary to ensure that the income and expenditure methods of measuring GDP provide the same total. It is an indication of the deficiencies and errors in the statistics.

Short run. The length of time in which at least one factor of production used by a firm is fixed. The short run is therefore not a specific period of time but is determined by the time taken by a firm to change one factor of production.

Stock appreciation. The change in value over a period of time of a constant amount of inventories or volume of raw materials. It is an item in the national income accounts.

Subsidy. A payment made by the government to the producers or consumers of goods or services. It can be regarded as the opposite of an indirect tax.

Substitution effect. The general tendency to switch demand towards a good whose price has become relatively cheaper than that of other goods. If the price of a good falls it is relatively cheaper than other goods and consumers will, *ceteris paribus*, buy more of it. If its price rises other goods will become relatively cheaper since it is now relatively more expensive, and the demand for it will tend to fall. The substitution effect is always positive, but the net effect on demand will be determined by the combined effects of the income and substitution effects. In some cases the positive substitution effect may be outweighed by a stronger negative income effect.

Super-normal profits. A rate of profit higher than normal profits. Super-normal profits would attract new entrants into an industry assuming there are no barriers to entry.

Terms of trade. The relationship between the change in the average price of imported goods and the average price of exported goods over a time period or between two dates. The terms of trade are said to improve if the average price of exports rises by more than the average price of imports, or falls by less, between two dates.

Transfer payments. A payment, usually made by the government, which is not a payment for economic activity or payment to a factor of production.

Utility. The satisfaction derived from the consumption of a good or service. All goods and services on which consumption expenditure is made have positive utility. It is assumed that marginal utility – the utility obtained from consumption of additional units of the same commodity – declines. It is not possible to measure utility since satisfaction is a psychological concept. It is possible to say that one good gives more satisfaction or utility than another without being able to say how much more utility. Work is regarded as having disutility since it deprives us of leisure.

Variable costs. The costs of employing variable factors of production.

Variable factors of production. Those factors, usually labour and raw materials, whose level of employment can be varied by the employer in the short run.

Varying proportions. The law of varying proportions states that successive applications of additional units of homogeneous variable factors of production to a given amount of fixed factors will lead first to increasing and then to decreasing returns.

Velocity of circulation. The average number of times each unit of money is used during a given time period.

Voluntary unemployment. Those who are unemployed by their own choice in that they choose not to work at the prevailing level of wages.

Index